HOW DO WE
KNOW
THEY'RE GETTING
BETTER?

HOW DO WE KNOW THEY'RE GETTING BETTER?

ASSESSMENT *for* 21st CENTURY MINDS, K–8

JOHN BARELL

CORWIN
A SAGE Company

CORWIN
A SAGE Company

FOR INFORMATION:

Corwin
A SAGE Company
2455 Teller Road
Thousand Oaks, California 91320
(800) 233-9936
Fax: (800) 417-2466
www.corwin.com

SAGE Ltd.
1 Oliver's Yard
55 City Road
London EC1Y 1SP
United Kingdom

SAGE India Pvt. Ltd.
B 1/I 1 Mohan Cooperative
Industrial Area
Mathura Road, New Delhi 110 044
India

SAGE Asia-Pacific Pte. Ltd.
33 Pekin Street #02-01
Far East Square
Singapore 048763

Acquisitions Editor: Hudson Perigo
Associate Editor: Allison Scott
Editorial Assistant: Lisa Whitney
Production Editor: Cassandra Margaret Seibel
Copy Editor: Barbara Corrigan
Typesetter: C&M Digitals (P) Ltd.
Proofreader: Theresa Kay
Indexer: Jeanne Busemeyer
Cover Designer: Scott Van Atta
Permissions Editor: Adele Hutchinson

Printed in the United States of America.

Library of Congress Cataloging-in-Publication Data

Barell, John.

How do we know they're getting better? : assessment for 21st century minds, K-8/ John Barell.

p. cm.
Includes bibliographical references and index.

ISBN 978-1-4129-9528-3 (pbk.)

1. Educational tests and measurements—United States. 2. Education, Elementary—United States—Evaluation. 3. Middle school education—United States—Evaluation. 4. Curriculum change—United States. 5. Education—Aims and objectives—United States. I. Title.

LB3051.B263 2012
371.260973—dc23   2011036700

SFI label applies to text stock

This book is printed on acid-free paper.

12 13 14 15 16 10 9 8 7 6 5 4 3 2 1

Contents

Appreciations

I deeply appreciate the help of all teachers who have so generously shared their classrooms with me. Their intelligent and creative experiences demonstrate how much our students can achieve if we engage them in inquiring about meaningful problematic situations. In this day and age, with educational issues often at the forefront of our daily news, you will find it a most rewarding and enriching experience to share in some of these teachers' marvelous challenges to all their students. I am deeply indebted to all whose stories appear herein.

I am especially thankful to those visionary leaders who have pioneered educating our students for the 21st century. Their extensive stories are told in Chapters 7 through 10:

Kerry Faber

Lorraine Radford

Mary Darr

Pat Burrows

Everybody is indebted to you all for the passion you bring to this, the noblest profession, and for disclosing how we can observe students' growth over time.

Thank you all very much.

Bravo Zulu!

About the Author

 **John Barell** became an explorer at age thirteen when he first read Admiral Richard E. Byrd's book *Little America*. From this story of intrepid adventurers camped out on the Ross Ice Shelf in Antarctica in 1928, Barell developed so many questions. He wrote Admiral Byrd, who not only answered with four letters but also invited him to visit at his home in Boston and urged him to explore Antarctica. Barell sailed to Antarctica on board Admiral Byrd's flagship, *USS Glacier*, and served as her operations officer during Operation DeepFreeze '63 and '64.

Subsequently, Barell became an educator attempting to explore the many possibilities for educating young people in nontraditional settings in New York City and at Montclair State University (New Jersey). His published writings reflect an attempt to challenge students and their teachers to take risks by adventuring into complex problematic situations to inquire, solve problems, and think critically. Antarctica, once a dream for a young reader, has become a metaphor for all educational inquiry, adventure, and discovery.

Now professor emeritus at Montclair State University, Barell worked from 2000 to 2007 as a consultant to the American Museum of Natural History in New York City, helping teachers and students become inquisitive about the wonders of earth and space.

As a national consultant, Barell works with schools in the United States and Canada to foster and assess those 21st century capacities needed for success and well-being in this new century.

John Barell's recent publications include *Why Are School Buses Always Yellow? Teaching Inquiry, PreK–5* (2007), *Problem-Based Learning: An Inquiry Approach* (2007), *Developing More Curious Minds* (2003), *Quest for Antarctica: A Journey of Wonder and Discovery* (2011, a memoir), and *Surviving Erebus: An Antarctic Adventure* (2008, a novel).

He lives in New York City with his wife Nancy.

Introduction

Growing Up With Radio

I grew up with radio, listening to reports from London and the Pacific theaters of World War II. The voices of Edward R. Murrow ("This . . . is London.") and H. V. Kaltenborn were my link to the outside world from Hartsdale, New York, where I was an elementary school student.

After the war came black-and-white television, with a huge magnifying lens mounted in front of the nine-inch screen (maybe a little more or less). I watched with intense inquisitiveness news events of the early 1950s such as the Army-McCarthy hearings about communists lurking in our government (Look it up if you don't remember these dramatic events from high school history class. It's worth it!) and the Democratic and Republican conventions of 1952. Eisenhower and Stevenson were nominated.

Finally, we got a color television, and I thought the whole world had changed. There were my favorite teams—the New York Yankees and the Notre Dame football team—and all our beloved comedians—Jackie Gleason, Milton Berle, Sid Caesar, and others—in vivid color.

Slowly, the technologies began to change even more.

While I was teaching at Montclair State University, my colleagues and I were called into an auditorium one day to see the latest: what a computer could produce on a screen. And what was that? The roster from a class at a California university, perhaps a class in science or the humanities. Shortly thereafter a colleague showed a friend and me, from her own desktop machine, pictures from various Parisian hotels, rooms, salons, dining areas, and the like. This was rather cool!

The World Wide Web had expanded from California to encompass so many wonders!

Now, my nephew Benjamin Gleason is embarking on a new adventure; with two children and a wife, he's in a doctoral program in educational technology at Michigan State University. He and I have had several conversations about what an exciting field this will be. (When I contemplated a similar doctorate at Teachers College, Columbia University, in the 1970s, what we had in the way of technology for educators was television—the sets [or monitors], the cameras, the portapacks [for remote recording], the lighting, the whole works!)

I mention this brief history because when I began this project on 21st century learning, I conceived of the skills or capacities requisite within our new century as the same as those of the 20th, the 19th, and the 18th centuries, on back to the age of Socrates. Yes, we had new technologies, but these were not my focus.

Now, I've reconsidered.

Daily, I receive news briefs, e-mails, notes about blogs, and so forth announcing how new technologies are transforming our classrooms. Students are using devices never imagined just a few years ago:

iPhones, Androids, and other smart devices;

iPads;

BlackBerry smartphones;

iTunes University;

Skype with one/multiple settings;

Google Docs;

Wikis;

Moodle;

Wordle (try it!);

Facebook;

LinkedIn;

Twitter;

Cloud computing (some schools and businesses use extensively); and

many more that haven't yet been invented.

What do we do with all of these means of communication? How should they affect the old models of teaching and learning? What will be their long-term effects for various kinds of students?

The National Association of Secondary School Principals recently (2011) noted, "As mobile devices become more powerful and more affordable, their potential for enhancing student learning has come into clearer focus. Social networking sites provide platforms for student creativity by enabling them to design projects using words, music, photos, and videos. In recent years, there has been explosive growth in students creating, manipulating, and sharing content online (National School Boards Association, 2007). Recognizing the educational value of encouraging such behaviors, many school leaders have shifted their energies from limiting the use of these technologies to limiting their abuse" (http://www.nassp.org/Content .aspx?topic=Using_Mobile_and_Social_Technologies_in_Schools).

Initially, there may have been abuses with these new ways of communicating. Now, leaders are realizing we must learn how to deal with access to infinite amounts of information and the responsibility to think critically about whatever we find there.

Indeed, we must ensure that from a very early age—some teachers say as early as kindergarten—our students begin to become aware that anything is permitted on the Internet. "Nobody is in charge!" as Tom Friedman (2008) has often noted.

This is what is so different and exciting about educating students for the 21st century—the access to unlimited amounts of information and being open to worldwide resources. I've had the pleasure this year of engaging in Skype conversations with teachers in a Pittsburgh Science, Technology, Engineering, Art, and Math project as well as with educators in Austin, in Syracuse, and in Edmonton, Alberta, while sitting at my desk here in New York City. Obviously, students can do the same. (Witness the commercial with Ellen Page, who enters an elementary school whose students are about to take a field trip to China. And then there they are on the screen!)

"AN EXPANSIVE CANVAS"

Schools are using Skype technologies to connect with one another in different states to learn about "Web 2.0 skills, digital citizenship, personal network building and social media responsibility and practice." Here is the "virtual classroom" (see http://www.edutopia.org/blog/web-20-21st-century-skills-collaboration-digital-citizenship). One teacher, Mrs. Miller, noted, "My students cannot stop talking about our connected classroom. They have made so many new connections and realize that their classroom is not simply limited to a room, but is an expansive canvas." Imagine the prospect of learning about different peoples, their varying points of view, and how that might positively affect your view of a subject, of yourself, of the world. And now we're on to Web 3.0 skills and concerns, such as working more with cloud computing.

So my nephew Benjamin and I have had interesting conversations about his forthcoming studies and about how this technology might affect how we learn, how we think, how we process information, what we think about old and new knowledge, and how we acquire it. Certainly kindergartners this year will graduate from high school thirteen years from now with vastly different ideas of what it means to learn, where we learn best, and how to become good thinkers and be responsible citizens.

> How will current technology affect how we learn, how we think, how we process information, what we think about old and new knowledge, and how we acquire it? How will our graduating seniors think differently from you and me? What do we need to do to ensure they use all these technologies responsibly and to their own and society's benefit? Most significantly, what effects will these newer technologies have on students' achievement over time? And do we even have means to assess their impact on student learning at present?

This project has set me on a fascinating journey, one that has taken me into schools I've never set foot in physically and back to ones that I've written about in the past (see Barell, 2007).

Even though at present I do not own an iPad2, I know that some districts in the neighboring state of New Jersey are about to field-test a new algebra curriculum using this device and a publisher's curriculum. Apple reports that there are 600 districts across the country that are introducing new curricula in other subjects, sometimes designed by the textbook publishers themselves. The benefits are numerous. In addition to being sleek, lightweight, and able to access more current information, "They include interactive programs to demonstrate problem-solving in math, scratchpad features for note-taking and book marking, the ability to immediately send quizzes and homework to teachers, and the chance to view videos or tutorials on everything from important historical events to learning foreign languages. They're especially popular in special education services, for children with autism spectrum disorders and learning disabilities, and for those who learn best when something is explained with visual images, not just through talking" (Reitz, 2011).

So the means of delivering content have changed, but will our ways of learning change with them? And even more importantly, will the content delivered on these miraculous devices be any different from what we currently find in our weighty textbooks?

We're moving away from a reliance on overweight textbooks to having access to information that may be far more current, but will that change how we educate our students to think about this content?

And what, in the long run, will be the effects of all this technology on student achievement as we currently assess it? Do we have the means to determine how use of, for example, iPads affects our learning of content?

One teacher, Kelly Taylor from Catalina Foothills School District, near Tucson, Arizona, introduced me to another technology, YouTube, as an assessment tool. She videotaped an evaluative discussion with one of her students, a reflection on a science project, and sent me a link to it on YouTube. Then I became intrigued and finally figured out how to post my own videos on YouTube (see www.morecuriousminds.com/videos.htm).[1]

The teachers I have had the pleasure of working with have not yet, by and large, introduced most of these communication devices into their classrooms. They might not have students Twittering among themselves about school subjects in class, but in one Vancouver third-grade classroom, Shauna Ullman has her students sharing questions and responses using Google Docs, and this is a change. It's a way of including all students, some of whom would rather not raise their hands to contribute. She also, as we'll see in Chapter 6, has had students experimenting with iPads and how they can provide access to even more resources. Shauna is opening her classroom so students can explore myriad possibilities within our globalized world.

21ST CENTURY CAPACITIES

What has made my own journey so rewarding is, of course, meeting many extraordinary teachers who have found ways to identify and monitor their students' thinking. The 21st century skills or capacities we have focused on during this adventure include the following:

inquiry,

problem solving,

critical thinking,

creative thinking,

reflection,

collaboration/teamwork, and

uses of information technology.

Lists of 21st century skills also include dispositions:

self-direction,[2]

leadership,

adaptability/resourcefulness,

responsibility, and

global awareness.[3]

These are, for me, the core intellectual processes we have required in the past, and we surely will require them in the connected, interactive classrooms of the globalized world where we learn from an infinite variety of sources.

RATIONALE FOR THIS BOOK

So why do we need this book? Why focus on these 21st century learning skills, or capacities, as I prefer to call them? *Skills* seems quite technical and limiting. Having a capacity to identify and resolve problems through inquiry is more far-reaching, more demanding of in-depth thinking than the skills of changing a tire, adding a column of numbers, or posting your videos on YouTube.

Even though many of us are not yet where educational leaders see us being in the near future, it seems to me that we are educating our students to grow and thrive within a world that is changing with "an ever increasing acceleration," as Admiral Richard E. Byrd wrote me many years ago about exploring the continent of Antarctica.

GLOBAL COMPETITION

Our students will have to deal with unlimited sources and kinds of information, some of that at lightning speed within a world where there is "increased global inter-connectivity" that puts "diversity and adaptability at the center of organizational operations."[4]

In other words, our students are going to have to compete with people all over the world. They will have to innovate, be critical problem posers and solvers, reflect, and be able to use all of the technologies and social media we've mentioned above. They already far surpass many of us more mature folks in using these technologies!

Recent research on innovation by Dyer, Gregersen, and Christensen (2011) suggests that the 21st century capacities we've identified are part of their DNA:

questioning,

observing,

networking, and

experimenting.

"Innovators," Dyer et al. (2011) write, "are consummate questioners who show a passion for inquiry. Their queries frequently challenge the status quo, just as [Steve] Jobs did when he asked, 'Why does a computer need a fan?' They love to ask, 'If we tried this, what would happen?' Innovators, like Jobs, ask questions to understand how things really are today, why they are that way, and how they might be changed or disrupted" (p. 23).

Innovators and 21st century citizens are people who are continually raising questions and seeking answers. They are very entrepreneurial, ready and willing to set off on different pathways, take risks, and explore new territories.

The DNA of innovators consists of the capacity to

question,

observe,

network, and

experiment.

When we engage in these behaviors as well as in what Einstein called "combinatorial play with ideas" (i.e., "Associating"), we foster innovation.

Source: Dyer, Gregersen, and Christensen (2011, p. 23).

We must ensure that we challenge all our students with "authentic" problem situations so they become better at thinking through complex, multifaceted issues such as climate change, pollution control, feeding the hungry, preventing disease, electing the most qualified candidates to office, preserving our democracy, fashioning the artworks that will inspire us all, and probing nature to ferret out its secrets.

With such challenges as they will face in the interconnected world of today and tomorrow, a curriculum full of pablum-like rote memorization exercises will never suffice. Our students need to think through problematic situations similar to those we confront outside of school every day.

Even if they do not apply for and receive patents for new creations, they will have to become innovators of how to do business, how to succeed, and how to prosper in this new century.

21ST CENTURY CITIZENSHIP

Looking at the political landscape at this writing (September 2011), it seems that our country is mired in public wrangling about so many issues—for example, the role of the federal government in our lives and how to solve problems of employment, health care, clean air, and national security.

Regardless of anybody's leanings or persuasions on these issues, it goes without saying that what America needs to survive as a democracy are people who are intelligent, who keep themselves well informed, and who raise questions about situations that are perplexing and intriguing. These citizens will, then, seek answers as well as pursue remedies for their own as well as the common good.

Benjamin Franklin is reputed to have told a questioner who asked, "Well, Doctor, what have we got—a Republic or a Monarchy?" upon leaving the Constitutional Convention in Philadelphia in 1787, "A Republic, if you can keep it."

That is the responsibility of all of us.

PERSONAL GROWTH

It's not just to enhance our competitive edge that we advocate for 21st century capacities. No, those of us who work daily within schools to enhance, say, students' curiosity, do so because we see how enriching such experiences are for all concerned. The teacher derives benefit from so many students' being engaged with artifacts or stories that are intriguing, interesting, and perplexing. And of course, our students become emotionally and intellectually engaged when they are posing their own questions and can see them become part of what we are investigating for the unit:

"My inquiry skills shot through the roof!" (see Chapter 8).

"STEM changed my life" (see Chapter 9).

Speaking from personal experience, my own questions about Antarctica (Barell, 2011) led to meeting Admiral Byrd; sailing south on his flagship; exploring the highest, driest, and windiest continent on the planet; and thence finding this profession, working with educators like you to foster the same kinds of inquiry and investigation. It is immensely enriching and satisfying!

For these tasks we need all the teachers you will meet here. We will need my nephew Benjamin Gleason as well as parents and principals who will help guide our journeys.

WHY NOT HIGH-STAKES STANDARDIZED TESTS?

But why attempt to observe, measure, and monitor progress, growth, and development?

I once asked educators, "How do we know students are getting better?" at critical thinking and was told we needn't be "reductionist about it." This meant to me that this principal was thinking of reducing growth to numbers.

Most assessments from the federal No Child Left Behind law, as well as state assessments in various subjects, are based on standardized tests. These "bubble tests" record what students are able to do within one subject at that moment. They do not, most of them, come close to reflecting the authentic learning challenges leading educators have been advocating for many years (see, e.g., Bransford, Brown, & Cocking, 2000; Newmann & Associates, 1996). To become a good inquirer, problem solver, and critical/creative thinker, one needs to encounter tests that are complex, intriguing, ill structured, and not given to any one right answer and that reflect what people do in the world to live and make a living. These kinds of authentic problems will not be found in standardized tests (except, perhaps, for assessments such as the College and Work Readiness Assessments that do challenge students with ill-structured problems to consider; see www.cae.org/content/pro_collegework.htm).

And we need to be able to assess students' progress over long periods of time, not in a one-shot test given within an hour or perhaps longer. The 21st century capacities and their associated dispositions grow over long periods of time as the result of maturation, environment, and encounters with authentic problems. Teachers here have disclosed to us ways of capturing this growth and development.

So you won't find numbers within these pages so much as various ways, from kindergarten through eighth grade, that teachers have observed their students' becoming better questioners, better thinkers, and more self-directed over time—during the year and within the span of five years.

But why even seek to observe growth?

Because if we assert that these 21st century capacities are so vital to our nation's survival (and I do believe they are), we should be able to say whether our students are improving beyond merely learning the content of various subjects.

Can they think about this content productively and creatively?

Are they learning how to adapt to changing conditions and forge adventures toward new horizons of learning and discovery?

> What I have attempted to share with you in this book is a disclosure model—a model that discloses various possibilities for observing growth over time and within a wide range of different settings.

What I have attempted to share with you in this book is a disclosure model—a model that discloses various possibilities for observing growth over time and within a wide range of different settings. I do hope that the possibilities described here launch your own inquiries about sharing with students, teachers, and parents how our students are growing and becoming better.

OUTLINE OF THE BOOK

We haven't been able to delve specifically into every K–8 classroom to find the rich textures of students' learning that came from four gifted teachers, Lorraine Radford, Kerry Faber, Pat Burrows, and the teams of Grade 6 through 8 teachers led by Mary Darr. However, I do hope we have sufficient examples from all grade levels to provide every reader with some valuable ways of observing and assessing students' growth in their development of 21st century capacities.

Here's an outline of what you will read:

Chapter 1: This chapter provides an overview of what teachers are doing.

Chapter 2: We address teacher self-assessment, a topic too seldom open for discussion. How do we ourselves think, inquire, and grow intellectually? "We were the blind leading the blind," said one Ohio teacher about her participation in a science, technology, engineering, and math (STEM) project. This may be the most important chapter in the book!

Chapter 3: The topic is designing the invitational environment. How do we ensure that our students are willing to take the risks to ask good questions, to break out of traditional ways of thinking?

Chapter 4: This chapter addresses basic principles of planning for excellence that affect our consideration of assessment. Planning backwards (planning with the ends in mind) has been with us for over a half century, and it continues to dominate our thinking

Chapter 5: I consider preassessment. How do we get an idea very early on of how good our students are at asking questions? Lorraine in kindergarten reports that her students mostly told stories. Pat in eighth grade tells us that early in the year her students were mainly "cookie-cutter A students," not asking questions and not giving good reasons for conclusions.

Chapter 6: Formative assessments, now seen as perhaps the most vital element of assessing how well students are progressing toward desired goals, are the topic of this chapter. Teachers' experiments as well as question-monitoring frameworks help monitor students' progress.

Chapter 7: I consider assessment of inquiry from a kindergarten class in West Vancouver, British Columbia. Lorraine Radford has an easily transferable system of tracking her students' growth in inquiry from telling stories to asking questions such as "If a game is designed for two, what do you do if three or more want to play?"

Chapter 8: This chapter explores assessment of inquiry as well as problem solving and critical/creative thinking based on Kerry Faber's fifth- and sixth-grade classrooms in Edmonton, Alberta. "My inquiry skills shot through the roof!" exclaimed Sydney.

Chapter 9: This chapter assesses problem-based learning within a STEM project for Grades 6, 7, and 8 in Sandusky, Ohio. "STEM changed my life," claimed one eighth-grade girl.

Chapter 10: We explore the process of students' becoming better critical thinkers. Pat Burrows has challenged her students to think deeply about issues in media, politics, and art. Here we describe how she helped Rachel grow from a "cookie-cutter A student" to one who is self-directed.

Chapter 11: This chapter deals with communicating with parents. I relate the story of Isidore I. Rabi, noted Nobel Prize in Physics winner, and his mother's influence on contemporary parents who took up the challenge to observe their son's growth during the early years.

Chapter 12: I review all curricular elements within these case studies to apply to Grades K through 8 in all subjects for all students. What do we do with all the assessment data we might collect from preassessments, formative assessments, and summative assessments?

John Barell

New York City

September 2011

jbarell@nyc.rr.com

www.morecuriousminds.com

ENDNOTES

1. Jose Vilson is a middle school math teacher, and he recently noted Lady Gaga's phenomenal popularity and her use of social media networking, YouTube, and Twitter.

> Some might say she's a product of social engineering, but if anything, she's the engineer. In the same way we already have come to the conclusion that learning can't just happen in class. Much of the mantra these days is still centered on teacher-direct instruction. While I do believe there's room for that, there has to be a sense that learning comes 24/7. It happens even when our students least expect it. . . . I wonder how often students find a context where they used the math they had just learned in class, drop it as a picture on a teacher's fan page, and had the teacher reply back to ask them another question on it? (http://future .teacherleaders.org/2011/05/lady-gaga-and-the-future-implications-of-connectivity/comment-page-1/#comment-293)

2. Ken Kay (2010), former president of the Partnership for 21st Century Skills, noted that one manager at Apple told him that "any employee who needs to be managed is no longer employable" (p. xxi).

3. For a more complete list, see "Framework for 21st Century Learning" at Partnership for 21st Century Skills: www.p21.org/index.php?option=com_content&task=view&id=254&Itemid=120.

4. Advertisement for the University of Phoenix in *The Atlantic*, July/August 2011, "Promotion" pages following page 84.

REFERENCES

Barell, J. (2007). *Why are school buses always yellow? Teaching inquiry preK–5*. Thousand Oaks, CA: Corwin.

Barell, J. (2011). *Quest for Antarctica: A journey of wonder and discovery* (2nd ed.) Lincoln, NE: iUniverse.

Bransford, J., Brown, A., & Cocking, R. (2000). *How people learn: Brain, mind, experience, and school.* Washington, DC: National Academy Press.

Dyer, J., Gregersen, H., & Christensen, C. (2011). *The innovator's DNA—Mastering the five skills of disruptive innovators.* Cambridge, MA: Harvard Business Review Press.

Friedman, T. (2008, October 18). The great Iceland meltdown. *The New York Times.* www.nytimes.com/2008/10/19/opinion/19friedman.html

Kay, K. (2010). Forward: 21st century skills: Why they matter, what they are and how we get there. In J. Bellanca & R. Brandt (Eds.), *21st century skills—Rethinking how students learn* (pp. xiii–xxxi). Bloomington, IN: Solution Tree Press.

Newmann, F., & Associates. (1996). *Authentic achievement: Restructuring schools for intellectual quality.* San Francisco, CA: Jossey-Bass.

Reitz, S. (2011, September 3). *Many US schools adding iPads, trimming textbooks.* Retrieved from http://denverpost.com/nationworld/ci_18822767

An Overview

O ur journey begins with brief introductions to the stories of several teachers who have learned about their students' abilities to inquire, think, and figure things out. We will note the wide variety of information-gathering approaches illustrated here as well as what the evidence suggests about students' growth in the 21st century capacities.

Why stories?

We all know the power of a story. When we hear about how a student became valedictorian of her class, how a student won a prize or a scholarship, or how a parent raised a child to succeed against terrible odds, we not only are enlightened intellectually but also feel good for that person. Of course, not all stories are happy ones, but they come with content knowledge, a structure (beginnings and endings), and associated feelings.

We remember these stories well because with their settings, plots, characters, sights, sounds, and emotions, we easily store them in what psychologists call episodic memory. This is different from knowledge of facts, semantic memory. Both constitute declarative memory. First identified or named by Endel Tulving, episodic memory allows us to "travel back in time" to re-experience what happened in the past (see http://eecs.vanderbilt.edu/cis/crl/episodicmemory.shtml).

The point is that it's more fun, for me at least, to read short vignettes about teachers working in schools to bring about major changes within the lives of their students than it is to read a set of abstract principles, view a few charts, and attempt to interpret columns of data. All of that is important because it provides structure, and you will find, I hope, sufficient intellectual structures and frameworks here to help interpret the short vignettes about these educators for the 21st century.

JOHN SELKIRK

John Selkirk teaches first grade in the Ottawa-Carlton school district. He shared with me his very high level of challenge for his students—to think critically about people in stories they were reading. His rubric for this task (see Figure 1.1) is most intriguing, and all year I wondered how well he was doing with helping his students draw reasonable conclusions about people's feelings as seen in pictures. Right off the bat, John started challenging students with making observations and drawing good and reasonable conclusions (see Chapter 5).

If we wish our students to think critically, what are our expectations for how they will engage each other intellectually and socially? This was a most important consideration for John.

JESSE MACKAY

Jesse Mackay started a new year at Coronation School in Edmonton with her second and third graders in a most unusual fashion.

On the very first day at her new school, Jesse decided to assess her students' inquisitiveness. Here's the way she described her experience with her combined Grade 2/3 class of fifteen students: "The very first thing I asked the students to do on the first day of school was to look around the room and after a few minutes come back to their desk with a question (or more). They could write it down if they liked or just remember it to ask for a whole class discussion. My assumptions about children and development were drastically challenged during this activity" (J. Mackay, personal communication, 2009).

What did Jesse learn about her students?

JENNIFER MONTGOMERY

Jennifer Montgomery teaches second grade at Parkside Elementary School in Austin. Since shifting their focus away from more traditional methods of teaching, she and colleagues claimed they saw marked improvement in students' performance on state assessments, especially in mathematics. Not only did she note these developments, but she also

Figure 1.1 Critical Thinking Assessment

Student's Name:_____

Levels	1	2	3	4
Makes relevant observations	rarely	sometimes	often	always
Identifies most important points	rarely	sometimes	often	always
Justifies conclusions	rarely	sometimes	often	always
Asks powerful questions	rarely	some "yes or no" or factual questions	some open-ended questions	many open-ended questions that generate a lot of info
Is open-minded	considers only one point of view	considers some points of view	considers many different points of view	makes up mind only after careful consideration of all different points of view

Source: © John Selkirk (2011). Used with permission.

recorded students' improvement in asking good questions during units on marketing and building animal habitats. To what did she attribute her successes?

JASMIN RAMZINSKY

Jasmin Ramzinsky teaches with Jennifer Montgomery at Parkside. She too altered the course of her teaching during a recent unit on the solar system. Following this shift from almost total teacher control, her students asked her the following:

> Mrs. Ram, that doesn't make any sense. Why would you ask questions about my planet? You weren't doing the research, I was.

> Mrs. Ram, I bet your kids kinda got bored with finding the answers to your questions.

I bet they did, indeed! As do many other students engaged in learning the way Mrs. Ram used to teach.

What did she do and with what kinds of assessments of students' growth?

SHAUNA ULLMAN

Shauna Ullman teaches third grade in West Vancouver at the Mulgrave International Baccalaureate School. During my visit to her school and in subsequent correspondence, I discovered how she has used modern technology in ways in which most students will soon be engaged. In addition to tracking her students' growth during various units using her own record-keeping system, she helped students share their own wonderings and searches for answers on iPads during a three-week time period.

Having students become more fully engaged by using this and other technologies (Google Docs, cloud computing, Google+, iPhones, and the like) is creating a revolution in our schools.

I was most intrigued to discover what Shauna observed about her students' engagement and responsiveness with this technology and how it might have fostered growth in 21st century capacities—beyond, of course, learning how to be very comfortable navigating an iPad.

These technologies have the potential for enhancing students'

personal engagement with content—stuff to learn;

peer-to-peer interaction, here and around the world; and

responsiveness to our curricular expectations.

We will see how several schools are, in effect, transforming their enclosed four-walled, textbook-bound classrooms into open-air communication centers where students can access infinite amounts of information and communicate with interested and valued resource persons around the globe at the touch of a finger whenever they choose. Our challenge under these circumstances is to guide their ability to question, analyze, and critique such information and draw reasonable conclusions.

LORRAINE RADFORD

Lorraine Radford also teaches at Mulgrave School. When I walked into her kindergarten classroom, I was amazed at the writings on the wall. Lorraine had students' questions in their own handwriting displayed as well as their later questions, formatted by Lorraine during a unit on sea creatures that involved group and individual research projects.

At the same time, Lorraine showed me one of the most elaborate means of recording students' questions over time that I've ever seen.

We will see how several schools are, in effect, transforming their enclosed four-walled, textbook-bound classrooms into open-air communication centers where students can access infinite amounts of information and communicate with interested and valued resource persons around the globe at the touch of a finger whenever they choose. Our challenge under these circumstances is to guide their ability to question, analyze, and critique such information and draw reasonable conclusions.

How does she take students who enter their all-day, yearlong kindergarten making statements and help them formulate a wide variety of questions, from "What if you're playing a game for two, and three people want to play?" to "Why does the mommy octopus die when her babies are born?" and "Does the angler fish think humans are fish?"

You will learn more about Lorraine in Chapter 7.

KERRY FABER

Like Jesse Mackay, Kerry Faber teaches in Edmonton, Alberta. She has most generously shared much of her work that leads students to question and seek for answers. I have had the good fortune to visit one of her classes (winter 2010) and, recently, conduct Skype conversations with another. Kerry has long been interested in students' growing in their abilities to ask good questions in all subjects, and she has done amazing work with students in all ability ranges.

One of the units she regularly undertakes with her students is called Evidence and Investigation, a study of how we conduct good investigations to solve problems.

A few years ago, she undertook this unit of study lasting about seven weeks with this diagnostic situation: "I thought for this first unit it would be best to begin getting them to develop inquiring minds. I gave the children a picture prompt. It contained a partial view of a classroom with children looking at an empty cage with a sign saying 'please close lid.' There are some sort of footprints leading from the cage to the door. There are also several other details included. I told the children that there was a problem(s) presented in this picture. In partners, they had to brainstorm possible problems based upon their observations and interpretations" (K. Faber, personal communication, November 2009).

Notice how Kerry has begun her unit, not with "Let's open our books to page 25 and read. Who would like to read for us?"

No, what she did forms the essence of problem-based learning (Barell, 2007a, 2007b): presenting students with an intriguing situation that leads them to ask good questions and present tentative conclusions that need more investigation.

What do you think are the benefits of Kerry's approach compared with the more traditional "Let's open our books"?

Now, what did Kerry discover from this diagnostic exercise conducted at the opening of her very first full-length inquiry unit in September? "I found that some students didn't understand what I meant by a 'problem.' They just listed things they observed in the picture" (K. Faber, personal communication, December 2009).

What a valuable lesson to learn right off the bat! Some students don't know or cannot articulate what we mean by *problem*.

This is not all that easy. Try asking your students for their definitions of a problem. They might say, "When things go wrong . . . something you don't like. . . ."

MARY DARR

Mary Darr is the coordinator of STEM projects in Sandusky, Ohio. STEM represents an initiative to develop more interest and competence in science, technology, engineering, and math. The reason for this emphasis at the federal level derives from American students' poor performance on many standardized tests when compared with students from various other countries. We rank way below number one, and recent, accepted state applications for federal Race to the Top funding included placing more emphasis on attempting to provide students with challenging learning experiences in STEM subjects.

The state of Ohio has what appears to be a highly developed network of schools fostering STEM projects, and I was fortunate enough to begin communicating with Mary Darr in Sandusky.

What you learn in Chapter 9 is how her students figured out how to build models of sky-high roller coasters for the Cedar Point Amusement Park right on the shores of Lake Erie.

There were some amazing results. "What were the most important aspects?" I asked students during telephone interviews and on end-of-project personal reflections.

"TEAMWORK" was the almost unanimous response.

How do projects for sixth, seventh, and eighth graders build such a united and positive response?

One student, Karla, actually went well beyond this assessment as well as those about learning how to think outside the box—creatively, that is.

Karla claimed, "STEM changed my life."

How did it do that?

PAT BURROWS

We all know them.

These are students whom eighth-grade literature and writing teacher Pat Burrows calls "cookie-cutter A" students.

These are very respectful students; some might be labeled as gifted. But what they are often gifted at doing is guessing what's on the teacher's mind and giving it back on various assessments. I remember some of them from my days of teaching the same subjects in New York City. When I challenged them to think on their own, they became befuddled because there were no right answers to put down on the test.

In Chapter 10, Pat tells us how she took Rachel from being such a student to being one who showed she had developed into a fine critical thinker, one who could tell the local bus company why their policy of dropping off students in the Catalina Foothills School District (Arizona) was less than optimal.

How did she do that? And how does she assess students' progress in one of the schools that exemplifies an emphasis on 21st century skills and capacities?

RANDY AND JENNIFER GRAGG

It all begins at home, and Randy and Jennifer Gragg are parents who took seriously the challenge laid down by the mother of world-famous nuclear physicist and Nobel Prize winner Isidore I. Rabi. Rabi's mother did not, like many other mothers in Brooklyn, ask him when he returned home from school daily, "So, did you learn anything today?" No, she asked a different question.

In Chapter 11 you will see how the Gragg family took Sheindel Rabi's challenge to heart and how they monitored the growth of their young son, Spencer.

MEANS AND RESULTS

Figure 1.2 represents the wide variety of means of information gathering used by the teachers who are here to share their stories. Analyses of this information give us insight into students' growth in many 21st century capacities.

A word of caution, however, is in order. My conclusions about students' growth are just that. And Pat Burrows's conclusions in accordance

Figure 1.2 Multiple Means of Assessment

Teachers in this volume will present us with a wide variety of means of assessment:

teachers' observations of classroom behaviors;

teachers' reflections/analyses of students' work (using districtwide or individual assessment criteria and rubrics);

students' journals, notes, and work products;

students' thoughts, ideas, and questions recorded on Google Docs, wikis, iPads and other electronic devices; and

students' reflections on their work—written, oral, and recorded on video.

These means will direct us to evidence of growth in the following 21st century capacities:

inquiry,

problem solving,

critical/creative thought,

cognitive development,

reflection,

teamwork/collaboration, and

self-direction/resourcefulness.

with the Catalina Foothills School District's 21st century scoring rubrics are hers. In all cases cited here, I agree with the teachers' conclusions, but you may have doubts and would want to raise questions about these conclusions.

Good!

Here's what to do with these questions:

1. Discuss them during a teacher study group considering assessment of these important capacities.

2. Jot them down in your own inquiry journal, and try to find some answers, preferably with your colleagues.

3. Ask the teachers themselves. If you send me the questions (jbarell@ nyc.rr.com), I'll forward them to the teachers mentioned herein.

4. Your ideas. . . .

RELIABILITY AND VALIDITY

We should always raise questions of reliability and validity when considering evidence or data that purport to tell us something significant. This is true for evidence about change or growth in our children's capacities to think, to inquire, to reason, and to grow stronger as persons. This is perhaps especially true when we are examining, as we are here, data primarily from teachers' observations, students' self-reports, and students' work projects. We are not relying on standardized tests. They have their all-too-significant role in our educational lives, but they do not in many cases provide us with the information we seek about 21st century capacities. They are limited, one-time glimpses at students' abilities in, for example, reading comprehension and mathematical skills. For this they have their value.

We are interested in growth over time that is not currently measured by these kinds of tests.[1] You will read in subsequent chapters about growth within distinct units, during a year and between Grades 1 and 5 (see Travel Journals in Chapter 6).

RELIABILITY

The reliability of a test refers to its consistency of measurement. Do we get the same results time after time? In different settings? At different times? This is a vital part of the scientific process, to redo the tests of somebody who claims, for example, that a meteorite presumably from Mars has evidence of ancient life. Or that chocolate (heaven forbid!) has deleterious qualities within it.

When we speak of the reliability of a particular service (e.g., energy) we want to know, Will it be there when I need it, consistently, safely?

When we speak of product reliability (a car or dehumidifier), we want to know if it will perform up to standards, consistently and safely. In other words, will it perform as advertised?

When we speak of the reliability of sources, we're asking, Is the information they are providing believable, trustworthy, unbiased? For example, if we read a restaurant review, we should ask, Are these objective, reliable sources, or are the reviewers the parents and children of the owners? Are the doctors we see on television reliable sources of information about the products they are selling—or are they, in fact, the creators of these products and therefore biased in their favor?

Are the teachers quoted herein trustworthy observers of their own students? Or are they biased because they want to see growth and development? We speak of interrater reliability in terms of grading students' papers. We could ask here if other teachers, people like yourselves, would interpret Rachel's work (see Chapter 10) in the same way. Would you conclude that she had developed her ability to construct good arguments using appropriate analogies and comparisons, for example?

And we need to ask, Are students reliable sources of information about their own thinking, feeling, and growth? Will they consistently provide us with information related to how well they can solve problems and work through complex situations? Or are they just telling us what they think will earn them credits and praise? Is Sydney a reliable source when she claims, "My inquiry skills shot through the roof" (see Chapter 8)? I think so, and so does Kerry Faber, because we have seen the evidence in the classroom over time and within several work products.

VALIDITY

And we should ask, Is the information from teachers and students valid? Validity here has to do with the question of whether we are actually observing what we think we're observing. A valid test of a drug claiming to lengthen life must actually evaluate its power to add months and years to our lives (the Fountain of Youth drug!).[2]

For data about inquiry to be valid means that we have to be observing students' spontaneously asking questions, their own questions, not their copying somebody else's questions. For information about critical thinking to be valid, we must be observing students actually engaged in thinking critically as defined by the teacher and/or the district—and doing so on their own, not merely in response to a given test or prompt.

For data to indicate that students are improving in problem solving, they must reflect students' actually solving problems they have never seen before, ones that call for them to use a variety of approaches on their own, without copying from a manual.[3]

Look at John Selkirk's and Pat Burrows's district rubrics for critical thinking (see Chapters 1 and 10). They give good, observable indicators of what they consider critical thinking, in part drawing reasonable conclusions with evidence to support them. Is this what you're seeing in Rachel, Pat's exemplary student? Or is it something else?

Self-reports are, it seems to me, good, reliable indicators of what students have experienced, and we too seldom consider them in attempting to understand what learnings have occurred. These may reflect what some have called the "collateral learnings," what students learn while being in our classrooms that might not be in our lesson/unit plans. Others have called these outcomes part of the "hidden curriculum."

We can rely on students' journals and the reflections therein if we think they are being straightforward and not merely telling us what we want to hear.

I am raising all these questions because we should approach all data like that in this book with that certain skepticism we define as critical thinking. I'm sharing the questions with you because I consider them valuable in and necessary to determining students' growth. We all should be raising these kinds of questions about interpreting data from students and teachers.

One final word about evidence gathering is in order: We should have a *representative* sample of *relevant* students' work. We cannot say that Rachel has improved in her critical thinking if we have only one essay to show parents. We need multiple sources of information gathered over time that reflect different kinds of challenges. This is another reason why we cannot rely on any standardized, one-time test to indicate students' growth in these all-important 21st century capacities. In figuring out the crime scene event in Chapter 8, Kerry Faber's students needed more than one piece of evidence. They required multiple pieces of information to confirm their conclusions.[4]

A DISCLOSURE MODEL

So why are these questions important? They are important because the purpose of this book is to suggest ways that we can gather reliable and valid information about students' growth with 21st century capacities. What I hope we have in this book is a disclosure model for certain 21st century capacities, a model that communicates ways of doing the following:

1. define what these capacities are within a sound educational, philosophic framework;

2. specify the observable, performance behaviors (often in rubrics), asking, What does it look and sound like in our classrooms, on the playground, at home? and

3. design ways of observing, monitoring, and drawing conclusions about these capacities.

With this disclosure model we want to be able to communicate results to our students (they should be in on the decision-making process as well), teachers, administrators, parents, and members of the community. We must be able to sit down with parents, members of boards of education, and the voting public to say, "This program [be it Partnership for 21st Century Skills (www.p21.org/), STEM, International Baccalaureate (www .ibo.org), or an inquiry-and-problem-based learning initiative] is worth our effort. And here are results we have to support our conclusions. We have gathered this information directly from students' reflections about and our observations of their own work. We can see evidence of students' growth from unit to unit and from year to year. It is vital we continue with these programs, provide needed resources, and support our teachers in pursuit of their goals."

We cannot rely only on standardized tests to provide the data we need. These tests (though easy to administer and grade with Scantron machines) often have deleterious effects when we are continually pressed to show specific results in a given time with a specific cadre of our students.

CONCLUSION

Each teacher has experimented with learning experiences that challenge her students in ways that reflect what they know and are capable of doing.

I hope that these vignettes will reveal several issues about assessing our students' abilities and understandings:

1. The nature, quality, and planning of assessment experiences are very important instructional decisions. We need to make many of them before we commence a unit, but not necessarily all of them. Planning for excellence (otherwise known as planning units of

instruction or curriculum development) and performance indica- tors (otherwise known as rubrics) are essential to any consider- ation of students' growth.

2. There is a wide variety of alternative, authentic ways to learn what our students are capable of and what they understand, far different from standardized or paper-and-pencil tests.

3. Who is assessed is an important equity issue. In other words, do we consider all students capable of the kinds of inquiry on which this book focuses? For years I've been concerned that we challenge only students within certain groups with the highest levels of inquiry, problem solving, and critical/creative thinking. All students deserve and need the kinds of challenges the teachers here are presenting.

4. How we use information gleaned from assessment experiences should guide our instructional processes and ought not to be used primarily for ranking students in accordance with national or state criteria. Ainsworth (2007) has called this use of data "predictive value."

5. The quality of the assessment experiences reflects the levels of intellectual challenge to which we hold our students. There are vast qualitative differences between the kinds of culminating expe- riences some of our students receive and those from a problem- or project-based learning environment. It is safe to say that we still have students who are assessed using tests of their abilities to memorize stuff, not to solve authentic, significant, and meaningful problems like the ones you are soon to read about.

6. Assessment is an ongoing process. We are always gathering infor- mation about what students do and do not understand and making appropriate adjustments. This occurs before, during, and after instruction because we are always taking in information, analyzing it, and drawing conclusions—perhaps within the blink of an eye!

These are just a sample of the many concerns and issues we shall encounter as we delve into various teachers' stories.

ENDNOTES

1. Indeed, there are standardized tests of critical and creative thinking designed by Torrance, Ennis, and others. I have used these, but it is very difficult to set up effective research using control and experimental groups, especially in high schools.

2. To be valid, patient selection must be randomized with comprehensive follow-up: "We'd want to see that the duration of follow-up was sufficiently long to see the outcomes of interest. It is also important that the investigators provide details on the number of patients followed up and if possible, on the outcomes of patients who dropped out of the study" (Centre for Evidence-Based Medicine, http://ktclearinghouse.ca/cebm/practise/ca/therapyst/validity2). My wife, Nancy, and I recently received such a pamphlet full of claims that human growth hormones would have these Fountain of Youth results. I wonder.

3. When we asked second and third graders how they would teach friends to solve problems, after they had worked on various authentic classroom problems for weeks (e.g., preventing graffiti in their bathrooms), they said, "Make it littler . . . get to the main problem . . . ask a friend, look at the problem from a different angle . . . work it out on a piece of paper . . . believe in yourself" (Barell, 1995, p. 168).

4. Some districts are administering the College and Work Readiness Assessment, a test that does present authentic problems to students. And we can look to this to give us some data about students' growth during high school, for example.

REFERENCES

Ainsworth, L. (2007). Common formative assessments: The centerpiece of an integrated standards-based assessment system. In D. Reeves (Ed.), *Ahead of the curve—The power of assessment to transform teaching and learning* (pp. 79–102). Bloomington, IN: Solution Tree.

Barell, J. (1995). *Teaching for thoughtfulness—Classroom strategies to enhance intellectual development* (2nd ed.). New York: Longman.

Barell, J. (2007a). *Problem-based learning—An inquiry approach.* Thousand Oaks, CA: Corwin.

Barell, J. (2007b). *Why are school buses always yellow? Inquiry preK–5.* Thousand Oaks, CA: Corwin.

Teacher Modeling

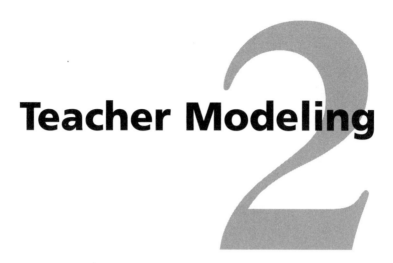

Teacher Inquisitiveness: "It was the blind leading the blind!"

FLIGHT 335 TO DALLAS

Recently, I was at LaGuardia airport ready to board a plane to Minneapolis. It was September 11, 2008. I hoped this would be a routine flight.

But what caught my attention was the gate attendant for a flight to Dallas who announced a limitation on the number of passengers able to fly.

"Flight 335 from New York to Dallas will be limited to 130 passengers. All those who can delay their flight plans will be provided with a coupon worth $300 anywhere in the United States. Please see me at the counter."

Now, that's odd, I thought. Why are they limiting the flight to a certain number of passengers? Does it have to do with excess baggage? With the weight of passengers?

What could be causing this restriction? I asked myself.

When the gate attendant had finished his commentary, I approached him.

"Excuse me," I said. "I'm just wondering why you're limiting capacity on this flight."

He replied, "Hurricane Ike is in the Gulf, and we must fully load the plane with fuel in case we have to take evasive maneuvers."

On hearing this explanation, what might have been your follow-up comments or questions?

My next question was, "You mean to tell me that planes leave here and elsewhere without a full tank of gas?"

"Yes," he replied.

More oddities. More assumptions questioned.

"How many passengers does the plane carry?" This was an MD-80, and its capacity was 140. So they were going to reduce their passenger load by 10 to carry the extra fuel.

My journal for this day recorded the following reflection on this event:

"Possible reasons for reduction [in passenger capacity]: 1. Too much luggage 2. Cost of fuel 3. Storage capacity?"

None of these explanations seemed adequate, so I later asked another desk attendant who said, "All flights must balance fuel and passengers."

This was a revelation as I was not too aware of just how airlines calculate relationships of fuel, baggage, and passengers.

The next entry was, "I wonder if WWII B-17s always took off with full load of bombs and fuel" for flights into Germany or over the Pacific.

I relate this story because of the importance of modeling whatever behaviors we wish students and children to engage in.

If we want them to grow up curious, we model asking good questions about the world, about people, and about their relationships.

If we want them to work cooperatively, we are always looking for opportunities to engage in sharing ideas and solutions to problems. "Let's see if we can figure this out together."

So when I do workshops on fostering inquisitiveness within schools, I always begin by sharing my own inquisitiveness.

MY INQUIRY JOURNAL

The above story and journal entries are typical of what I share with educators.

And then I began looking over some of my entries during the course of one or two years, all kept in various notebooks I always have with me.

What I learned recently was that my journal entries often look for causes by asking, "Why?"

Why can the plane carry only 130 passengers when its capacity is 140?

Why did security in a different country allow a man to avoid sending his bag through the x-ray machine? ("Diplomat," I was told, except that the briefcase had no markings on it to designate such a mission.)

Why did we fall into a deep financial abyss in 2008, leading to the worst recession since the Great Depression?

How could we have missed the Christmas 2009 bomber with explosives in his underwear so many years after 9/11?

I'm very intrigued by how things come about, what causes things to happen.

So in workshops, I'm always providing participants with opportunities to ask questions about artifacts I share with them.

OBSERVE, THINK, AND QUESTION ARTIFACTS

These exercises work best if students are examining stuff related to their current studies, be they sea shells, pictures of various topographical features, different hats, original documents, or the like.

An exercise like this could also be the prelude to a larger unit of study, say on habitats, change, predator/prey, and growth.

Participants examine these artifacts using the Observe, Think, and Question framework (see Figure 2.1). What do you see, feel, hear, taste (well, not so often), and smell? What do these observations remind you of in your prior knowledge? What concepts, ideas, facts, and feelings do you have that relate to what you're observing? Then, what questions do you have?

Figure 2.1   Observe, Think, and Question

Observe: Look closely at the artifact (whether it be a three-dimensional physical object, a passage from a book, or an episode within a video). Note what you can verify as true for all observers, that on which everybody can agree (e.g., it's round, it's green, and it has lines encircling it). Be sure to distinguish between these verifiable observations and inferences.

Think/Feel: Of what do your observations remind you? What connections are you making between the observations and that which is in prior knowledge? What feelings does the artifact engender?

Question: What curiosities do you have about the object? Which questions would you ask an expert if you wanted to understand this object, its context, source, consequences, and the like?

And yes, sometimes we pose questions immediately. Where are they from? Who found them? What are they made of? And that's fine. Note questions whenever you experience them. But I'll want to know what observations led to the questions.

This is also an excellent opportunity to school folks in the differences between observations—that on which we can all agree, that are verifiable—and those thoughts that are clearly inferences: "Something lived inside . . . they're very old . . . they lived in shallow tropical waters. . . ." These thoughts reflect tentative conclusions based on the direct observation of evidence about the shells themselves.

Very recently, I've used the seashells that I've picked up on our beaches in Southampton, New York. Nancy and I collected many over the years to the point that all of our windowsills were covered. But then some years ago, the shells disappeared from our beaches.

Why?

Participants ask questions using the Observe, Think, and Question format. Then they select their best questions.

Next we ask, "What do we do with all these questions?" Teachers suggest that we classify, find similarities and differences, prioritize, and conduct research.

Workshop participants then read several paragraphs about these shells to see which questions are answered and to generate new ones.

Next, we move into unexplored territory by consulting the Three-Story Intellect (see Figure 2.2) and asking questions we haven't asked. "I see that we have no comparison questions, as in Level II. We have no what-if/speculative questions as in Level III."

"Let's ask a question, in our groups, that we haven't asked before."

Then, of course, we share all our findings.

During the whole process, we have been writing in our inquiry journals. Recent research from Singapore (Towndrow, Ling, & Venthan, 2008) indicates that when students regularly write questions in their journals and discuss them, they improve. After just six weeks of this recent study, researchers found that students' questions became "bolder and more adventuresome" (p. 282). They also discovered that inquiry led to understanding the scientific content, the nature of matter.

WHAT HAVE WE LEARNED ABOUT OUR OWN QUESTIONING?

As a final exercise, I ask participants to respond to this question: "What have you learned about your own questioning processes here?" This is, for me, an essential question, one stemming from many years of personal

Figure 2.2 Three-Story Intellect

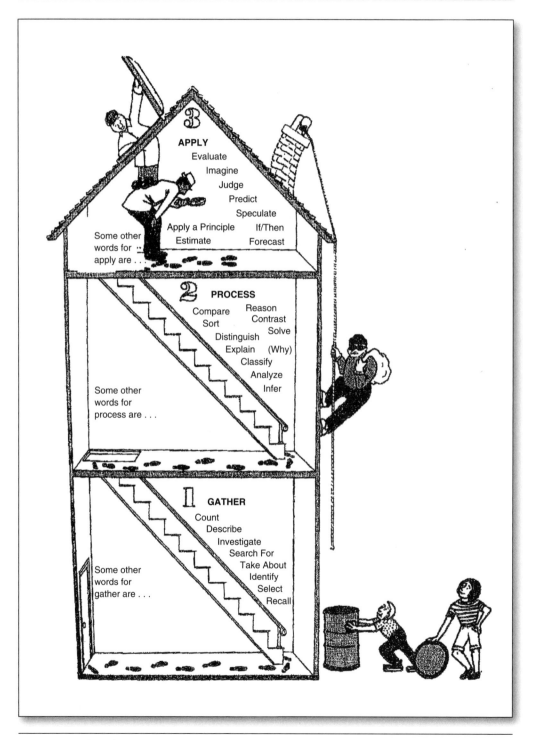

Source: Fogarty (1997).

reflection but also one mindful of what Socrates is supposed to have said: "The unexamined life is not worth living." It also stems from what John Dewey (1938) described as having "an experience," that is, what we learn by reflecting on what we've done, searching for causal links, patterns, connections, emerging feelings, and the like.

Reflection of this kind is what puts us in control of our ship of state because we learn what we're doing and not doing, what we're good at, and what we might want to get better at.

Here are some of the participants' responses:

"I work best when listening to others' questions."

"Questioning isn't one of my strengths. Don't do it enough."

"We found that one question led to another. Building upon each others' [sic] thoughts." (Participants work in observational groups.)

"I usually ask Level I questions and then proceed to more complex as we discuss them."

"I'm not comfortable working in a group. Too distracting. I can't concentrate."

"We get a lot of different perspectives this way."

"Having time to ask questions is great, but where in the day do we find the time?"

"I don't care about shells and didn't find this interesting."

"Wasn't very interested initially, but as we listened, bounced ideas off each other I found myself becoming more intrigued by these shells."

"I start off with Level I questions and often move to more complex ones."

"Sometimes, if I'm not interested, I'm not very good at asking questions."

"I hesitate to ask questions in public thinking they might be stupid."

As you can see, there are several issues raised by these observations.

But what's even more important to me here is that educators are reflecting on their own inquiry and investigative processes. We are learning how we observe, think, and question—the kinds of questions we do and do not ask without prompting.

Why is this important? It's vitally important if we want to encourage inquiry and investigation within our classrooms to be able to share with our students, to model our own ways of asking questions, some of our frustrations (e.g., not everybody is interested in what we're studying), and how we benefit from sharing our observations and questions with colleagues. It's not really effective (nor is it, I think, fair) to challenge students to pose questions when we do not do so openly ourselves. We model what we want students to do.

FAMILIARITY WITH INQUIRY

"Questioning isn't one of my strengths." We might make this observation as an adult without realizing that growing up, for most of us, was a continual process of inquiry, from our first days of looking at mobiles suspended above our cribs or seeing something very strange and trotting off to explore it—a fish tank with tropical black mollies and silver-tinted angel fish inside.

Some of us lead lives so full of having to get things accomplished—teach classes, raise children and drive them hither and yon, work full-time in an office—that we do not pause to reflect on what we've been doing with a quizzical bent. (Smell the roses, watch the stars, and wonder.)

I mentioned above that I usually keep notes in a journal. In fact, I keep more than one journal going, one for daily notes and reflections and one for a particular project. These provide me with a reminder to take some time to ask the following:

What happened today that I think is important and why?

How do I feel about these events?

What might I want to do about it?

What am I noticing that is strange, perplexing, different, or problematic, and what action do I want to take?

What did I learn today?

What are my projects, and where do I wish to take each one of them—what are my goals?

Did I ask a good question today?

The latter question, of course, comes from Sheindel Rabi. Every day on her son's returning from school (at a young age) she would ask him, "Izzy, did you ask a good question today? That difference—asking good questions—made me become a scientist" (Sheff, 1988, p. A26). And asking good questions could transform how we conduct our lives in classrooms and at home.

ASKING LEVEL I QUESTIONS

This is the most logical place to start when we're investigating something that is new or different, something that challenges our assumptions about life, something that is just intriguing:

What is it? Where does it come from? How does it work?

At the Museum of Natural History, there is a film on the fourth floor where all the dinosaur fossils are (TRex, Barosaurus, and others) about the evolution of life on earth narrated by Meryl Streep.

In an early sequence, we see very strange animals that lived hundreds of millions of years ago (strange whale- and fish-like creatures in the oceans), and then we see fossils emerging from sandy soils, perhaps in the Gobi desert where so many dinosaur bones have been found.

Streep asks, "When did they appear? Where have these animals come from? How are they like others?"

Then she says, "These are the questions paleontologists ask." She refers to very introductory, fact-finding questions that require us to gather a lot of information and then engage in the more complex, Level II process (see Figure 2.2 on page 33) of analysis to determine age, relationships, and perhaps times of extinction.

So as with all new phenomena, we need the facts—just as we are taught that in writing a lead for a news article, we must answer the questions suggested by Rudyard Kipling in the *Just So Stories* (1902):

I keep six honest serving-men

(They taught me all I knew);

Their names are What and Why and When

And How and Where and Who. (www.kipling.org.uk/poems_serving.htm)

Sometimes we can answer these questions immediately, as with reading a news story.

But for interpreting the origins and nature of fossils from the Gobi, it will take more complex thinking to arrive at reasonable conclusions. Here, for example, is a fossil found very close to the South Pole. It's this long, this wide, and with these colors and textures. But we aren't immediately certain what this one bone is related to in terms of the animal's overall bone structure. We aren't sure to which others it might be related.

With some more complex thinking we can determine that this Antarctic fossil is related to other dinosaurs from 200 million years ago.

What conclusions might we draw beyond this identification?

Finding a fossil in Antarctica leads us to conclude that dinosaurs lived on several continents: North America, Asia, and Antarctica. Antarctica's climate was once hospitable to warm-weather animals such as dinosaurs. And we think that Antarctica was once located way north, nearer to where the state of Texas is today (about 700 million years ago in a landmass known as Rodinia).

So facts are important. We cannot reason without them, although you will certainly be able to find those adults (perhaps in media and politics) who seem to violate this rule daily. As former senator from New York Daniel Patrick Moynihan said, "You have a right to your own opinion, but not to your own facts."

But if we stop here at Level I, gathering information, then we have short-circuited our mind's desire and ability to use this information to reason toward conclusions.

For example, the other day I was guiding two of my friends through the Hall of Planet Earth at the American Museum of Natural History. We were in that section given to how the earth creates mountain ranges and changes. On either side of us were models of the different plate boundaries, showing subduction of one plate beneath another (as in the Chilean earthquake of 2010); divergent boundaries, where the plates spread away from each other as in the Mid-Atlantic Ridge; and transform boundaries, where they grind past one another perhaps at the rate of one inch a year. The latter boundary is exemplified by the terrible 2010 earthquakes in Haiti.

In this area, there were three high school students from one of the city's more prestigious private schools. Suddenly one asked me, "What's convection?"

Before I could ask them questions in return, my friend read the definition from a nearby plaque, one explaining how plates move by convection currents generated by heat at the center of the planet, just like what happens when water boils on the stove.

Then I asked what they were going to do with all the information on the fill-in-the-blank forms attached to their clipboards.

"We'll turn it in then go on to doing a project on something we're interested in," said one of the young men. They were interested in investigating various kinds of volcanoes or the sulfide chimneys where, in total darkness, more than 200 species of animals thrive.

The pattern to note here is gathering information at an exhibit (or from a book, iPad, or newspaper) and handing in the papers for the teacher to grade without any analysis of what convection is, how it operates, why it's important, and how it might affect other aspects of life on the planet. In this case, getting the facts needs to lead to more thoughtful engagement with the content. Allowing students to gather information and just hand it in without engaging in Level II processing of data could lead to quick forgetfulness and lack of deeper understanding.

Sometimes Kipling's How and Why questions require lots of thought and do not necessarily appear in the first paragraphs of the news story because they take time to figure out: Why did we suffer such a colossal economic meltdown in 2008?

GROUP PROCESS FOSTERS INQUIRY

When we engage in inquiry as I've described above, collectively examining artifacts, generating questions, asking different ones, and reflecting, we will often note how our questioning and thinking have been modified by the group.

Different Perspectives

One of the most important observations from those I've cited is the one referring to different points of view: "We get a lot of different perspectives this way." What we know about working in groups is that we want them to be heterogeneous for problem solving for this very reason. We want to hear different points of view on the same topic. We know from research about creativity that better solutions come from flexibility of thinking, that is, taking and offering varied perspectives on a problematic situation. We learn from others' unique backgrounds and insights.

"I'd never thought of it quite that way," is something we will often hear during the reflective experiences mentioned above.

Confirmation Bias

The other side of this coin, however, is what we call "confirmation bias," or the tendency in many of us to prefer information or perspectives that agree with our own ideas. Thus, we might believe only evidence that confirms what we already believe in or seek company of those who agree with us. The latter is a most common human trait. We'd rather dine and converse with those who generally agree with us than with those whose point of view is quite different. We'd rather read editorials that support our general outlook on life.[1] We spend precious little time asking, What's the other side of this issue? What am I missing? It's worth our time and effort to do so.

The other comment that we hear very often is that the inquiry process is definitely fostered by working in groups where people hear others' ideas and build on them, thus taking the thinking in new and unexpected directions.

"We were building upon each other's ideas."

This is the kind of inquiry process we wish to foster in all of our classrooms:

We listen . . . think and reflect . . . add on or build on others' ideas.

You will hear comments like these again from some of the Sandusky students reflecting on their science, technology, engineering, and math (STEM) projects.

We might also provide ideas and evidence that contradict somebody else's offerings. And we should be encouraged to offer the other side of the coin, a different angle on the same situation. You will learn about students' becoming better at raising these kinds of questions in Kerry Faber's classroom during crime scene investigations (see Chapter 8).

This is how we grow intellectually, by challenging our own well-developed ideas and perspectives, not by resting on what's familiar.

IT'S TIME CONSUMING

Another comment heard very often during these hectic days of fulfilling all sorts of local, state, and national mandates is, "Where do we find the time to luxuriate in this kind of questioning?"

Yes, indeed, where do we find the time to allow students to examine artifacts closely, generate questions, share them, and then, building on each other's ideas, go on to ask better questions that can then guide investigations toward a summative product?

The answer is in the planning. We must plan for excellence. The process might take place during one forty-minute segment of a day's teaching or stretch over the course of several days. But if we do not think of it beforehand, if we do not carefully map out time for these experiences, they likely will not occur. Additionally, we must identify those performance indicators (rubrics and frameworks) that give us guidelines for the qualities of achievement we wish our students to attain.

In Chapter 4 we will describe a curriculum-planning process that will take these comments into account. Suffice it to say here that during our curriculum-planning meetings with teammates or on our own, we must think of what we want students to be able to do by the end of a unit and by year's end as well.

Once we have an idea of our intended outcomes, we plan how we will achieve these and plan access to resources (e.g., artifacts); time for inquiry, thinking, and drawing conclusions must be part of this.

One participant recently noted, "Questioning processes like these are *legitimately* time consuming."

Yes they are, and we need to be diligent and mindful during planning to create opportunities to engage with stuff—artifacts and the like from which students can generate meaningful observations, reflections, and questions.

In sum, the social processes we have described are excellent for students' beginning to feel comfortable posing questions, challenging each other's ideas, and generating new perspectives on experiences. These are the kinds of experiences we can and should be working on at the beginning of each year so by the time we embark on a lengthy inquiry unit, students know how to ask questions and feel comfortable sharing them and then working in groups to find answers and draw reasonable conclusions to share with others (see Chapter 3).

Just before asking participants to share their inquiry journals about what they've learned about their own thinking, I refer to another reflection of long standing.

Years ago I read an item about then CEO of Microsoft Bill Gates. He used to get all kinds of upbeat reports from various divisions of the company: from Word, Excel, and PowerPoint; from sales, marketing, research, and the like. They would often be very positive about productivity, how well Microsoft was doing.

But—and perhaps this is why his company has succeeded so phenomenally well—he pushed back from his computer and asked a question: "What aren't they telling me?"

In other words, What's the other side of the coin? What evidence contradicts what they're telling me? What are the challenges not mentioned? What are the areas where we need to improve?

When I mentioned this during one workshop in Texas (at the convention for teachers of the gifted and talented), one gentleman reminded us all of how this comment reflected what one quarterback in the NFL said. "We may have a 14-0 record, but we need to look at the areas that need improvement," said Drew Breese before leading the New Orleans Saints to victory in Super Bowl XLIV.

I recognize my own confirmation bias, especially when it comes to socializing with friends, and I sometimes struggle to see the other side of any story that reflects well on candidates and policies I favor. It's hard work to look at both sides of an issue.

We get morning newspapers (yes, we still read real newspapers), and each represents a different political point of view. It's important to know both sides, but I'm not here to say it's at all easy to read ideas and gather information that tends to contradict one's favorite point of view.

"I DON'T LIKE THIS!"

Sometimes I hear from folks who are uncomfortable with the exercise, with asking questions, with sharing them in public or with colleagues. It is possible that more people have these feelings than share them with me during a school or large-group session.

This may reflect their own discomfort with being inquisitive. They may have grown up in a culture that does not reward or encourage questioning. I've heard, as I'm sure you have, of parents who want their children to be obedient, not to ask rude questions, especially of adults.

We know there are differences in how children are raised. Richard Nisbett (2009) has recently summarized some of the foundational research by Betty Hart and Todd Risley, psychologists who conducted extensive observations in the homes of professional and working-class parents and their interactions with children. They found significant differences in the language used by different groups of parents.

For example, professional families "talk to their children more than working-class parents do . . . include the child in conversations . . . speak about 2,000 words per hour to the child" (Nisbett, 2009, p. 86), whereas working-class parents speak about 1,300. Professional families read to their children "much more than does the working-class parent. . . . From a very early age the middle-class child expects to be asked questions about books and knows how to answer them" (p. 88).

In some families, "the child is supposed to pay attention, and comments or questions are regarded as interruptions" (Nisbett, 2009, p. 89). In some families you hear questions such as What? Why? and What if? whereas in other families you hear more commands and directions.

Thus, some of us might grow up with encouragement to ask questions, to allow our imaginations to play with characters in stories, to engage in speculative questioning about possibilities. Kids love this kind of word play. But some parents do not encourage it. (I am reminded of stories from Richard Wright's childhood in *Black Boy*. His questions about family, race, and culture were seldom encouraged and often actively discouraged.)

Some of us grow up without the encouragement I received from my grandfather, a scientist who delighted in pointing out discrepancies and puzzles to me such as "Why do you suppose the sun appears larger while setting on the horizon than at its zenith?" We loved playing these question games—"Did you ever wonder?"—together.

"MY QUESTIONS MIGHT BE STUPID"

Lindsay's honest reflection leads us to consider how we feel about our questions. Some of us, myself included, have had feelings that a question we have within a social group might be interesting but that others might consider it stupid. So we maintain our silence.

I felt this way in graduate school at Columbia University. Sitting in a class full of New York City teachers, all of whom were working toward master's or doctoral degrees, I would think of a question, my heart would immediately begin to pound, and I would shelve the question until after class for a one-on-one with Ann Lieberman or Gary Griffin.

After many weeks of small-group work during which I could listen to others' questions and respond to them, I realized that my questions were just as good as anybody else's, so my apprehensions gradually waned, and I spoke out more often.

We hope that we, and our students, will spend sufficient time in groups with others of like and different backgrounds and experiences that we will learn that we can make very positive contributions and not be overly worried about asking "a stupid question."

TEACHERS WHO MODEL INQUIRY IN THE CLASSROOM

Here are the reflections of outstanding educators who have spent a long time modeling inquiry and their own curiosities for students. Each reflects the value of this required first step for herself as well as for students.

Kerry

Kerry Faber from Edmonton (Ekota School) recently shared with me the following about her own inquiry processes. She now teaches sixth graders.

> I know I ask more questions—deeper ones. Ones that have to be mulled over for a while and then discussed with someone else or [that might] result in a search in literature or an online source (like a newsletter/journal). I know I model more curiosity with the kids. I am also not afraid of their questions or intimidated by them if I haven't a clue as to what the answer could be OR if there is an answer. Our questions can take us on some wonderful "rabbit trail" searches that open up doors to learning I

hadn't planned on when starting out. (K. Faber, personal communication, March 2009)

Notice that Kerry says, "I am also not afraid of their questions or intimidated by them if I haven't a clue as to what the answer could be OR if there *is* an answer [italics added]."

I vividly recall my days teaching *Othello* to freshmen at Montclair State University. One day a young lady asked a question about Desdemona. I hadn't a clue about how to answer her question and dodged it by saying something evasive like "Let's take that up tomorrow."

Obviously, I needed time to become much more familiar with the play.

That was a long time ago. Now, I hope that I'm more like Kerry and others and can say, You know, I never thought of that. Let's find out, shall we?

At the time, I thought I should know the answer to the question, but I had reread the play only twice prior to embarking on the unit in English 101. So part of our growth is certainly due to comfort with the subject as well as with sharing our wonderings with our students.

Liz

Liz Debrey, a fifth-grade teacher from Whittier International Baccalaureate School in Minneapolis, was one of the first educators to share with me progress students had been making on becoming better inquirers. Here she shares with us the importance of being a good observer:

To be curious, you have to notice things. Once I started becoming a better observer, the questions came. This did not come naturally for me. My family has always dubbed me The One Who Never Notices Anything. As an adult learner and a teacher of inquiry, I have started to notice and observe my surroundings more. Simply by paying attention to my environment, I have come to take more of an interest in certain things that might not have interested me before. An example is the placement and size of the white pines in the Superior National Forest by my cabin. Once I started noticing the density of the forest versus the sparseness of the forest, I was able to ask questions of myself about fires that have ravaged the area and when maybe they had occurred in the past. I am then motivated to find answers to the questions that genuinely interest me. The important thing for me now is that because I have become more of an observer, and inquirer, I am able to model and encourage observation in my students which, in turn helps them to ask better questions. (L. Debray, personal communication, September 2011)

As we have noted, curiosity is often the result of very careful examination of our surroundings. Liz's observations and subsequent questions reflect what every scientist, reader of good literature, and art lover realizes, that when we look very closely at stuff, we are likely to be struck by little or large oddities that will intrigue us.

STEM TEACHERS—"THE BLIND LEADING THE BLIND!"

As you will discover in Chapter 9, sometimes we as teachers are challenged to engage projects that are quite different from what we're used to. We do not bring a whole lot of experience to the task.

This past year, teachers who supervised the STEM projects on building model roller coasters and habitats on Mars and creating marketing plans for the Cleveland Indians baseball club found themselves out of their elements.

"The teachers were out of their comfort zone. This was a super learning experience—to work outside of our own comfort zones," one teacher from Sandusky, Ohio, told me in a telephone interview.

"It was the blind leading the blind! We worked through this with the students," another person said.

I find these shared reflections to be amazing and heartwarming.

I find them amazing because it isn't very often that we as educators are in the position of being out of our comfort zones. Several years ago I joined Outward Bound for a week's adventure in the Penobscot area of Maine. One of its mantras was stretching us (we were all educators of various stripes) beyond our comfort zones.

And I find them heartwarming because I'm considering what these teachers are modeling for their students. I can just hear several conversations in the team planning groups: "Well, I don't know any more about designing a roller coaster that will draw a specific g-force on the human body than you do, Tony! What do you think we should do here? Let's dig into what might attract teens and tweens to the ballpark together. I'm no marketing expert [an art, math, literature, or PE teacher might say]. We're in this together, pal!"

Imagine how you would have felt had you been assigned to a team with your seventh-grade teacher and you observed these behaviors and sentiments.

Let's work it out together! We're all in the same boat.

You would have felt that your own insecurities had been validated, and more important, you might have felt very powerful—"We're in this together. Let's find some ideas and answers."

You would never forget that teacher, I bet.

This is, in part, what learning is all about, stretching our thinking beyond our knowledge boundaries, going out of our intellectual and emotional comfort zones, to experience the novel, intriguing, and mysterious.

CONCLUSION

When I ask teachers what the purpose is of modeling our own inquisitiveness, they invariably point to many good reasons:

1. Students model what we do;

2. We want to reflect our own inquisitiveness, openness to new ideas, persistence in searching for answers, and ability to listen and collaborate;

3. It's OK not to know everything—nobody does;

4. We are vulnerable; and

5. We are still very curious, wondering people.

Our wonderings are what make us vital, alive, and human, capable of taking a question of interest and pursuing it into new, unexplored territories.

And modeling our inquisitiveness is a *sine qua non* of establishing that open, invitational environment wherein students feel comfortable taking the risk to raise their hand to ask you or a classmate a question.

Some of my unanswered questions now are, How do I become more open to perspectives and ideas different from my own? How do I move beyond my own biases? When is it important to be open to others' ideas? and, from a very successful hedge fund manager, "What am I missing?" (Cassidy, 2011, p. 2).

ENDNOTE

1. In 1921, James Harvey Robinson wrote in *The Mind in the Making* that "most of our so-called reasoning consists in finding arguments for going on believing as we already do" (p. 41). He called this process of self-confirmation "rationalizing."

REFERENCES

Cassidy, J. (2011, July 25). Mastering the machine. *The New Yorker, 87*(121). www.newyorker.com/reporting/2011/07/25/110725fa_fact_cassidy?currentPage=2

Dewey, J. (1938). *Education and experience.* New York: Macmillan.

Fogarty, R. J. (1997). *Problem-based learning & other curriculum models for the multiple intelligences classroom.* Thousand Oaks, CA: Corwin.

Monastersky, R. (1991, April 27). Married to Antarctica—New theory proposes an ancient wedding between North American continent and the lonely polar continent. *Science News, 139*(17), 266–267.

Nisbett, R. E. (2009). *Intelligence and how to get it: Why schools and cultures count.* New York: Norton.

Robinson, J. H. (1921). *The mind in the making.* New York: Harper & Brothers.

Sheff, D. (1988, January 19). Letters to the editor. *The New York Times,* p. A26.

Towndrow, P. A., Ling, T. A., & Venthan, A. M. (2008). Promoting inquiry through science reflective journal writing. *Eurasia Journal of Mathematics, Science & Technology Education, 4* (3), 279–283.

Creating the Invitation-to-Risk Environment

During this study of students' growth in 21st century capacities, I have had the pleasure of working with kids in Grades 1 through 6 in the United States and in Canada.

As I reflected on what I've attempted to do in each of these classrooms, it occurred to me that I was walking into learning environments where teachers had done an exemplary job of creating settings where students were very willing to participate, to ask good questions, to listen and respond to each other, and to risk expressing their ideas about whatever topic we were discussing.

This is important because without their preparation I wouldn't have enjoyed myself as much as I have.

In two of the schools, I was videotaped modeling different inquiry-based lessons. At Mulgrave International Baccalaureate School in West Vancouver, British Columbia, I taught in Grades 3, 4, and 6. At Parkside Elementary School in Austin, Texas, I taught Grade 4 and made presentations on my Antarctic exploring experiences. You can see these videos at www.morecuriousminds.com/videos.htm.

What I hope these episodes demonstrate are different inquiry approaches to be discussed at great length subsequently:

modeling my own inquisitiveness;

using Observe, Think, and Question with artifacts and pictures;

using problematic situations to foster inquiry and achievement;

using KWHLAQ (see Figure 4.2 in Chapter 4);

listening and responding to each other's ideas and comments;

thinking critically about content;

working productively within small groups and teams; and

being nonjudgmental.

MODELING OUR OWN INQUISITIVENESS

When I ask teachers what are the significant ways we have of fostering students' growth in these 21st century capacities, skills, and mind-sets, many invariably respond, "Modeling."

I usually share my own story of growing up curious, fascinated with Antarctic adventures and the expeditions of Admiral Richard E. Byrd; meeting Admiral Byrd; and sailing south on his flagship *USS Glacier* (AGB-4) during Operation Deep Freeze.[1] At Parkside, Kim Connor invited me to share this experience with all K–5 students, and this was a terrific challenge. It was most exciting because not only was I able to model my own questions about this most fascinating, intriguing, and mysterious continent (Do you know where she's been on her wanderings across the planet for the past 700 million years?) but I was also able to encourage the students to ask a lot of questions on their own ("Why don't fish and penguins freeze in the water?").

I share with educators, in addition to these experiences, my many fascinations with current events, nature, and books:

How do we accept more responsibility for the well-being of the planet and all creatures thereon?

How did we get into the financial messes we're still living with?

Why is current fiction so dominated by stories about vampires and the supernatural (making it very difficult for writers of regular adventure stories to get published)?

How will we ensure productive use of our new technologies (e.g., iPads) in schools?

What will happen to the ice in Antarctica as the result of global climate change?

These are the questions that come to me today, July 15, 2011, as I work on this chapter here in New York City.

THINKING JOURNALS

I always have my journals ready to hand. I do not write in them every single day, but when I'm relaxing and in a pensive mood, I will take one of them up and jot down current projects, my short-term and long-range goals, and any questions I have about these subjects. And I'm always on the lookout for situations that pique my curiosity: "Why does the Towhee bird like to eat from the ground and not fly up to the bird feeder we have near our patio? Other birds that regularly visit, the Black-Capped Chicadee, the Chipping Sparrow, the Cardinals and Blue-Jays, they all use the elevated bird-feeder up six feet off the ground.[2] I assume it has to do with this species' ways of adapting and evolving over time."

Jodi Baker, a good friend and curriculum coordinator, worked at a school where the principal agreed that teachers' learning about their own inquiry processes was important. Their decision was to purchase for all their teachers modest but respectable journals and to encourage all to use them during special faculty meeting sessions each month. In this way teachers became more aware of the kinds of questions they asked and from whom they had learned about being inquisitive (see Barell, 2007).

QUESTIONING, LISTENING, AND RESPONDING

When I was on a visit to Heights Elementary School recently, Gayle Baisch asked me to model how we can get students to interact among each other more positively.

During lessons with faculty and with fourth graders about Mars exploration, I found myself asking questions and then engaging in the following:

JB: What do we know about the planets?

Mark: Neptune is like Jupiter.

JB: How?

Mark: They both have storms. They are both gas planets.

JB: Who agrees with Mark? [Sally, David, and Emily raise their hands.]

JB: OK, Sally, why do you agree with Mark? [Sally explains, speaking to the teacher.] Sally, please tell Mark. [Sally, somewhat shyly and taking a second breath, redirects her attention to Mark.]

JB:	Who else agrees with Sally and Mark? Why? [We continue the process of students' listening and responding to each other, not to the teacher.]
JB:	What else do we know about planets?
Jessica:	I know how Saturn got its rings.
JB:	Oh, that's interesting. How did Saturn get its rings? [Jessica gives her reasons.]
JB:	Emily, do you agree with Jessica?
Emily:	Yes, I agree with Jessica because . . . .
JB:	Anybody else?
Harry:	Well, I disagree because . . . .
JB:	Please tell Jessica.[3]

And so it goes. We attempt to create a web of social responsibility and interaction where the old game of asking, telling the teacher, and asking again is broken. It's like kids playing basketball, tossing the ball among each other, not just back and forth between two players.

CREATING A PROBLEM-ORIENTED CURRICULUM

Kerry Faber teaches Grade 6 at Ekota School in Edmonton, Alberta. During the first two or three days of school she presents her students with a number of problematic situations to figure out. This she does because the whole year is going to present challenges to question, analyze, and figure out how to respond to complex, intriguing, perplexing, problematic situations. In Chapter 4 we will work these into the curriculum, but here, in the first days of a new year, we want to communicate to students what our high expectations are.

Recently, Kerry played Twenty Questions with her students, a game she plays early and often to introduce good questioning in pursuit of figuring something out. After placing a magnifying glass in a box, she invited the students to determine what was inside by asking good questions. Kerry shared this observation with me: "There were questions like, 'Can it be placed in a drawer?' and 'Would you use it to make something look bigger?' I had to think for awhile when asked, 'Is it commonly found in a family home?' I know a lot of people have one but I have many ethnic groups represented and some of them might not have one as a standard tool in a home. I ended up saying, 'Yes'" (K. Faber, personal communication, September 8, 2011).

Kerry uses this kind of game to help students become more adept at asking good questions, using the Three-Story Intellect as a guide (see Figure 2.2). In Chapters 7 through 10 you will see how others use more complex problems to challenge students to inquire and think productively.

But very early on in her class, Samantha learned an important lesson: Samantha said, "She's not answering us, guys. We have to ask her the right questions to get her to ask some questions so we can figure out the answers to our questions."

> "She's not answering us, guys. We have to ask her the right questions to get her to ask some questions so we can figure out the answers to our questions."

Kerry's summative comment was, "Wow— only four days have gone by—they catch on quickly!"

The lesson for her students is that they're going to have to learn how to think for themselves. They're not in class to sit quietly, hands folded, listening, taking in information, writing it down, and repeating it on Friday's quiz.

This understanding comes as the result of four days of constant modeling and challenging students to think through various kinds of problems, including how to order school supplies from a catalogue. Already one student, Jona, has asked, "What challenges are going for this year?"

SMALL-GROUP TEAMS

In Chapter 9 we will have occasion to visit with teams of sixth-, seventh-, and eighth-grade students engaged in solving authentic problems as part of their science, technology, engineering, and math (STEM) project. STEM projects are a high national priority right now for a variety of educational and political reasons. In Chapter 9 we will see students grappling with learning to work with others. This concept of teamwork is very important today because so much work involves working with others. I love the story of former president Gerald R. Ford's interviewing candidates for positions in his administration. He had one very important criterion: ability to work on a team. He judged applicants' credentials, in part I'm sure, on whether they had ever served during World War II[4] or had been on a varsity sports team. He had done both with distinction.

We need to consider the criteria for successful teamwork. What do they look like in our classrooms?

SETTING HIGH EXPECTATIONS
FOR CRITICAL THINKING

John Selkirk teaches first grade in Ottawa, and he has a notable goal: challenging students to think critically. Figure 1.1 on page 17 represents his rubric for this process.

He challenges students to interpret pictures of people expressing themselves, showing their feelings.

"What can you tell me about this character?"

"She's feeling sad."

"How do you know?"

And the child gives her reasons. At the beginning of last year (2010) he had about six students who could do this.

During the year he was watching and listening for students to learn how to ask questions of each other:

"She's feeling sad?"

"How do you know?" another child would ask.

We can report as of this writing that some students did learn how to use evidence to draw conclusion and others began reflecting John's modeling by asking each other, "How do you know?"

LEARNING ABOUT OUR OWN
21ST CENTURY CAPACITIES

The general principle here is that if we believe in educating for 21st century capacities, we must model them in front of our students. This will mean doing the following:

1. identifying the 21st century capacities we deem important;

2. observing them in our own lives, perhaps through keeping our own inquiry journals;

3. reflecting on our own practices of inquiry, problem solving, and critical/creative thought. (How do we pose and solve problems and think critically about stories in the media? Are we, for example, good at identifying the other side of the coin, evidence that contradicts our own points of view? To what degree are we comfortable

recognizing and questioning assumptions that challenge traditional ways of doing things? How often do we identify perplexing, intriguing situations that might represent problems within established ways of thinking and doing? In other words, what do we do well, and what do we struggle with? What do we wish to improve on?)

Unless we become very familiar with how our own minds engage 21st century skills, we are not able to model these skills for our students.

SHARING CONTROL WITH OUR STUDENTS

"What does the sun look like from other planets?" This question from Jasmin Ramzinsky's third-grade class at Parkside Elementary School in Austin reflects how any classroom can be turned around almost on a dime by simply challenging students to assume more control of their own learning.

How do students do this? They do this by being encouraged to ask good questions and pursue purposeful investigations about problems or intriguing questions.

And how do we encourage students to get interested and excited enough to pose questions about a subject we have to teach?

First of all, teachers must be willing to model their own curiosities about the subjects we teach. If we aren't curious, why should our students be? Modeling tells our students that we are inquisitive, that we don't know everything, and that asking good questions and searching for answers is very exciting! And this is what we do throughout life.

For a unit on the solar system Jasmin's students read a short book, and she wondered, "Why is Pluto no longer considered a planet? What is a 'dwarf planet'?" These questions led off the unit with the guiding question, Is Earth the only planet with life?

These teacher wonderings sparked other curiosities from students:

"How did the sun get into space?"

"How many galaxies are there?"

"What's a nebula?"

"How big do asteroids get?"

"How many seasons are there in space?"

"Is it legul [*sic*] to color with markers on the moon?" and, my favorite,

"What does the sun look like from other planets?"

You can imagine their excitement, total engagement, and purposefulness as they researched questions to which they wanted answers.

Before Jasmin adopted this inquiry-based approach, she would assign students questions; they would then dutifully conduct the research and write one- or two-page papers as directed.

After completion of this solar system unit, Jasmin asked her students to comment on how this new approach compared with what they did previously and answer questions she posed for them. Here are some of their comments:

"Mrs. Ram, that doesn't make any sense. Why would you ask questions about my planet? You weren't doing the research, I was."

"Mrs. Ram, I bet your kids kinda got bored with finding the answers to your questions."

"Mrs. Ram, how did you know what your kids wanted to research? Did you ask each kid before you wrote the list of questions?"

Indeed, why do we assume we can dream up the kinds of questions our students would be intrigued by? (Because we have stuff to teach, to "cover"?)

Teachers who afford students an opportunity to pose their own questions related to the designated content report that students become

1. more highly motivated,

2. more engaged intellectually and emotionally, and

3. more in control of their own learning and, thereby, more responsible for achievement.

As a matter of fact, this problem-based/question-based approach led one student to tell her mom that now she was "in charge" of her own learning.

Jasmin's story has a lot to do with establishing the welcoming, invitational environment. She has created instructional challenges where students feel comfortable not only posing good questions but also gently chiding her for the assumptions she has been making all along (http://morecuriousminds.blogspot.com)!

21ST CENTURY CONCLUSION

So why do we need to be concerned if we want our students to grow up to be inquiring problem posers and solvers who can think creatively and critically without being told what to do at every moment?

The answer is just this: We need to model and create those structures and opportunities for students to take risks that will lead them to new territories where we all make mistakes but where we always learn.

Later on in this volume you will read about many amazing educators at all levels of schooling, those who have challenged their students to inquire, solve problems, think critically and creatively, and grow in the process. Had they not established the invitational environment, their students, in the case of Pat Burrows's eighth graders, would not have grown from "cookie-cutter A" students who avoided risks and just tried to guess what was on the teacher's mind to become much more self-directed, self-assured risk takers whose growth we can observe in a wide variety of ways.

The invitational environment is something we must attend to in the first weeks of school if we wish to see students growing and developing their 21st century minds.

So during the first days of school we can do the following:

1. model our own inquisitiveness;

2. challenge students to ask questions and help them figure out differences in intellectual demands made by each (Factual Recall, Deeper Analysis, Speculation);

3. communicate high expectations for students to solve problems collaboratively and alone;

4. provide opportunities for students to work together and learn about best practices within small groups;

5. coach students in responding to deeper, more probing questions and not resting comfortably with short, one-word (and too often) "correct" answers—for this we must ask questions at more complex levels;

6. help them listen to and respond to each other, not just to the teacher; and

7. encourage them early on to reflect on and write about their learning experiences for the day, guided, of course, by your priorities: What am I learning about math/science/books/art? What am I learning about my own questions and ways of thinking/solving problems? and What do I wish to improve on during the year?

ENDNOTES

1. You can read this story in *Quest for Antarctica: A Journey of Wonder and Discovery* (Barell, 2011). See www.morecuriousminds.com for paper and e-book references.

2. According to the Cornell Lab of Ornithology, "Eastern Towhees are birds of the undergrowth, where their rummaging makes far more noise than you would expect for their size" (www.allaboutbirds.org/guide/eastern_towhee/id).

3. For this creative retelling, I have used the actual statements and questions from Coral Boudin's fourth-grade classroom at Heights Elementary. The class was part of a KWHLAQ (see Figure 4.2 in Chapter 4) assessment of students' prior knowledge about the solar system and Mars in particular. And this is a process I learned from my Montclair State University colleague Matt Lipman, creator of the excellent critical thinking program Philosophy for Children.

4. Like most men and women of "the greatest generation," we seldom heard about President Ford's heroic actions to save his aircraft carrier, USS *Monterey,* from sinking during a terrible typhoon in the Pacific. His actions helped save the ship.

REFERENCES

Barell, J. (2007). *Why are school buses always yellow? Teaching inquiry preK–5.* Thousand Oaks, CA: Corwin.

Barell, J. (2011). *Quest for Antarctica: A journey of wonder and discovery.* Lincoln, NE: iUniverse.

Curriculum for the 21st Century

PEOPLE WHO CAN INVENT

Noted *New York Times* foreign affairs columnist Tom Friedman is often one of this country's leading advocates of 21st century skills and capacities. That is, he's one of the few telling us that we must leave the old models of stand-and-deliver content behind and prepare our students for a very different world.

For example, recently he wrote about "the start-up you." Jobs in this country will (and now do) call for young employees to be able to do more than merely fulfill the requirements of any job: showing up, filling the job description adequately, and the like. More is demanded now in this globalized economy: "Employers are, in the current recession, 'increasingly picky. They are all looking for . . . people who not only have the critical thinking skills to do the value—adding jobs that technology can't but also people who can invent, adapt and reinvent their jobs every day, in a market that changes faster than ever'" (Friedman, 2011, p. A47).

He goes on to say that employers will be asking, "Can he or she help my company adapt by not only doing the job today but also reinventing the job for tomorrow?" (p. A47).

In other words, you must add value by helping to create new practices, processes, and products. You have to be entrepreneurial and innovative. These are the information careers of today and tomorrow.

IMPORTANCE OF A PROBLEMATIC SITUATION

What this means is that education for the 21st century must lead our students toward being citizens like those in the Sandusky, Ohio, projects (see Chapter 9) who were constantly thinking—to use their term— "outside the box," having to be creative as they worked to redesign the roller coaster or create a habitat for living on and exploring Mars.

All the teachers you have already read about and will meet in this volume have a core set of beliefs about education, ones founded on current research. And what this research says is that to become a productive, thoughtful contributor to society, one must encounter challenges that stretch one's thinking and being beyond what might have been expected. Again, as one teacher from the Sandusky science, technology, engineering, and math (STEM) projects said, teachers and students were stretched and pushed beyond their "comfort zones."

Other teachers, such as Lorraine Radford, Kerry Faber, and Pat Burrows, have learned that to enable their students to think, to invent, to be critical, they have to challenge them with problematic situations that encourage them to ask questions and conduct purposeful research.

> "Learning should be organized around authentic problems and projects that are frequently encountered in non-school settings" (Bransford, 2000, p. 77).

As John Bransford (2000) has noted, "learning should be organized around authentic problems and projects that are frequently encountered in non-school settings" (p. 77).

These "authentic problems" are designed within a structured learning environment complete with goals, assessments, strategies, resources, and technologies.

"DOING IT IN THE MARKET IS BETTER THAN IN A TEXTBOOK"

Jennifer Montgomery teaches second grade at Parkside Elementary School in Austin, Texas. This past year (2010–2011) she claimed amazing results by introducing problematic situations to her students. Not only did they become highly engaged inquirers, but their performance on state assessments improved.[1]

First with a unit on creating a market economy, then with one designing zoo habitats for African animals, Jennifer saw her students' participation and learning improve quite dramatically compared with their performance with more traditional (less problem-oriented) ways of teaching these subjects.

In a unit that integrated science, social studies, math, and language arts, Jennifer's students were charged with the problem of building "zoo exhibits for each continent. Our class is responsible for African animals. And when we're finished, we will teach what we have learned to our first graders."

How different this is from reading textbooks about these animals, drawing their pictures, and describing them to classmates.

Jennifer has presented a problematic scenario, a complex situation that challenges students to ask good questions, conduct purposeful research, and arrive at conclusions (see Figure 4.1).

Figure 4.1 illustrates a model problematic scenario, that of saving the ocean plant and animal life. Such scenarios or problematic situations generally have these characteristics: They are

ill structured—there is no clear path toward one correct solution;

open to multiple interpretations—each student may approach this differently;

characterized by doubt, difficulty, and uncertainty[2]—this is what fosters thinking: not knowing precisely how to approach or solve something;

complex—it contains many facets and important elements;

robust—embedded within the scenario are important curricular concepts, ones reflecting essential questions and understandings;

fascinating, intriguing—it sparks our interest because of its novelty, and novelty leads to wonder and exploration; and

researchable—we can find information to help us solve the problems.

So creating a zoo exhibit presented to Jennifer Montgomery's young students this kind of challenge: to inquire, to think, to solve the problems, and to create something to be proud of. She might have worded it thusly: "Our current zoo is way overcrowded, and animals are, therefore, in some danger. You and your teams are responsible for creating a new zoo habitat for African animals. Your new habitat must be safe, be suitable for each different animal, and demonstrate your understanding of how each survives. You will share your models and thinking with representatives of the Austin Zoo and Animal Sanctuary." (In fact, Jennifer's students became "zookeepers" and shared their new knowledge about animals and habitats with their first-grade friends.)

The first time Jennifer embarked on this kind of construction research project with aquatic animals and their habitats, she said, there was no problematic situation, and the questions were "small details and they had

Figure 4.1   Model Problematic Scenario

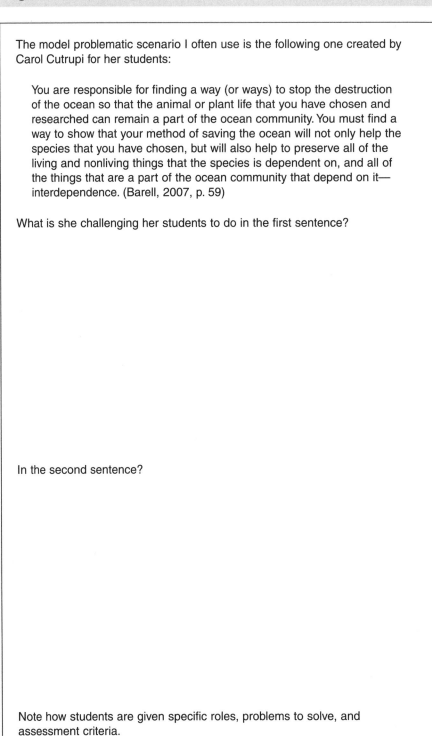

The model problematic scenario I often use is the following one created by Carol Cutrupi for her students:

> You are responsible for finding a way (or ways) to stop the destruction of the ocean so that the animal or plant life that you have chosen and researched can remain a part of the ocean community. You must find a way to show that your method of saving the ocean will not only help the species that you have chosen, but will also help to preserve all of the living and nonliving things that the species is dependent on, and all of the things that are a part of the ocean community that depend on it—interdependence. (Barell, 2007, p. 59)

What is she challenging her students to do in the first sentence?

In the second sentence?

Note how students are given specific roles, problems to solve, and assessment criteria.

no questions about important topics like 'Where does this animal live?'" That project had "no world purpose/problematic." (See Appendix A for an appropriate rubric for this and other problematic challenges, especially related to the mathematical aspects of creating fact plaques for each exhibit.)

> But by this time a year later, her students were full of enthusiasm for the project, and the first day saw these activities: "There were lots of questions about the project itself (what materials will I use?, will I have a partner?, etc.) and questions about animals (What do they look like? Which animals live in Africa? How do they protect themselves?) Kids wrote their own questions on sticky notes, we sorted them into questions about the project and questions about the animals. We learned about the continents and labeled a world map during social studies and did zookeeper math problems during math. (J. Montgomery, personal communication, May 2011)

Jennifer had an approach that met a need for students to go beyond their initial curiosities. During the research she would pause and ask her students, "What do we know now?" and "What do we still want and need to find out?" (see Figure 4.2 for an example of a long-range inquiry approach that incorporates Jennifer's questions).

Jennifer is here illustrating that we can use a rich inquiry approach such as KWHLAQ at any time during a unit. She has used it at the midpoint of the inquiry to give students an opportunity to ask deeper questions and ones that have resulted from their research.

Figure 4.2 KWHLAQ Framework

Here is a long-range inquiry approach that can be used at any time during a unit of instruction.

K What do we *think* we already know?

W What do we want and *need* to find out?

H How will we find our answers?

L What are we learning?

A How can we apply what we've learned?

Q What new questions do we have? (Barell, 2007).

"That's where the deeper questions came up. They needed to know about their animal first before they could wonder 'Why is it on the endangered list?' or 'How is this animal like another animal?'" (J. Montgomery, personal communication, May 2011). Very important questions.

And what of the results of their research, building the zoo exhibits for African animals? "The other big news is that they were able, for the first time, to take their questions/answers (notes) and write informational text that is interesting and organized. This text became part of the 'fact plaque' at each exhibit. That was our main literacy goal for this unit, so we're thrilled!"

You can imagine that at higher grade levels the challenges would have been appropriate for students' abilities and interests. But here the problematic got Jennifer where she wanted to be.

PLANNING FOR EXCELLENCE

Obviously, it takes more than a good, intriguing, and challenging problematic situation and rich resources to engage students like Jennifer's to such a degree. It takes sound planning.

For years we have been hearing about the rewards of "planning backwards," of "planning with the end in mind." These are sound curricular concepts that were articulated many years ago by Ralph Tyler in a seminal work titled *Basic Principles of Curriculum and Instruction* (1949). The slim volume was written, as I understand it, for one of his courses in curriculum development, and I used it as one resource in my own graduate courses by the same title.

What Tyler identified were basically four questions:

1. What educational purposes should the school seek to attain?

2. How can learning experiences be selected which are likely to be useful in attaining these objectives?

3. How can learning experiences be organized for effective instruction? and

4. How can the effectiveness of learning experiences be evaluated?

This is the table of contents of Tyler's important book.

By "educational purposes" he means educational "objectives," and these "objectives . . . become the criteria by which materials are selected, content is outlined, instructional procedures are developed and tests and examinations are prepared. All aspects of the educational program are really means to accomplish basic educational purposes" (Tyler, 1949, p. 3).

All of curriculum development since 1949 has been strongly influenced by Tyler's framework.[3]

The important differences we see today include stating our intended outcomes—our learning objectives—first and then considering how we would assess these objectives.

What kinds of assessment experiences can we plan, and what kinds of evidence will we require?

Wiggins and McTighe (2005) and others have rightly placed strong emphasis on teaching for understanding. How will we know that students have not only mastered facts about zoos and animals but understand, for example, why certain animals are on the endangered species list? One of Wiggins and McTighe's important notions is that from the very beginning of a unit we must think like assessors, asking, "What would be sufficient and revealing evidence of understanding?" (p. 151). Indeed, what will be sufficient and revealing evidence of students' growth in 21st century capacities?

My own interests have been in line with those of these educators ever since a math teacher told me that her students could get all the right answers but did not understand the basic concepts.[4]

Figure 4.3 is a planning document I use with educators, one derived from years of attempting to identify key elements in challenging students to think. You will notice that we start with a significant curricular concept, map out all of its potentially important elements or subtopics, and then decide which we wish to incorporate based on our assessment of students' needs and interests, which in turn is based on our knowledge of local, state, and national standards and our own sense of what's important.

LOCAL, DISTRICT, AND STATE/PROVINCIAL STANDARDS

It is here that some speak of fundamental standards, the ones that get to the heart of the subject.[5] Ainsworth (2007, basing his conclusions on Popham, 2003) identifies what he calls "power standards," those that are "high-impact" and "critical for students' success in school, in life, and on all high-stakes tests" (p. 87). Each subject will have its own power standards: in literature, for example, being able to read, comprehend, and analyze complex written materials and in science, being able to recognize problems, ask key questions, establish hypotheses, set up experiments, and test and evaluate results.[6]

It seems to me that our 21st century capacities would be examples of power standards within each subject, ones that challenge us to think

Figure 4.3   Planning for Long-Term Curriculum Development

"How do we plan for students' questions, use of local/state standards, objectives, strategies, and authentic assessments?"

I. Identify major content topic/issue/concepts within your unit.

(consult state curriculum standards)

II. Web out (draw a concept map of) major elements/factors you might teach:

III. Identify concepts/ideas/principles of major importance and lines of inquiry and enduring understandings—ones you must teach—consulting local, state, and subject matter standards as well as those you wish to add in accordance with students' needs, interests, and abilities.

IV. State your objectives, such as "Students will be able to . . ." (include intellectual challenges from Levels II and III of the Three-Story Intellect; see Figure 2.2).

V. Identify initial problematic scenarios ("You are a paleontologist . . .") that create interest, contain major content concepts—are "robust"—challenge students to think at Levels II and III, and can serve as summative assessments.

VI. Create assessments that are directly related to and dependent on the problematic scenario. What kinds of evidence will we use to establish that students have achieved deep understanding of the major concepts within the problematic scenario?

VII. Use the following strategies:

A. Initiating Experiences: How will we engage students' interests? How can the use of problematic scenarios generate early questions?

B. Core Learning Experiences: These include organizing our investigations, conducting research, thinking critically about results, and teaching different subjects directly.

C. Sharing Results and Assessment Experiences.

Note: This is a workshop material of my own creation.

deeply about the important ideas and concepts therein. For science, these key concepts might include force/motion, energy, and the structure and properties of matter. In language arts we would include literary genres such as poetry, the novel, short stories, myths/legends, and literacy processes such as expressing main ideas or themes, appropriately using figurative language, and presenting persuasive arguments.

Notice that I have not suggested creating a problematic scenario at least until we have thought thoroughly about the basic ideas and concepts to teach, ones that make the content robust. It seems to me that we should also think about what we want our students to be able to know and to do before designing an important problematic scenario.

Consider once again Carol Cutrupi's model problematic. What are the key concepts and ideas embedded within this scenario? What are the specific objectives she wants students to accomplish? How will they demonstrate the depth and quality of their understandings?

Here is a template for creating a problematic scenario:

Creating a Problematic Scenario

Grade Level   Subject

1. Identify major curricular concepts/ideas/principles/skills you wish students to engage. These will be embedded within the scenario.

2. Identify major intellectual processes students will use in working through the problem (Consult Levels II and III of the Three-Story Intellect; see Figure 2.2):

   a. problem solving,
   b. decision making,
   c. hypothesizing/creating experiment/testing, and
   d. creating a product.

3. Identify possible roles, settings, and circumstances for the scenario.

4. Create a "You are . . ." situation.

5. What are specific objectives within this scenario? How does it provide for various summative assessments?

Note: This is a workshop material of my own creation.

ASSESSMENT

With a problematic scenario (what others call a "performance task"; Wiggins & McTighe, 2005), we have our goals in mind. Now, we can think constructively about what kinds of information we will elicit from students to demonstrate deep understanding and, we hope, growth in our 21st century capacities.

What might these kinds of evidence be?

Students' work:

Input Evidence. What do students bring to the unit? What is the extent of their prior knowledge? In Chapter 5 we will consider several teachers' ways of conducting these investigations that provide initial foundations on which to build.

Process Evidence. How are students proceeding to figure out solutions to problems? Kelly Taylor in Catalina Foothills (Arizona) sent me students' notebooks (Grade 6) as they worked through problems in science, and she made a video of one exemplary student sharing his thinking (in dialogue with her) about how he arrived at his research findings. And in Chapter 7 you will see Lorraine Radford's exquisite method of collecting and recording kindergartners' questions during units on life in the sea. Oral evidence can be most revealing in whatever form it comes, and we can plan for it.

Other kinds of process evidence will come from students' artwork, graphic organizers, and the notes that accompany them.

Travel Journals. In Chapter 6 we will read about Jill Levine's use of travel journals with every student for every unit for every year of her K–8 school. These can be invaluable resources for units on any subject (solar system, writing poetry) as well as for important projects such as STEM (see Chapter 9) and the International Baccalaureate (www.ibo.org) exhibitions. Students, as you will see, kept these journals not only on paper but on wikis, Google Docs, and their iPads. They can be personal, informal, and reflective as well as highly structured (What did we learn today? What questions do you now have? How can we answer them? What learning experiences would be helpful now?).

Teamwork. What can we look for as groups of students collaborate on problem solving and research? What criteria of good group participation can we establish with our students?

Practice, Trials, Dry Runs, and Rehearsals. STEM students (see Chapter 9) had to do trial runs with their roller coasters and presentations to the

Figure 4.4   Graphic Organizer for Essential Question: How Is Space an
Active, Changing Environment?

We can use students' ongoing graphic organizers as real evidence of change
over time:

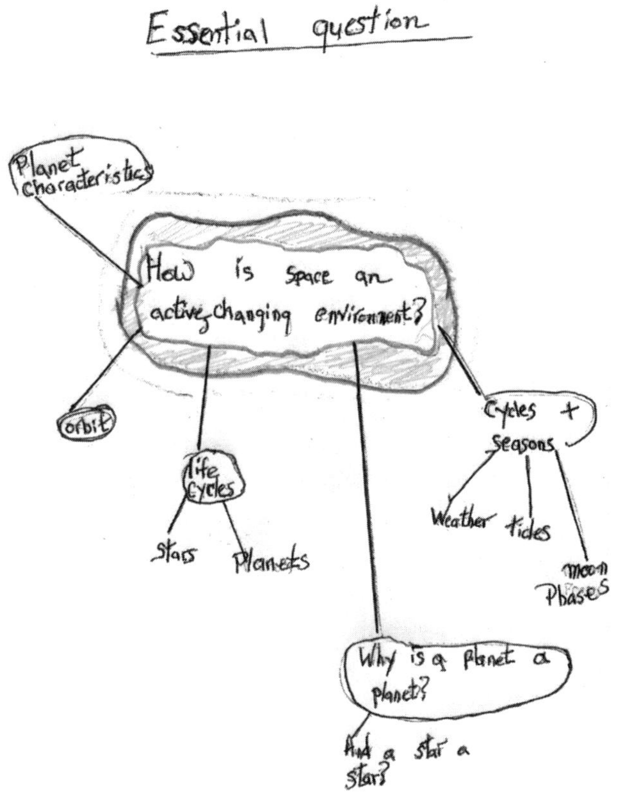

Planetary characteristics   Cycles + seasons [weather, tides, moon
                             processes]

Orbit   Essential question

                             Life cycles [stars, planets]

Why is a planet a planet? [And a star a star?]

As the unit progresses, Michael can add to this graphic, and we have
evidence (to be confirmed) of his changing ideas.

Source: Graphic by Michael Genovesi, Normal Park Museum Magnet School (2011). Used with
permission.

Cleveland Indians baseball team. These rehearsals, Grant Wiggins (1998) reminds us, are what adults do in the world of work, and they provide us with good formative assessments of students' progress as recorded in their performances, their journal reflections, and their teamwork.

Output Evidence. Anything students generate can provide us with evidence of growth: written essays, oral presentations, videos, websites, interviews, stories, culminating projects, and so forth. These are all examples of final products. We need to look within each one to identify the specific evidence we will need. Consider how Pat Burrows determined that one of her students had grown in the area of critical thinking. Consider STEM reflections on problem solving.

STRATEGIES

I have identified three aspects of our strategies: initiating, core, and summative/sharing experiences. The first may be the most important. How do we engage students' interests in oceans, zoos, civic responsibilities, ecology, or stories about heroes?

Initiating Experience. Most of us cannot just walk in and ask, "What do we know about coral reefs or heroes?" We need to create interest through any of the following means:

sharing of personal stories, trips, and wonders;

pictures, videos, and websites related to the unit;

visits to places such as museums or aquariums (see Chapter 7);

guests with experiences related to the unit (see Chapter 9);

close examination of artifacts related to unit concepts (I usually travel with my own set to introduce a unit on ocean ecologies).

Core Experience. After the initiating experiences, students are engaged in what International Baccalaureate calls "purposeful research." Here students are continually learning new information about which they need to think critically:

What am I being told?

Do I believe it and why?

Is this a reputable/reliable source?

Are the claims presented valid?

What evidence contradicts/disagrees with what I'm finding out? and

What conclusions can I draw?

Our core learning experiences will comprise some or all of the following:

small-group investigations and collaborations;

access to media, museums (see Chapter 7 for an excellent field trip), and personnel resources from the community;

large-group discussions of progress and new questions;

direct teaching of unit concepts and critical thinking skills;

initial reports from groups and feedback from others; and

rehearsals of final products and revisions.

Notice how Jennifer continued, during the core learning experiences, to ask students what they were learning and whether they had new questions. This is part of the KWHLAQ framework—to be continually reflecting on our initial questions and, perhaps, generating new ones.

Summative Assessments. These will consist of students' responses to the problematic scenarios, including whatever other forms of self-evaluation and teacher evaluation we need to use to determine students' depth and quality of understanding. The problematic Jennifer presented to her students—becoming zookeepers—and the performance with first graders was not her only assessment. She used the math rubric (see Appendix A) for this purpose. She also might have used a self-reflective format for students' writings as well as a group participation guide. In other grades, of course, we can use expository essays to accompany students' work with animals and their habitats.

CONCLUSION

Curriculum planning, or planning for excellence, requires time, and this is always at a premium.

Sometimes after I model a thirty-minute exploration of an artifact in a classroom, teachers will ask, "How can we get so much time for students to observe, think, and question?" (See videos of fourth graders' explorations of land erosion (www.morecuriousminds.com/videos.htm) with students in Jennifer's school.)

It is evident after such a question that long-range planning has not been as effective as it might be. Many units range in time from four to six weeks, and certainly within that time frame we can plan for initiating our students into the wonders of creating zoo habitats or exploring life in the oceans. We can do this with artifacts, slides, videos, and the problematic situation. But this takes time to plan.

If we are going to build curricula on John Bransford's (2000, p. 77) observation about the primacy of engaging students with "authentic problems and projects" (saving the oceans and designing new roller coasters—Chapter 9), then we need to plan, plan, and plan some more!

This requires that we identify the following:

1. What's really important within this unit that we want our students to inquire and think about over a period of time? What are the very important ideas, concepts, and essential questions that make the unit robust?

2. How will we go about initiating our students into an exploration of these ideas, these essential questions? What will engage their imaginations and their curiosities?

3. How will we organize our time effectively, allowing students plenty of time for inquiry, purposeful investigations, critical thinking about findings, and sharing our conclusions?

4. How will we observe and monitor students' daily, weekly, and monthly progress? As Crystal Martin (Grade 5, Heights Elementary, Ft. Myers, Florida) is now asking her students, "How do we know we're learning?" (C. Martin, personal communication, September 2011).

ENDNOTES

1. I understand that students' performances improved dramatically following the introduction of a problem-oriented math curriculum.

2. John Dewey (1933, p. 12) claimed that "reflective thinking . . . involves (1) a state of doubt, hesitation, perplexity, mental difficulty, in which thinking originates, and (2) an act of searching, hunting, inquiring to find material that will resolve the doubt, settle and dispose of the perplexity."

3. Most educators now recognize the importance of laying out what we want our students to be able to know, be, and do. During my graduate work I encountered one theorist (Dwayne Huebner) who objected to adults' overly controlling these intended outcomes to the detriment of students' having a

voice in their own learning. Hence, my own emphasis is on the important concept of control—who makes which decisions and when, believing with most educators in this volume that students deserve and need to have opportunities to make good decisions about their own learning.

4. Barbara M'Gonigle of Dumont High School led me toward working on approaches that would document the degree and depth of students' understanding. One experience we especially enjoyed was challenging her students to create analogies and metaphors for important concepts such as "the limit." Pat Burrows, Chapter 10, does the same with teaching critical thinking in eighth grade.

5. We know there are too many standards in each subject for us to deal with productively. So we have to be selective, choose the important ones for our students in our district, and add those of our own creation based on our knowledge of our students and the subject. These standards, as we are often reminded, are minimal standards. We can certainly exceed them.

6. As a college professor, I used to enjoy asking my colleagues this question: If you had one week to teach your entire course, what would you focus on? I think whatever they said would have reflected what they considered to be the power standards for that subject.

REFERENCES

Ainsworth, L. (2007). Common formative assessments: The centerpiece of an integrated standards-based assessment system. In D. Reeves (Ed.), *Ahead of the curve: The power of assessment to transform teaching and learning* (pp. 79–102). Bloomington, IN: Solution Tree.

Barell, J. (2007). *Why are school buses always yellow? Teaching inquiry preK–5.* Thousand Oaks, CA: Corwin.

Bransford, J. (2000). *How people learn—Brain, mind, experience, and school.* Washington, DC: National Academy Press.

Dewey, J. (1933). *How we think.* Lexington, MA: D. C. Heath.

Friedman, T. (2011, July 13). Op-ed. *The New York Times*, p. A47.

Popham, J. (2003). *Test better, teach better: The instructional role of assessment.* Alexandria, VA: Association for Supervision and Curriculum Development.

Tyler, R. (1949). *Basic principles of curriculum and instruction.* Chicago, IL: University of Chicago Press.

Wiggins, G. (1998). *Educative assessment: Designing assessments to inform and improve student performance.* San Francisco, CA: Jossey-Bass.

Wiggins, G., & McTighe, J. (2005). *Understanding by design.* Alexandria, VA: Association for Supervision and Curriculum Development.

CHAPTER 4 APPENDIX

Here's a rubric that Jennifer Montgomery and colleagues, Grades 2–5, used for problem solving. It can be used for math as well as for the kinds of problematic scenarios she created for the zoo habitat.

Problem-Solving Rubric: Grading
Grades 2–5

	4	3	2	1
Problem-solving strategy	___ Develops 2 or more strategies to solve problems using pictures, objects, numbers, and/or words	___ Develops appropriate strategy using pictures, objects, numbers, and/or words	___ Develops a strategy that does not work to solve the problem	___ No strategy is evident
	___ Extends understanding by using multiple strategies to solve the problem	___ Demonstrates complete understanding of the problem	___ Demonstrates little understanding of the problem	___ Demonstrates no understanding of the problem
	___ Shows advanced organization	___ Shows clear organization	___ Shows partial organization	___ Shows no organization
Communication of mathematical thinking	___ Clearly explains all the steps used to solve the problem with multiple strategies	___ Clearly explains all of the steps used to solve the problem	___ Explains most of the steps used to solve the problem	___ Explanation is somewhat confusing
	___ Explanation justifies why the answer is reasonable in multiple strategies	___ Explanation justifies why the answer is reasonable	___ Explanation somewhat justifies why the answer is reasonable	___ Explanation has little to no justification as to why the answer is reasonable

	4	3	2	1
Answer	___ Answer in complete sentence with a correct label	___ Correct label	___ Any label	___ No label
	___ All computations are correct	___ All computations are correct	___ No computational errors, but strategy does not lead to the correct answer	___ Computational errors that lead to an incorrect answer
	___ Correct answer	___ Correct answer	___ Incorrect answer	___ Incorrect answer
	I can teach it.	I know it.	I am still practicing.	I need help.
Scoring	[ ] × 4	[ ] × 3	[ ] × 2	[ ] × 1

Comments:

Action Plan: I will improve my work by:

1.

2.

3.

Grading Scale

WOW! : 100

27–25 points: 90
25–22 points: 85
21–18 points: 80
17–14 points: 75
13–10 points: 70
9–7 points: 65
6–0 points: 60

Source: Permission granted from Math Department, Parkside Elementary School, Leander ISD, Texas.

Preassessments

SITTING BY THE JUDGE

In considering how to commence this discussion about how we initially assess our students, I thought it would be fun to go to the dictionary. In this case I used the *Random House Dictionary of the English Language* (1967) we've had in our family for many years.

The meanings include, in this order: (1) to estimate officially the value of (property, income, etc.) as a basis for taxation; (2) to fix or determine the amount of (damages, a tax, a fine, etc.); (3) to impose a tax; and (4) to estimate or judge the value, character, etc. of; evaluate. . . .

Very interesting that the dictionary is speaking mostly of economics here, assessing the value of my house or damages thereto.

Where does the word come from? is always a question I'm intrigued by as my grandfather was keen on word derivations, or etymology.

"To assess" comes from the Middle English meaning to "assess a tax," derived from the Latin meaning "sitting beside a judge," from *assidere* ("sit by").

This is very intriguing. What does our current use of the word, especially in education, have to do with "sitting by" or to "assist in the office of a judge"?

Perhaps we use that word to reflect the work of an assessor, one who helped a judge affix value, blame, or extent of penalties (as in assessing a penalty in a sport).

How do we use the word *assess* now? To take a reading on students' knowledge and understanding of subjects. To gather information about what they know before, during, and after we teach.

Some of us, myself included, will not cotton too much to sitting next to a judge, because we do not much care to be considered primarily, or solely, a judge and jury about our students.

Therefore, current literature (Popham, 2008) asserts that students can play a "dominant decision-making role in determining whether to adjust their learning tactics" (p. 79).[1]

So we are not speaking here as judges but as coaches or guides leading the way into strange and wonderful lands of exploration and discovery.

COMMON PREASSESSMENTS

Engaging in determinations of value, worth, strength, and likeability is something we do on many occasions:

entering a new restaurant,

sizing up a new player on the team,

meeting a potential friend or date for the first time, and

seeing a new model automobile.

We are always assessing and making judgments. Experts, of course, do it very quickly using a wealth of background knowledge to form an almost instant judgment, as Malcolm Gladwell (2005) has pointed out in *Blink: The Power of Thinking Without Thinking.*

In education, when we make a preassessment, it almost sounds like one of George Carlin's comedy routines in which he poked fun at our uses of language, for example, when the gate attendant speaks of preboarding the airplane. (This makes no sense when you think about it!)

What we are speaking of here are our initial assessments, judgments about our students' abilities in many areas of knowledge, skills, and dispositions.

In this chapter, I would like to share a variety of preassessment experiences, ones that focus on inquiry, problem solving, and critical thinking. Then we will examine different forms of gathering information, from using PowerPoint presentations to introducing an inquiry question guide such as KWHLAQ (see Figure 4.2 on page 61).

WHOLE-CLASS ASSESSMENT OF INQUIRY

Jesse Mackay is a second-grade teacher I first met at the George P. Nicholson School in Edmonton, Alberta, Canada. While I was visiting the school to model inquiry in classrooms, she challenged me right off the bat to get her students to ask "deeper, more philosophic questions."

Needless to say, she gave me a very high challenge, and during a thirty-minute session during which students were studying comparative cultures—that day, Korea—I did my best.

But it wasn't until after we'd exchanged a few e-mails that she figured out that one way to get her average students to ask the kinds of questions she wanted was to give them ample time to take an important question, What if Mexico City turned into an ice cube? and discuss it among themselves to discover what they really wanted to know.

The new question, What would happen if the weather we experience in Edmonton suddenly happened in Mexico City? resulted from lots of back-and-forth discussion among these second graders. Recall our discussion of the efficacy of adults' working in groups during question experiences—how they became more interested and developed "deeper and more philosophic" questions as a result of their social interactions.

I mention Jesse's experience at the outset of this book on assessment to let you know just how demanding she is in setting very high expectations for her students.

Jesse eventually relocated to another school in Edmonton, Coronation School, an International Baccalaureate school where inquiry is a high priority.

On the very first day at her new school, Jesse decided to assess her students' inquisitiveness. Here's the way she described her experience with her combined Grade 2/3 class of fifteen students:

> The very first thing I asked the students to do on the first day of school was to look around the room and after a few minutes come back to their desk with a question (or more). They could write it down if they liked or just remember it to ask for a whole class discussion. My assumptions about children and development were drastically challenged during this activity. I had jars of candy, a water table with various materials around it and many interesting things on the walls and around the classroom. They didn't know anything about me either so I was expecting a flood of questions. (J. Mackay, personal communication, November 2009)

Jesse expected she'd be surrounded by students eager to know about stuff in the classroom as well as about her. She came into the class assuming that all kids this age were brimming with curiosities and all we needed to do was to provide an opportunity for them to share these questions with us and with others. But that's not what she discovered.

Some students had real difficulties forming questions, and others asked questions such as "Where are spiders?" and "How many motorcycles are there?"

REFLECTIVE PAUSE

Here I shall ask you to stop and reflect on what you've just read to formulate your own ideas and tentative conclusions. I offer these pauses every once in a while to emphasize the importance of considering what you've read and to think about it in relation to your own experiences.

What do you like and wonder about in terms of starting off the school year in this fashion?

What can we learn about the responses that Jesse observed?

What do you notice about the questions?

Perhaps you thought to yourself about the nature of the opening day experience—that it might be a good way to find out some important information about your students.

I'm sure you also have noted something about the nature of the questions these second and third graders asked her. What impresses you?

This is one of the important concerns we will discuss later: What are we learning from our assessments, and how do they suggest instructional learning experiences for the future?

Subsequently, I asked Jesse to share a few more details from this experience: "I don't remember all of the questions, but the two related to the map were 'What is the population of Quebec?' and 'How do you say "Yukon"?' The only other question I remember is 'I wonder who will tuck me into bed tonight?' Yes, they were all Level I of the Three Story Intellect. Truthfully I don't know how to account for what I observed" (J. Mackay, personal communication, November 2009).

We should note right here that presenting this experience to new students on the first day of instruction is a challenge to them for a variety of reasons, not the least of which is their comfort level with a new teacher. Perhaps they aren't used to thinking and behaving in this fashion. Maybe they don't yet feel comfortable with their new teacher to share what they really are curious about. Perhaps they are more comfortable (as were some of my high school students!) with step-by-step learning experiences, not ones wherein they could take the risk to ask a question. Some students like copying stuff from the board, and I can still remember the positive feelings I had very early on with filling out workbook pages.

WHAT TO DO?

In Chapter 3 we discussed how others establish a classroom culture that invites and fosters inquiry, that creates a risk-free environment within which all feel comfortable participating. All the actions I suggested, from modeling inquisitiveness and challenging students to solve complex problems to asking good questions and listening and responding to each other, can serve as preassessments of students' abilities. This is exactly what Jesse has done, introduced her students to the inquiry classroom with her search-and-question approach and taken a measure of their comfort levels with asking questions about what they found intriguing or puzzling.

What does she need to model? What kinds of routines will she establish, and how will she involve her students in the creation of the community of inquirers? For some of Jesse's students, what Lorraine Radford does with her kindergartners (see Chapter 7) will be most beneficial, modeling our own inquisitiveness and introducing the language of questioning. You'll see how Lorraine does it.

These are steps Jesse undertook upon reflection on the results of this Day 1 experience.

CRITICAL THINKING

John Selkirk teaches first grade in Ottawa, and I met him at a conference when he offered a definition of critical thinking he uses with his students: drawing inferences or conclusions and giving reasons. As he noted in an e-mail, he thought his students thought of it as, "You can say what you want but you have to give a reason for saying it." Figure 1.1 on page 17 is a rubric John uses to guide his instruction.

Early on, he told me, he had about six students who could draw inferences when the task was to look at a picture of a person and tell what he or she was feeling. For example, early in the year, "The other day we were looking at a book together and one student said that the person looked disappointed or sad. Another student asked how she knew that. The first student said that she could tell by looking at her 'eyes.' (Window to the soul and all that). They are young but the kind of comments they are making make it obvious that they can handle this type of learning and enjoy it" (J. Selkirk, personal communication, February 7, 2011).

John's preassessments came from reading stories, examining pictures, and having specific intellectual goals in mind for his students—to be able to improve at interpreting literature and, perhaps, human interactions in class through analysis of facial features and expressions. This involves the critical thinking process of drawing reasonable conclusions and being able to support them with evidence, one of the most significant 21st century capacities.

As the year progressed, John noticed that some students not only could draw inferences but also would follow through with the all-important question, How do you know? obviously from his modeling.

GRADE FIVE—FLYING PENGUINS

During a unit on polar exploration, Kerry Faber showed her fifth- and sixth-grade students a video of penguins flying through the air and landing in some faraway place. She allowed students to respond.

A few students right off the bat had doubts about the veracity of this film. They knew penguins had wings but doubted their ability to fly. Others were less skeptical, asking questions about where they were going and how long they flew.

A definition of critical thinking I often refer to is that of John McPeck: "Critical thought involves a certain skepticism, or suspension of assent, towards a given statement, established norm or mode of doing things" (1981, p. 6).

"A certain skepticism" suggests that we ask questions when we encounter claims, stories, or artifacts full of those doubts, difficulties, uncertainties, and perplexities that lead to thinking. It's similar to what scientists say they experience that leads to the statement, "That doesn't seem right." They say that, and the questioning about the natural world begins.

Which questions did Kerry's students ask about this video? Here are some of their responses:

Dani: How do they make it look so real? Are those real penguins? How do they record the penguins landing in a tropical island?

Sydney: Is this fake and if it is, how did they make this?

Shannon: What kind of penguins are those and are they real? Did they do that with computers and wires?

Jessica: What kind of penguins did this? My reaction—NOT REAL.

Rebecca S.: Are they actually flying and if so how?

Sarah: How did they get a shot of penguins near a warm island?

Rebecca L.: Why are the penguins flying to a hot tropical island?

Brendan: How could a penguin fly and what would he need to do this?

Kyle: Why did the people make this?

Because Kerry Faber had been modeling asking good questions during the entire year, I'm not sure we can count this as a preassessment except in the sense that it might have been a good application of all they've learned up to that point, an application of knowledge and capacities to an entirely new situation. In this case, it would have served as a good formative assessment.

CRITICAL QUESTIONING

We can give our students other problematic situations that might lead to assessments of critical thinking and questioning. For example, here's an intriguing situation: Your friend hit a ball through the neighbor's window.

You might ask your students, "What would you do in this situation?"

Think to yourself how you would respond (as an adult) in this circumstance.

If your students are like most adults to whom I give this situation, there's a bit of laughter and you can hear them saying, "Run!"

Once you receive some of their courses of action ("Go apologize; get your friend to apologize"; ask, "What's in *your* wallet?"; etc.), you will know whether anybody thought about this critically, to wit, did anybody ask, "Was the window open?" If it was open, then no glass was broken. The groans and looks of chagrin appear within the room.

Somebody else might ask, "When did this occur?"

Then you might share with your students McPeck's (1981) definition of critical thinking as a "certain skepticism" and see how many critical questions they can ask to analyze the situation, to determine what the real problem is.

Eventually, you might get students to challenge all of their assumptions about the nature of the window, your presence at the site of the accident (maybe you were at home), and when this occurred (maybe two years ago and you're just learning about it now on the telephone or in an e-mail).

Here are some other situations:

The classroom is too noisy for the teacher.

You arrive home and find the door locked with no one home.

You get lost in the mall.

While driving to Grandma's home for dinner, you have a flat tire and have no spare.[2]

We can assess critical thinking in so many ways that we're limited only by our desire to introduce students to this fascinating aspect of being an inquirer.

We need to prepare our students for all their roaming around the Internet, all their Google searches as each of them becomes—what one teacher in Edmonton called herself—"a real Googler."

STATE AND LOCAL STANDARDS

In elementary school here in New York City, we expect good readers to be able to

"Make and support warranted and responsible assertions about texts;

Support assertions with elaborated and convincing evidence

And draw the texts together to compare and contrast themes, characters and ideas." (http://schools.nyc.gov/offices/teachlearn/docu ments/standards/ELA/index.html#toc)

Thus, being able to analyze text, make comparisons, and draw reasonable conclusions about themes, characters, and ideas is part of what critical thinking is all about. What is too often left out of any mention of comparing and contrasting is the necessary subsequent step, that of drawing conclusions. That's why we compare and contrast, to make a decision about something, whether it is about texts or buying a new car.

Any of these critical thinking experiences can be used as preassessments, including the following experiences with websites.

CRITICAL THINKING
ABOUT DINOSAUR WEBSITES

I once sat next to a sixth grader here in New York City in Coney Island. He was interested in dinosaurs, so we did a Google search. As I reflect on this experience, I realize it could have been used as a good assessment of his ways of critiquing different sites.

We found one site similar to www.amnh.org where there were descriptions of dinosaurs living from the Triassic era (245 million years ago), through the Jurassic era (remember *Jurassic Park*), to the Cretaceous era and their extinction some 65 million years ago as the result, we now think, of a gigantic asteroid's crashing into the Yucatan Peninsula (probably aided by concurrent multiple volcanic eruptions).

On the next click of the mouse, however, the student came upon a site that claimed dinosaurs cohabited the earth with human beings and lived up until recently.

Both sites looked professional, well documented, and well organized. What was he to believe?

How would he determine which one to believe? Which one was presenting the latest scientific point of view and conclusions? I didn't ask on that occasion, but I would now.

After working with a few of these kinds of situations, supplemented by others you create and ones you find in newspapers, in magazines, and on TV, you can gather students' good questions and collate them into a class list: questions we can ask when trying to determine what to think, say, or do.

Among them might be questions about sources, evidence, dates/times, locations, motivations, definitions of terms, goals, and the like.

How do we know that what we're reading is in fact true?

What's the source, and when was this document prepared?

Who made the statement, and what are his or her qualifications?

What is the nature of the evidence presented in both sites?

Are there links to corroborating sites with similar kinds of evidence?

In *Why Are School Buses Always Yellow?* (Barell, 2007), I shared teachers' sets of questions gleaned from students:

I—Information?

W—Who/what does it involve?

O—Opinion or fact?

N—Natural impact?

D—Do we know enough about this?

E—Evidence/elements?

R—Real or not real?

These questions from Kerry Faber's fourth-grade classroom in Edmonton served her students as a guide when they were analyzing important situations.

ASSESSING INDIVIDUAL STUDENTS' CONCEPTUAL UNDERSTANDING

Michelle Thoemke taught at Elizabeth Hall International Elementary School in Minneapolis. While visiting there once, I stopped by her kindergarten classroom to see what she was doing with her special education students. We all sat on the floor, and some of the kids shared what they had been learning about the human body, even taking to acting out their excitement about bones and skeletal structures by stretching, rolling around on the carpet, and rather raucously having a merry old time.

Early in a subsequent year, Michelle related a lengthy conversation that tells us how we can assess individual students' thinking about a certain topic. In this case the story concerns what Michelle learned about a student's understanding of the concept of magnetism:

> We were doing a whole group activity, putting together a train track. I had been pulling the pieces out of the tub and putting them on the floor so the students could see what was there. There were lots of wooden tracks and 2 train cars.
>
> David noticed there were magnets on the trains and asked about them:

S: Do they stick like magnets?

T: Good question; how could we find out?

He put them together so the magnets were touching.

T: Are they magnets?

S: Yep.

T: How do you know?

S: They just is.

T: So you pushed them together and they are touching, but how do you know it is a magnet?

S: 'Cause they're stuck.

T: How do you know they are stuck?

S: 'Cause.

T: What could you do to show they are stuck?

S: [No response.]

Michelle continued, "I took two pieces of train track and pushed them together so they were touching."

T: Are these magnets?

S: No.

T: How do you know?

S: They aren't stuck?

T: But they're touching just like the train cars.

S: They're not magnets.

T: How do you know?

S: [No response.]

T: What could you do to show that they aren't stuck?

S: I could move them.

T: If they are magnets, what would happen?

S: They'd be stuck.

T: Try to move them.

He did and showed they weren't stuck.

T: OK. Let's look at the train cars again. What could you do to show they are stuck?

He reached forward, and Michelle encouraged him to pull on the first car.

T: That's a good idea; you could pull it like you pulled the track.

He did and showed they were stuck.

Having been in Michelle's classroom, I can picture her on the blue carpet with this student whom I'll call David, surrounded by the other kindergartners in her class, perhaps ten or more. From the walls are hanging large posters showing the human body, posters advertising Reading First, and early students' work.

REFLECTIVE PAUSE

What do you see Michelle doing here? What is she learning about her student's thinking?

One thing I noticed on reading this excerpt is that Michelle is challenging her student, David, to figure things out for himself. She did not say, "This is and this is not a magnet." She wants to see if he can solve the problem himself, thus holding out the highest levels of intellectual challenge for one of her special education students.

"How could we find out?" leads him to think to himself, *What do I do now? She's not telling me the answer as I expect her to do!*

THINKING AS A SCIENTIST
ABOUT MAGNETISM

Another exciting element of this little dialogue is that Michelle is introducing the essence of science: We develop hypotheses and then do experiments to answer our own questions. David thinks that because things are touching they must be magnetized.

"What can we do to find out?"

"I could move them." Yes.

"If they are magnets, what will happen?" She asks him to make a prediction. This question tests his knowledge of what a magnet is and how we know something is or is not a magnet—two substances will stick together. Unless, that is, they repel because they are of the same polarity.

This is a superb example of a high level of intellectual challenge for any student—to figure out on your own a natural phenomenon in nature.

Michelle told me, "I like to let the students explore on their own, but I also try to get them to verbalize their thinking, both to model it for other students and to help them be more aware of their thinking."

Notice the importance Michelle places on students' exploring and verbalizing their own thinking. She is engaged in what Brookhart (2008, p. 20) identifies as different kinds of feedback: about the task, about the process, self-regulation, and about oneself.

Why do you think this is so important?

Taking time to explore on our own is a luxury we afford ourselves when we are excited about a topic, object, or experience. Granting students time to explore is what we do when we know that an object or concept is important for them to learn.

I regularly hear from teachers that time is just so constrained by high-stakes tests and local mandates. But Michelle obviously thought that understanding magnetism was very important. She also thought that a child's thinking was important for her to assess.

Notice that she also indicates that she was doing this little exploration in front of the other kindergartners—all ten of her charges sitting cross-legged (or not!) on the carpet designed with the world map.

Why? "To help them be more aware of their thinking."

So here are little five-year-olds learning what so many high school and college students have little awareness of—their own thought processes. Or at least, we are not asking these older students to reflect on their own thoughts in this way. These metacognitive reflections on thought processes, feelings, and what we know and do not know lead to more control of our intellectual lives and, we expect, to higher achievement (if we set that as our goal).

Like Jesse, Michelle wants to discover how her students think. Jesse sent them out to explore, observe, think, and question (see Figure 2.1, Observe, Think, and Question on page 31). Michelle encouraged one student to explore possibilities with tracks and train cars and the magnets that may have been attached to either or both.

So what did Michelle's assessment tell her?

1. David was willing to experiment, to learn.

2. He had initial conclusions about magnetism that she wanted him to demonstrate, namely, that magnets are things that get stuck. Magnetism requires more than touching. Things must stick together to be magnets.

3. He could test out his own thinking by setting up an experiment.

4. He could make a prediction based on his understanding of magnetism. He used his background knowledge to provide him with evidence that led to a conclusion—the essence of critical thinking. David's expressing his prediction told Michelle he knew something important about the effects of magnetism.

5. In many ways, this student with special intellectual and emotional challenges behaved like any other kindergarten student.

What I like so much about this vignette is that Michelle has taken the time with her kindergartners to model a process of exploration and discovery. She didn't just say, "The trains are magnetized, and the tracks are not" and leave it at that. No, her objective was to teach about a very important concept and to model for all students that they can figure things out for themselves.

She is doing what psychologists might call "potentiating" higher levels of achievement, setting the bar high by not telling students the answers.

If we deem a concept important enough for students to understand, then we will take the time to assess their understanding and, perhaps, allow them to figure things out for themselves.

Finally, what I appreciated about this vignette is how often Michelle asked David, "How do you know?" On what are you basing your conclusion? She challenged him to support his ideas with direct observations. And his responses told her something about his reasoning processes—his ability to think critically.

This episode reminds me of the time I told my mother that stars were being born in the Eagle Nebula, some 6,500 light years distant. I was showing her a picture of the famous Pillars of Creation. On hearing my statement, she challenged me, "How do you know?"

I replied, "Look, it says here [on the website] that astronomers think this is a stellar nursery."

"Well, how do *they* know?" she asked quickly. Then I had to rely on my rudimentary knowledge (very rudimentary) of astrophysics to explain. I'm not sure I convinced her.

But "How do you know?" is a vital question in most realms of human thought, and responses will tell us about people's ways of thinking and believing.

WHOLE-CLASS POWERPOINT PRESENTATIONS ON MARS

In Coral Boudin's fourth-grade classroom, Heights Elementary School, Ft. Myers, Florida, I showed a PowerPoint presentation consisting of slides of the solar system and several pictures of Mars taken from the rovers Spirit and Opportunity, as well as the probe circling overhead, Mars Reconnaissance Observer (http://marsprogram.jpl.nasa.gov/missions/present). I was intrigued by some of their observations and questions (Using Observe, Think, and Question):

1. "I think there might be life on Mars."

   "They might live underground."

I was also intrigued by their engagement with other planets:

2. "How can two planets both be blue?"

   "Is it because the sun isn't close and they are cold?"

3. "I think they all have something in common because they are in the solar system."

   "The outer planets are far away because they are big."

4. "I think the gods made the planets."

   "I know Neptune and he lives on Neptune."

Here we have prior knowledge directly related to the current probes on Mars—searching for evidence of water that might indicate current or previous life on the red planet.

We also see a connection between gods and the planets. One student recalled that they'd learned about the Greek gods and that these gods lived on the planets.

The observation I find very intriguing is that all the planets "have something in common because they are in the solar system." That in itself—belonging to our solar system—is a common trait. But there's probably more there that I didn't delve into while eliciting the students' comments and writing them on the interactive whiteboard.

What could we have asked this youngster?

How do we build on this platform of prior knowledge for a unit on our solar system? How do we elicit even more observations and questions?

ASSESSMENTS OF UNDERSTANDING—KWHLAQ

Once when teaching a unit on exploration to fifth graders, I used a KWHLAQ (see Figure 4.2 on page 61) approach, asking first, "What do we *think* we know about exploration of the Americas?"

I received these statements:

"Columbus was redheaded."

"He was married to Queen Isabella."

"Came from England."

"There were lots of convicts on board."

"They got lost."

"They had three ships."

One of these statements we know to be a fact—*Nina, Pinta,* and *Santa Maria* were, indeed, his three ships. The others are based on some kinds of misconceptions students brought to the classroom that day. The observations about his birthplace and his marital status were quickly corrected by a fellow student, even though I had written the observations on the board.

The next question, "What do we want to know about explorers?"[3] led to deeper probing of students' understandings of who the explorers were, what their motivations were, what they discovered, and what the consequences of these explorations were.

If students mention only Columbus, then we know the whole array of other Europeans who participated, plus those from China and possibly South America, are a blank slate.

We expect at the beginning of units to discover the areas students are unfamiliar with, and that's why it is good practice to use this KWHLAQ format to tap into prior knowledge. We can discover areas of ignorance as well as misunderstandings to be corrected. And yes, I display on a whiteboard or interactive whiteboard all the observations, including the misunderstandings.

Why?

Some will say it's not good to leave false observations on display because kids will learn misinformation. But my experience (and others') suggests that students will be able to correct these false statements. And our research should uncover the truth about others as we move along during the unit. We can label some misstatements with question marks, either from us or from students, to indicate we aren't sure yet. We ought not to walk away from misunderstandings, even factually incorrect statements, especially if we have ways of correcting and modifying them during a unit.

A college professor of physics once asked me, "Why ask students what they already know about electricity? I know what they don't understand—about electrons and 'flow.' Why waste time? I'll just teach them what they need to know."

What do you think of his reasoning?

PROBLEMATIC SCENARIOS—SERVING YOUR COUNTRY

I once presented this problematic scenario to fifth-grade students studying the U.S. Constitution: "The president has determined that we need all high school graduates to serve up to two years either in the military or in some form of public service."

After the howls of complaint subsided, I asked, "What do we think we need to know about our form of government to respond intelligently to this situation?"

Here we elicit the extent of students' knowledge about the three branches of government and about democracies, republics, rights and responsibilities, the Bill of Rights, and so forth.

When it comes time for them to ask questions to understand this governmental command, we might hear these questions:

Does the president have the right to do this?

Who's job is it? Who's in charge?

Can I take this to the Supreme Court?

Isn't that against the law?

What makes a law?

Doesn't that violate my rights? What are my rights?

Depending on the grade level and the extent of prior knowledge, students' statements about what they think they already know and their questions will tell us a lot about their understanding of the national government, about misconceptions, myths, and factual misunderstandings. We should get all of these out on the table early on so we know what students are bringing to our discussions.

VIDEOS

Film can be an excellent introduction to a unit of study.

Given my fascination with Antarctic exploration, I have often had occasion to share with teachers clips from Discovery Channel programs. One in particular showed the amazing story of how emperor penguins spend their winters, miles from water, huddled in masses keeping each other warm. Prior to *The March of the Penguins*, this program depicted how mothers laid eggs in the dead of the Antarctic night, gently transferred them to fathers, and then took off during the polar darkness of −70 degree temperatures and trekked sixty or so miles to open water to forage for food.

I showed this to engage teachers in observing, thinking, and questioning and was often interested in the kinds of questions that were asked in the absence of much background knowledge. Questions ranged from "What keeps them warm at −70 Fahrenheit?" to "How are the emperors different from other species?" Their observations were also interesting: "I thought penguins lived at the North Pole." And there was usually, "Where are the polar bears?"

These questions can serve to diagnose

1. level of prior knowledge about animal life in the polar regions (penguins live down south, and polar bears reside only up north),

2. levels and kinds of questions asked,

3. willingness to ask a question, and

4. ability to listen to and build on others' questions/interests.

PROBLEM SOLVING

One of my major challenges during this journey has been to determine the answer to the question, How do we know students are getting better at problem solving?

I've communicated with several teachers around the country who have provided me with a wide variety of end projects that, for them, illustrate students' accomplishments. And indeed, they show mastery of various concepts and principles, for example, knowledge of Newton's Three Laws of Motion, knowledge of the action of lasers on prisms, and the ability to solve various types of mathematical problems.

But what has been puzzling is figuring out whether students have acquired anything more than knowledge of certain concepts. Do they, for example, know what to do when there is no solution immediately evident? When they have to think through a series of steps that might lead to solutions?

Here is a preassessment we administered at one New Jersey elementary school a few years ago. It was suggested by my colleague and friend Irving Sigel, then of Educational Testing Service in Princeton, New Jersey, the very folks who create the College Boards. "Bobby received a new train for his birthday. It worked well for a few days and then just stopped. Please write a story about how you solve this problem" (Barell, 1995, p. 54).

We were looking for a variety of problem-solving behaviors, and here are two that reflect such a spectrum:

Student A: If I was in bobby's case I would ask my dad for help with the train and if there was something I broke I would get it repaired but if it was broken when I brought [*sic*] it I would bring it back to the owner to fix. But before that I would look for a gaurantee [*sic*].

Student B: Suddenly, my train stopped moving. It just stopped where it was. I got up and checked the tracks to see if something was blocking the train. (Nothing was.) I checked the train wheels, they were fine. I even checked the batteries and tested them in my walk-man. They worked perfectly. What could be wrong? I didn't know what to do (Barell, 1995, p. 55).

Student B continues to consider the consequences of asking her parents. "They would have a fit about me being careless. But maybe they wouldn't" (Barell, 1995, p. 55).

Reflective Pause

What differences do you see between these two sixth-grade students?

What problem-solving processes are evident in each?

Here are the set of problem-solving capacities or processes we were looking for. The ability to

Analyze a problem.

Search for causes. Challenge assumptions.

Generate a number of hypotheses and solutions.

Test and evaluate proposed solutions. Search for evidence.

Project possible consequences of solutions.

Decide, test and evaluate.

Imagine himself/herself within a problematic situation.

Have confidence she/he can figure things out on her/his own. (Barell, 1995, p. 54)

Perhaps you find these criteria suitable for analyzing your own or somebody's ability to solve a problem. What might you add? Conduct a broad search for suitable resources? Access these resources? Think critically about evidence and information gathered? Reflect on own thinking?

We find several of these characteristics in Student B's response. What do we see in Student A? Which student would you prefer having in your class and why?

And how would you now design learning experiences to help Student A develop some of the capacities evident in Student B's response? Would this be a desirable goal?

We can ask students to think through and respond to a situation similar to the case of Bobby's train, although today we would probably use something a little more current but without the complexity of an iPad, iPhone, or PlayStation.

PROBLEM SOLVING AND MODEL BUILDING

One of the best ways to assess problem solving is to give students a problem to tackle and see how they do. This will, of course, depend on the student's age and maturity.

In a unit on Newton's Three Laws of Motion, Janice Somerville of Catalina Foothills School District in Arizona gave her students this problem: "Build a Rocket Racer using the supplied materials, Styrofoam, 4 pins, straw, scissors and a small party balloon."

This was a preassessment on the degree to which students could "plan, build, test and evaluate."

From any complex experience like this we can elicit valuable information about

how students analyze a complex task;

the kinds of questions they do/do not ask: gather more information, challenge assumptions, seek causes;

relating to similar problems;

reducing to smaller parts;

representing graphically;

reflecting on different points of view/contrary evidence;

solution generation and critical analysis of consequences;

decision making and implementation;

teamwork, error correction; and

how well they test and evaluate their results.

To assess problem solving, we can and should present students with content-free problems (such as "Ball through the window"). Then we can use ever more challenging ones related to our units to see how students can use any of these approaches:

identify problems;

analyze the problem: pose questions;

represent graphically;

relate to similar problems encountered;

reduce to smaller parts;

reflect on assumptions and different points of view;

research for more information, causes;

reason toward acceptable causes, possible and viable solutions;

recognize our feelings in dealing with complexity;

generate alternative solutions/perspectives;

critique possible solutions/establish solution criteria;

decide and implement; and

reflect on outcomes.

We may seldom use all of these research-based problem-solving approaches, but they might help to analyze how we and our students approach complex situations.

Source: Based on Barell (1995, p. 179).

Presenting students early and often with these kinds of challenges may be one of the best ways to acclimate them to a new vision of the curriculum as well as to help them feel comfortable with ambiguity—not knowing and loving to figure things out for themselves. We can, in fact, use their initial approaches, say, drawing a diagram or asking good questions, as a classroom guide, posted on chart paper, and add to it as the year progresses. Thus, it becomes a graphic guide to problem-solving approaches we are learning as we grow in our ability to tackle ever more complex situations. I much prefer eliciting good strategies from students rather than directly teaching a list like the aforementioned. This is, in effect, what we did in that second-grade classroom (see Chapter 2) where kids gave us over twenty problem-solving approaches: "Make it littler and littler . . . draw a picture . . . discuss it with a friend" (Barell, 1995, p. 168).

CONTINGENCY THINKING— GENERATING POSSIBILITIES

Related to problem solving is the ability to generate or consider a wide range of possible contingencies, as Student B did with the train before her (imaginatively, of course).

Here's a simple test created by E. A. Peel (1974) that neatly helps us determine students' abilities to consider related "contingencies," or factors that might have affected a situation: "Only courageous pilots are allowed to fly over high mountains. This summer a fighter pilot, flying over the Rocky Mountains, collided with an aerial sky ride cable and cut it, causing some sky ride cars to fall to the rocks below. Several people were killed and many others had to spend the night suspended above the rocks. Was this pilot a careful airman? Why do you think so?"

First of all, how would you respond to this situation?

Here's how some eighth graders responded:

Student 1: No, because before you go flying anywhere you should know the rules of the sky and be careful at all times.

Student 2: No, because the pilot was probably going too fast. . . .

Student 3: No, but their two side to every story . . . he mite have been a great pilot but their mite have been a storem [sic]. . . .

Student 4: It depends on the situation he was in. Maybe he was being very careful but something happened to his plane. Then again he could have been very careless. . . . You can't really answer this without knowing more about the situation. (Barell, 1995, p. 59)

Here again, we see a range of responses. What do they tell you about these students' abilities to analyze a complex situation?

What do these responses indicate about students' cognitive development, their transition from what Piaget called "concrete thinking" (reasoning only from what is immediately evident in front of us) toward what he called "formal operations" (more abstract thinking, the ability to imagine possible causes not readily evident)? Where in these responses do we see evidence of black/white/absolute or "it depends" kinds of reasoning?

Using these and other problematic situations, we can get an idea of how good students are at dealing with complex, ill-structured situations. They might not know what the word *problem* means. What's your definition?[4]

CONCLUSION

There are many ways to assess the quality of students' thinking and inquiring:

classroom exploratory experiences;

any artifacts: objects such as sea shells, videos, newspaper articles, websites, and the like; and

problematic scenarios and claims to be analyzed.

What can we do with this information?

1. Organize and draw conclusions that will affect instruction.

2. If students are exemplifying behaviors that we wish to develop, for example, in inquiry, then we need to make explicit the kinds of questions students are asking. Figure 2.2 on page 33 (Three-Story Intellect) is a framework I've worked with for many years (developed by Art Costa and Bena Kallick). If Jesse's second and third graders are not asking anything more complex than "What's the population of Quebec?" then she will model the kinds of questions she wants to develop. In Chapter 7 we will meet Lorraine Radford of Vancouver who has developed a very practical way of helping students grow from making statements to asking questions.

3. If students are not problem solving and thinking critically, then we can follow the lead of Gilbert Highet (1954): "Put problems before them. Make things difficult for them. . . . Produce things for them to think about and question their thinking at every stage. They are inventive and original" (p. 40).

> "Put problems before them. Make things difficult for them. . . . Produce things for them to think about and question their thinking at every stage. They are inventive and original" (Highet, 1954, p. 40).

Share with students our own thinking through such problems and "produce things for them to think about" often. Indeed, challenge them to bring such problems to class on a regular basis, and let's have a real sit-down with them and learn from each other how to approach and resolve many kinds of problems.

This is precisely what so many of the contributors to this book have done: created problems for students to inquire about, think about, and figure out what to do about. You'll read about crime scene investigations in the classroom, figuring out how to attract more teens and tweens to a Major League Baseball stadium, and how to build a world-class roller coaster in Sandusky, Ohio. Each of these tasks presents students with significant challenges, especially if embedded within them are concepts/principles and factual information about which we deem it important to think deeply.

ENDNOTES

1. We will revisit this theme of students' having a say in their assessment in Chapters 6 and 10.

2. I received a list of such situations from a special education teacher in New Jersey whose students had difficulty identifying the problem in ambiguous situations such as these. Notice that such ambiguity can be seen as an element in problem-based learning scenarios that are ill structured and open to various interpretations.

3. Now, in 2011, I would have phrased the question in this fashion: "What do we *need* to find out if we are to become experts in exploration? . . . if we are going to establish an Explorers' Museum?" or a variation that presents the students with a challenge wherein they must gather data, solve a problem, make decisions, and create a novel product.

4. "Any question or matter involving doubt, uncertainty or difficulty" (*Random House Dictionary of the English Language*, 1967). Derivation? From the Greek "to lay before," and equivalent to "to throw." Now, how did the Greeks come up with this concept, and how is a problem something we "lay before" or "throw"?

REFERENCES

Barell, J. (1995). *Teaching for thoughtfulness: Classroom strategies to enhance intellectual development* (2nd ed.). White Plains, NY: Longman.

Barell, J. (2007). *Why are school buses always yellow? Teaching inquiry preK–5.* Thousand Oaks, CA: Corwin.

Brookhart, S. (2008). *How to give effective feedback to your students.* Alexandria, VA: Association for Supervision and Curriculum Development.

Gladwell, M. (2005). *Blink: The power of thinking without thinking.* New York: Little, Brown.

Highet, G. (1954). *Man's unconquerable mind.* New York: Columbia University Press.

McPeck, J. (1981). *Critical thinking and education.* Oxford, UK: Martin Robertson.

Peel, E. A. (1974). A study of differences in the judgments of adolescent pupils. In Z. Cantwell & P. Svajian (Eds.), *Adolescence: Studies in development.* Itasca, IL: Peacock.

Popham, W. J. (2008). *Transformative assessment.* Alexandria, VA: Association for Supervision and Curriculum Development.

Random House Dictionary of the English Language. (1967). New York: Random House.

Formative Assessments

Gathering a "Wealth of Information"

RECORDING OUR STUDENTS' QUESTIONS

During a unit on plants in Shauna Ullman's third-grade classroom in West Vancouver (Mulgrave School), Harry asked these questions:

May 9 How [do] the sun and rain affect plants? [Off the top of my head . . . Causation]

May 19 How do the sun and rain affect the germinating stage of the life cycle? [Digging deeper . . . Causation]

May 26 Does the climate affect the plant and its failure? [And deeper . . . Causation]

June 13 What will happen if you keep cutting down trees? [Questions left hanging . . . Responsibility]

Tish Jolley, Mulgrave's Primary Years Programme International Baccalaureate coordinator, shared these questions (personal communication, June 2011) as she analyzed the inquiry-tracking tool Shauna had been using with her students (see Figure 6.1). She commented on Harry's performance: "Harry's questions and those of many others seemed to show a developing interest in a particular area, as the knowledge and understanding grew. A wealth of information about the student can be gleaned just from looking at their questions!"

Figure 6.1 Tracking My Questions

Name _____ Unit of inquiry: _Plants_

Off the top of my head...	Digging deeper...	And deeper...	Questions left hanging...
Date: May 9, 2011	Date: May 19, 2011	Date: May 26, 2011	Date: June 13, 2011
Question: How does the sun and rain affect Plants	Question: How do the sun and rain affect the germinating stage of the life cycle?	Question: Does the climate affect the plant and its future	Question: what will happen if you keep cutting down trees
Key Concept: Causation	Key Concept: Causation	Key Concept: Causation	Key Concept: Responsibility
Question: How does fungi glow	Question: What will happen if people don't take care of the environment?	Question: What will happen in the future of plants	Question: how are vegetables connected to fruit
Key Concept: Function	Key Concept: Responsibility	Key Concept: change	Key Concept: Connection
Question: How do flowers grow	Question: What will happen to the flowers and plants?	Question:	Question: how are trees seeds connected to fruit seeds
Key Concept: Function	Key Concept: Responsibility	Key Concept:	Key Concept: Connection
Question:	Question:	Question:	Question:
Key Concept:	Key Concept:	Key Concept:	Key Concept:

☆ Interested in growth + conditions for growth
☆ Good incorporation of new vocabulary.

Name _____ Unit of inquiry: Sharing the planet _____

Off the top of my head...	Digging deeper...	And deeper...	Questions left hanging...
Date: May 9, 2011	Date: May 19, 2011	Date: May 26, 2011	Date: June 15, 2011
Question: How do plants get fur?	Question: Why do flowers have pollen?	Question: How do plants get sunlight to grow?	Question: Do bigger plants produce more oxygen?
Key Concept: Function	Key Concept: Causation	Key Concept: Change	Key Concept: Function
Question: How do thorns form?	Question: How do we know that most plants produce oxygen?	Question:	Question: what would happen to plants in the future?
Key Concept: Function	Key Concept: Reflection	Key Concept:	Key Concept: Change
Question: Why are some plants squared shape?	Question: Why are flowers different colours?	Question:	Question: What would happen if we keep on cutting trees?
Key Concept: Causation	Key Concept: Causation	Key Concept:	Key Concept: Responsibility
Question: Why do some plants curl?	Question: Does any flowers have prickles on their pedals?	Question:	Question: What would happen if different flower patten get together?
Key Concept: Causation	Key Concept: Perspective	Key Concept:	Key Concept: Connection

Question:
Why are some roots big and small?

Key Concept:

Causation

☆ Interested in flowers + pollen

Figure 6.1 (Continued)

Name _____ Unit of inquiry: <u>Sharing the Plants</u>

Off the top of my head...	Digging deeper...	And deeper...	Questions left hanging...
Date: *May 9, 2011*	Date: *May 19, 2011*	Date: *May 26, 2011*	Date: *June 13, 2011*
Question: *How do plants grow?*	Question: *How do plants produce oxygen?*	Question: *How many kinds of carnavorcous plants are there?*	Question: *When did humans find food on plants?*
Key Concept: *Function*	Key Concept: *Causation*	Key Concept: *Reflection*	Key Concept: *Reflection*
Question: *How many kinds of plants are there?*	Question: *How do thorns form*	Question: *Is the biggest plant carnavorcous*	Question: *Do bigger plants make more food*
Key Concept: *Form*	Key Concept: *Function*	Key Concept: *Reflection*	Key Concept: *Causation*
Question: *How long do plants live?*	Question: *How do plants affect living things lives?*	Question:	Question: *Do bigger plants make more oxygen?*
Key Concept: *Change*	Key Concept: *Connection*	Key Concept:	Key Concept: *Causation*
Question: *How long can a plant grow*	Question:	Question:	Question: *How many plants are there?*
Key Concept: *Causation*	Key Concept:	Key Concept:	Key Concept: *Causation*

☆ *Interested in growth + oxygen*

Name _____

Unit of inquiry: *Sharing the Plants*

Off the top of my head...	Digging deeper...	And deeper...	Questions left hanging...
Date: *May 9, 2011*	Date: *May 19, 2011*	Date: *May 26, 2011*	Date: *June 13, 2011*
Question: *How long can trees live?*	Question: *How does sap form?*	Question: *How did we know what foods we can eat and can not eat many many years ago?*	Question: *When plants die does anything else happen instead of new plants growing?*
Key Concept: *Change*	Key Concept: *Function*	Key Concept: *Reflection*	Key Concept: *Function*
Question: *How does a tiny seed turn into a HUGE TREE*	Question: *Eat a life cycle stop.*	Question: *If the world around too many plants will that effect our lives*	Question: *How do carnauvocous plants know when to eat a bug if they don't have brains*
Key Concept: *Change*	Key Concept: *Function*	Key Concept: *Connection & Perspective*	Key Concept: *Function*
Question:	Question:	Question:	Question: *If a plant is healthy can something still go wrong*
Key Concept:	Key Concept:	Key Concept:	Key Concept: *Change*
Question:	Question:	Question:	Question:
Key Concept:	Key Concept:	Key Concept:	Key Concept:

☆ *Interested in life cycle*

(Continued)

Figure 6.1 (Continued)

Name _____

Unit of inquiry: _Sharing the planet/Plants_

Off the top of my head...	Digging deeper...	And deeper...	Questions left hanging...
Date: May 9, 2011	Date: May 19, 2011	Date: May 26, 2011	Date: June 13, 2011
Question: Are minerals in plants and flowers?	Question: What happens if the seed breaks before the plant grows out of it?	Question: How do plants affect our lives?	Question: How have plants changed?
Key Concept: ①Form	Key Concept: ②Function	Key Concept: ⑤Connection	Key Concept: ④Change
Question: Do weeds kill plants	Question:	Question: Why do some seeds decompose before the plant grows out of it?	Question: Why do some plants produce pollen and may be nectar?
Key Concept: ②Function		Key Concept: ④Change	Key Concept: ②Function
Question:	Question:	Question: How do plants make food?	Question: Do plants produce pollen while inside the seeds
Key Concept:	Key Concept:	Key Concept: ②Function	Key Concept: ②Reflection
Question:	Question:	Question:	Question: How do plants decompose?
Key Concept:	Key Concept:	Key Concept:	Key Concept: ③Functions

☆ Interested in <u>seeds</u>

Source: © Shauna Ullman (2011).

Indeed, Shauna found a wealth of information about Harry:

The quality and complexity of his questioning, said Shauna, "showed a genuine interest in our topics of investigation and a developing ability to ask questions from different perspectives that show a new understanding of the interconnection of all living things. . . . Mid-way through the unit his understanding had expanded from plants as individual specimens to plants being part of our larger environment and by the end of the unit he had begun to consider how the actions of humans can affect plant life" (S. Ullman, personal communication, August 2011).

Harry's use of the term *responsibility* refers to a set of concepts used by International Baccalaureate programs like that at Mulgrave (the Primary Years Programme) to guide students' inquiry.[1]

What brought about these perceived significant changes? Shauna told me that Harry was able to ask, "Does climate affect the plant and its future?" for the following reasons: "I don't believe he would have gotten to this more sophisticated point of questioning without having read and experimented with plants during the three weeks prior to this point. At this point in our unit of inquiry we were exploring the importance of plants in relation to our environment and the various ways people use plants. Students were working in small groups using iMovie to produce public service announcements teaching people about different reasons why plants are important to people" (S. Ullman, personal communication, August 2011).

I mention Shauna's question-tracking approach to illustrate what formative assessment is all about—that is, gathering information during a unit to help guide us toward students' achievement of the goals and objectives stated therein. We previously have dealt with preassessment, that is, gathering information about what students already know or think they know before a unit commences. And in the four subsequent case study chapters (7–10), we will present a variety of summative assessments, those we undertake at a unit's conclusion to determine the extent and quality of students' learning.

RATIONALE

When I started teaching in New York City many years ago, I'd never heard of formative assessment, but obviously, like every teacher, I gathered information about students' learning in a wide variety of ways: their comments and questions during discussions, responses to my direct questions, short quizzes, writings in inquiry journals (mainly later as a college teacher), and drafts of essays in English literature classes.

Why is formative assessment so important? "The function of formative assessment is to help teachers and students decide whether they need to make any adjustments in what they're doing. If a teacher's instruction is dazzlingly wonderful, and if students' learning tactics are marvelously appropriate, then no adjustments are needed" (Popham, 2008, p. 51).

But if we are falling short of our marks, then we adjust. We as teachers do this all the time when we discover, from students' answers and comments, that they're just not understanding a concept or mastering a skill. We adjust our instruction right on the spot, in the middle of the lesson.

As Dufour, Dufour, Eaker, and Many (2006) point out, what happens after an assessment determines what we call it: "The response that occurs after the test [or other information-gathering experience] has been given will truly determine whether or not it is being used as a formative assessment. If it is used to ensure students who experience difficulty are given additional time and support as well as additional opportunities to demonstrate their learning, it is formative; if additional support is not forthcoming, it is summative" (p. 77).

These formative assessments, the authors continue, should be "frequent, common, high-quality." By *common,* they mean that teachers should agree among themselves what measures they will use to observe students' growth during units of instruction (Dufour et al., 2006, p. 55).[2]

So formative assessment is built into our profession. We are always asking ourselves, Are they getting it? If the answer is no, we adjust. Those teachers who are flexible, who can and do adjust to changing students' needs, may be the more effective ones.[3]

OTHER FORMATIVE ASSESSMENTS

Besides tracking students' inquiries, as Shauna does, there is a wide variety of other means for gathering information and providing feedback:

students' reflective journals after specific learning experiences;

students travel journals during the year;

quizzes and tests of various kinds;

students' use of wikis, Google Docs, iPads, and blogs;

KWHLAQ inquiry processes at any time;

games such as Magic Bag and Twenty Questions;[4]

work on projects at any stage;

question frameworks (e.g., Three-Story Intellect); and

Evidence of Inquiry format.

STUDENTS' REFLECTIVE JOURNALS

Kerry Faber (Ekota School, Edmonton) teaches fifth and sixth graders and has long used reflective writings and journals. Within these journals she has been able to capture students' growth over time, not only with respect to unit objectives but also related to yearlong threaded goals such as becoming more reflective and becoming better inquirers. In the excerpts presented below I think we can see Rickey struggling with building a habitat for specific animals. He's trying to figure out how to solve various problems (another long-term goal), and he's learned something about self-reflection: "Today I hot glued my WCU (water containment unit) together and filled the gaps, with plasticine. Then, I decided to do an experiment to see how well the WCU would contain water. The first test was inconclusive because of spillage. The second test showed that the plasticine worked well but there were gaps in it. I managed to fill them. I enjoyed putting down the plasticine. Inquiry—*What if I'm wrong, and the plasticine doesn't hold up?* [italics added]."

Here's what Rickey wrote the subsequent day:

> Today I completed the "plasticining" of my WCU. Well, one of them (I have two). Then, I did another test to see if it would hold up. I was really hoping it would hold, or else I would have to scrape off all of the plasticine (NOT FUN!). The first test was inconclusive due to spillage. Test #2, however, was a success. That's right! No plasticine scraping today! Actually, I had to do a bit more plasticine-scraping and finish off the second WCU. I had a plan to do a couple of rocks, sticking out of the water for this one. I managed to finish off the rocks before we had to shut down for the day. My favourite events during all this? The tests on my WCU. Inquiry: *Will my WCU hold up over time? How much plasticine will I need to finish this off?* [italics added]

REFLECTIVE PAUSE

Now, just from reading Rickey's journal entries, what can we say about what he's learning about his own progress? What can we say about his approach to problem solving, testing once and twice?

Here's what Kerry told me: "I am finding a higher level of confidence with measuring out and building their enclosures than I found with my kids last year. I had to walk last year's group through step by step procedures much more" (K. Faber, personal communication, November 17, 2010).

This habitat-building project was guided by Alberta Provincial Standards, among which were the following:

Solve problems involving whole numbers and decimal numbers;

Represent and describe patterns and relationships, using graphs and tables;

Express a given problem as an equation in which a letter variable is used to represent an unknown number." (http://education.alberta. ca/media/645594/kto9math.pdf)

On the same zoo habitat–building project, Natasha, an ESL student, wrote the following in her reflective journal: "Today I started glueing my enclosure together. I'm having trouble with putting it together. My problem is trying to put the glue on and glue the enclosure together. How can I put together the enclosure straight. What stagery [sic] can I use to get things done quickly. My enclosure parts are coming a long really slow. That is my biggest problem is work slowy [sic]" (K. Faber, personal communication, November 6, 2010).

Natasha knows she has a problem and will consider different strategies to help her solve it.

Here's Kerry's reflection on the whole process: "As you can see the kids are already starting to use some of the vocabulary that I have been modeling since the start of the year. It is so calm and focused when they write their reflections after we have stopped the active building process. *This is a huge change from two weeks ago.* [italics added] Anyone who doesn't think there are big enough benefits to taking time to do this can look at my students writing before the project and compare it to now—significant differences" (K. Faber, personal communication, November 6, 2010).

Note the kinds of information she is gathering: Students' knowledge of and use of problem solving approaches (testing, retesting for verification); the readiness to assess their own learning by asking themselves questions related to their own progress. Notice it isn't Kerry Faber saying, "This is what you've got to do. . . . Do that!" No, it's Rickey and Natasha who now have that responsibility. And I received these e-mails in mid-November. The semester was only two and one half months old!

As Figure 6.2 indicates, these students are in the process of self-monitoring their progress toward a problem-oriented goal—building a zoo habitat for a specific animal—something that most of them did not accomplish easily.

Figure 6.2 Planning, Monitoring, and Evaluating

A very useful formulation here is the triad of reflective questions that will help us as well as our students gain better control of our own learning.

Planning—"What's my problem, and how will I solve it?" This calls for students to specify their objective and how they plan on reaching it.

Monitoring—"How am I doing? What should I do differently to reach my goal?" These are tracking or monitoring questions designed to give us an idea of our progress toward a goal.

Evaluating—"How well did I do in reaching my objective, and what would I do differently next time and why?" This calls for a task analysis after the fact with new approaches to improve performance.

Source: Barell (1995).

TRAVEL JOURNALS

An inquiry journal of a different, longer-term kind is a travel journal like those kept from kindergarten through eighth grade at Normal Park Museum Magnet School in Chattanooga, Tennessee.

On my last of three visits, the large oak tree in front of the school was lying spread out on the front lawn, full of dying brown-green leaves, the victim of terrible hurricanes that had swept up from Alabama a few days before. Jill Levine, principal, had led students down into the darkened basement of the elementary building where they sat quietly, nervously awaiting the all clear. (Interestingly, the only way teachers could communicate during the tornado was by using Facebook. In preparing for Hurricane Irene—in September 2011—residents of New York City were instructed to activate their Twitter accounts.)

But learning proceeded apace shortly thereafter, and part of that process was students' recording in their travel journals whatever observations they may have made about this terrible and natural event. The journals seemed to bring a brightness to everybody's day and drove the clouds away.

PURPOSE

Students view these journals as a way to record what they have been learning. "It's a textbook of all we've been learning," said Annie. Robert added, "We're building our own textbook. You can make this a teaching tool with which you could teach someone else."

Their teachers variously saw the travel journal as a way to record students' learning as they worked toward understanding the unit's essential questions. It is definitely a learning resource, a notebook of sorts, where students record learning in their own words. They are encouraged to imagine creative ways of illustrating various ideas such as the nature of the sun.

One teacher said the journals represented a way for students to "connect concepts with their own world," that is, to apply or transfer new learnings to their outside-of-school experiences. Thus, students get the idea early on in their schooling that learning is all the time, not merely between 9:00 and 3:00 in a classroom.

Why have I been interested in these journals for the past several years?

I've been interested because they serve as inquiry journals. Students often write down their initial and ongoing questions in an attempt to understand the essential questions of a unit. Grace said, "Any questions you have you're supposed to answer." But another student, Henry, said he preferred answering the questions later, "to see if I can answer them."

Students with whom I spoke in all grades seemed to treasure the fact that these were their own creations—they were encouraged to add pictures that they drew or that came from other sources to illustrate what they were learning. Looking back as an eighth grader at her first-grade travel journal, Alice said she was proud that there was "a lot more color and design" as she grew older.

In terms of their growth with questioning, students made these comments:

Peter: The questions become a lot harder to answer. [He had curiosities about the westward movement in the United States.] You try to picture it in your mind.

Victoria: The essential questions make you think more. . . . They are broader. . . . There's more to figure out.

You can imagine how such journals could be used for formative assessments within units of instruction during a year. For example, third graders were encouraged to write down what they were learning (with questions if they had any) and illustrate their ideas. Some shared with me a few of their questions and comments from recent units on geography, mixtures, and the solar system:

> "There are seven continents." (accompanied by a picture of the globe)

> "Here are four cloud formations." (with pictures)

> "This is the solar system . . . [with pictures] and layers of the sun."

What does this drawing (Figure 6.3) tell us about how well Michael understands the sun's structure?

This drawing was accompanied by his questions: "Why is the sun a star? How hot can the sun get to?"

What can and should we do with illustrations of the sun such as Michael's? How do they serve as formative assessments? If we think it is accurate, what do we do? If we consider that there are misperceptions and/or misunderstandings, how can we proceed to modify our instruction?

Figure 6.3 Michael's Drawing of Layers of the Sun—Grade 4

Source: Michael Genovesi, Normal Park Museum Magnet School (2011). Used with permission.

GROWTH FROM GRADES 1 TO 5

So here again, we have a potentially powerful record of a student's growth not only during a unit but from unit to unit, from beginning of the school year to end, and from kindergarten to Grade 8.

Here are Julia's questions—not all of them, but a representative sample—from Grades 1 to 5:

> Grade 1: I want to see a tree frog. What's the difference between these 2 places—Rain Forest and Chattanooga?

> Grade 2: I wonder why the [writing not clear] live on cliffs? What do they do for fun?

Grade 3: What is Pluto made of if it's not a planet?

Grade 4: Why do we never see the back of the moon?

Grade 5: What does it mean to be free?

REFLECTIVE PAUSE

What changes, if any, do you see in Julia's questions from first to fifth grade? Consider them in terms of

kinds of questions—asking for reasons/causes (Why?);

asking, What is it made of?

asking for definitions;

making comparisons/contrasts;

asking about something not seen, not concrete and immediately present, or abstract;

elaboration—adding details to explain;

linguistic complexity—going beyond simple questions; and

thinking—questions that require complex reasoning.

As you can see, Julia's questions could be a most valuable assessment of her growth over time, from limited, very concrete questions to ones that are more intellectually demanding as well as ones that focus on abstract concepts such as freedom.

One other student, Michael, a fifth grader, asked, "Is it possible to change a planet to be like Earth?" How is this different from one of his third-grade questions, "How far is it to Pluto?"

EVIDENCE OF INQUIRY—TEAMWORK

Over the past two years I have worked with a few educators to assess students' growth in inquiry using an Evidence of Inquiry form (see Figure 6.4). This is a protocol with which students can record their initial questions at the beginning, middle, and end of a unit, together with noting the instructional approaches used to achieve unit objectives.

Chapter 8 describes in great detail how Kerry Faber used these forms over a two-year period during several units of instruction.

Figure 6.4 Evidence of Inquiry

Evidence of Inquiry Questions Leading to Understanding (For teacher observation and students' self-report)	Inquiry levels: I—Gather II—Process III—Apply	Student: _____ Teacher: _____

A. Questions/Statements/Wonderings:

Date: _____ Topic/Unit: _____ Questions (level): _____

Sample of questions:

B. Major Teacher/Student Inquiry Strategies:

Modeling, OTQ, KWHLAQ, journals, small-group problem solving/investigations, students' own self-directed approaches	Date: _____ Strategy: _____ Notes on involvement:

C. Kinds of Investigations Chosen:

Books, personal interviews, web searches, real/virtual field trips, video conferences, use of iPads/other tablets, smart devices	Date: _____ Form of investigation used: _____ Time spent _____ Student or teacher choice (circle) Questions arising from investigations:

D. Evidence of Achievement/Understanding: based on culminating performances

Projects, presentations with Q&A, essays, artwork, formal teacher tests, use of inquiry vocabulary, quality of journal reflections (What I learned about subject, self, inquiry . . .), ability to express awareness of personal growth, taking action/application of concepts/ideas	Date: _____ Form of evidence: _____ Rating stage: Beginning or Improving or Proficient Comments:

(Continued)

Figure 6.4 (Continued)

E. Change/Development in Inquiry Over Time:	
Improvement in question levels of complexity (Three-Story Intellect); frequency, flexibility, elaboration; time travel; use of concepts such as International Baccalaureate concepts (form, function, causation/connection, change, reflection); problem solving—alternate solutions, consequences, critical thinking—questioning sources/assumptions, kinds/reliability of evidence, other points of view, contrary evidence, drawing reasonable conclusions; openness to novelty, ambiguity; reflecting compassion for others; persistence; cooperation/teamwork	Date: _____ Teacher/Student Comments:

F. Summary of Growth Comments/Observations:
Date: _____ (Consider the degree to which students' questions/problem solving/critical thinking contributed to involvement during the unit and to their understanding major concepts/ideas.)

Source: John Barell and Kerry Faber (2012).

Here I would like to share some students' reflections from Anna Hodge's use of these forms during fifth-grade exhibitions in her International Baccalaureate School in Rock Hill, South Carolina.

I have selected examples from two years' data to share what some of Anna's students wrote about teamwork, that very important 21st century capacity—to be able to work well within a group of very different people to achieve a goal:

Colton: My knowledge of my group's weaknesses and strengths has allowed me to help them improve. . . . We have been practicing our presentation on family and friends at home. I am growing on learning about my group mates and guiding them along.

Susan: I feel that I need to ask more questions and observe more so I can see what people are doing wrong and help them.

Maria: I . . . think that the cooperation in the group has risen also. I've learned that when you have more cooperation and more teamwork you get your work done quicker and better because you have multiple ideas that come from the group.[5]

And an observer of a group that functioned differently said the following: "Most girls in our group tend to play around and talk about boys. They could have a less a care of the world [*sic*]."

Douglas Reeves (2010) has noted that in the future, we will be judged on the quality of our teamwork: "When [today's] students enter the world of work, society, and life in the 21st century, their hyper-competitive habits of mind will be sadly out of place. Leadership will stem not from rank but from influence and service. Performance will be measured not by the success of the individual, but by the success of the team" (p. 310).

So what are the elements critical to being successful in a team?

What are the significant elements of teamwork? They might include the following:

accepts/supports group's goals;

listens to others' ideas;

builds on others' ideas;

makes positive contributions;

is able to assume different roles (leader, recorder, gatekeeper, etc.);

presents alternative points of view, contrary evidence;

works toward consensus (including others' ideas);

is mindful of time and other constraints; and

continuously reflects on progress and need to make adjustments.

What would you add?

Kerry Faber in Edmonton also used this form (see Figure 6.4) during an extensive unit on the Iroquois Nation and its use of the consensus model of decision making—an exemplary model of teamwork. Several students commented on the efficacy of reenacting this consensus model: "The Grand Council took the longest and it was the funnest. We really had to think about our decisions [how to solve our problematic scenarios for survival] and we needed to come to a consensus. We needed to think about the next seven generations that will come and how our decisions will affect them." Which content concepts are reflected herein? Are students making good progress in understanding how these Native Americans lived (and how they influenced our own governance practices)?

Following is feedback Kerry gave to one other student on this Evidence of Inquiry form (February through May, 2011; Section E, Change/Development in Inquiry Over Time): "I like your comment, 'Consensus model sounds nice but I don't think everybody could get along in one.' You are taking a more realistic approach. You are demonstrating this in your problem solving on the issue posed to your nation. I heard you raise questions when a group member suggested a solution that you didn't think was entirely workable. I wonder if you went deep enough with your critical thinking based on the simplicity of your written explanation. What do you think?"

You can see the value, I hope, of students' continually writing and reflecting on their progress through a unit. One of the major pluses is what we see here, a teacher's providing positive and constructive feedback for a student—share more of your thoughts in writing and think more deeply. Perhaps this meant the student should ask more questions, challenge others' points of view (which this student was good at) and other team members' assumptions.

WIKIS, GOOGLE DOCS, iPADS, AND OTHER FORMATIVE HELPERS

My introduction to using modern technological wizardry for purposes of assessment came when Mary Darr, leader of the Sandusky, Ohio, science, technology, engineering, and math projects at Pearson Middle School, directed me to the school's wikis. The project was designing a model roller coaster at Cedar Point Amusement Park (see Chapter 9). The students were divided by teachers into teams of CEOs, engineers, marketing managers, legal eagles, and architects.

Natalie was one of the CEOs, and here is an early set of posts on wikis: "Architects, you need to find out a lot of information for our financial and marketing officers. They need to know an estimated time and how much land you will be using for the roller coaster. I know this can be stressful but if one person doesn't do their work in this project we all will not get a very good grade."

Marketing involved creating an appealing brochure. Once again, here are Natalie's comments: "The marketing officers were supposed to get their brochures done soon but our groups brochure is hardly done. They are doing good work by taking very good notes. I believe they could work a little harder."

REFLECTIVE PAUSE

Now, if you were a faculty advisor to Natalie's team, what initial judgments (formative assessments) would you make about

Natalie's leadership abilities;

information gathering by architects;

teamwork: cooperation, initiative, and problem-solving abilities?

I'm sure the teachers working weekly with each team were constantly observing progress, noting challenges and difficulties, and determining where there needed to be adult intervention, such as accessing more information, perhaps from a specialist at Cedar Point.

iPADS

Shauna Ullman was afforded a golden opportunity to experiment with iPads in her third grade during the spring of 2011. Students loved using them, experimenting with different apps (such as Garage Band to compose music, StoryPatch, and PuppetPals) and having a means of communicating with each other. Here's Shauna's assessment, sent to me in an e-mail:

> One day, during our three-week iPad trial period, it occurred to me, on the spur of the moment, to have a group of students use the iPads to have an online discussion about a book they were reading called *Astronaut: Living in Space,* by Kate Hayden. The students were already familiar with accessing our online discussion forums, which we have located on class pages on our school's website.
>
> I quickly set up the thread and away they went. What struck me was how independently they worked and how focused they were on the task at hand. I wondered if they would be able to respond to one another or if they would each be posting their own thoughts with no regard for the other comments. I was pleased to see they were attempting to respond to one another and were using the book to help them sort out their responses. It proved to be a great example of gaining, applying and synthesizing information. (S. Ullman, personal communication, July 8, 2011)

Unfortunately, we have no recordings of the students' interactions on this occasion, but we could use a brief transcript from what they posted on their school blog about plants to give us an idea of how such student-to-student communications might be used for formative assessments. The unit focused on understanding plants and how they grow:

By Nancy Initial post: 5.26.11 do plant give oxygen

By Chris Initial post: 5.26.11 I know that trees do

By Susan Initial post: 5.26.11 NO plants do not give oxygen, but trees do give oxygen.

By Katie Initial post: 5.26.11 can a life cycle of a plant stop.

By Lorelei Initial post: 5.26.11 Temperatures that are too cold and the incorrect amount of water. Read more: http://wiki.answers.com/Q/What_two_things_could_stop_the_life_cycle_of_an_individual_plant#ixzz1NTTHHQPR

By Annie Initial post: 5.26.11 If there was only food plants how would it affect our lifes?

By Wallie Initial post: 5.26.11 no 'cause all plants make healthy foods (vegies & fruits) so we would just eat fruits & vegies our whole life

What criteria might we use to assess these interchanges?

Accuracy of information

Understanding of major concepts (plant growth, photosynthesis . . .)

Use of students' own words (or are we highlighting, cutting and pasting from a website?) (S. Ullman, personal communication, July 8, 2011)

Other?

It seems to me that here in this exchange among students we have the beginnings of a more self-directed student engagement with the stuff to learn, a precursor of the classrooms of tomorrow. Students are assuming more control over their own learning, a situation devoutly to be embraced.

In the classrooms of the second decade of the 21st century, we are bound to see so many more students with iPads and other computing, communicating, and researching tablets as part of their regular routines. Mary Darr, Shauna Ullman, and countless others are experimenting with them as ways not only for students to conduct research but also for them to communicate among themselves and with their teachers.[6]

Almost weekly during the past few months, I have received notices through various media outlets (ASCD SmartBriefs, Edutopia, Technology

Bits, Bytes and Nibbles, and the like) of experiments in classrooms with new media, iPads (and iPhones and iPods) chief among them. What some teachers are doing is putting these tools in each student's hands and, as Shauna has done, challenging them to work through their understandings of plants, the solar system, or *Charlotte's Web* by communicating with each other. Everybody is now engaged, and the teacher can safely monitor what is being said, what students' understandings are.[7]

As of this writing (September 2011), there are hundreds of experiments with iPads downloading new curricular applications. Let's just hope that what we have here represents new ways of learning and working with content, not merely a substitute for pencils, paper, and memorizing stuff from heavy textbooks.

DEALING WITH ANSWERS TO QUESTIONS

Another third grader at Normal Park Museum Magnet School in Chattanooga, Jacqui, asked a lot of questions about dinosaurs: How did they die? Fossils—how did they form? (See Figure 6.5.)

One of her travel journal answers was, "Some of the dinosaurs died because the paleontologists animals [handwriting not clear] ate the eggs. Asteroid fire, dust, ash, sickness. Nemesis sun comets and comet showers. And a meteors hit. And paleontologist may never no [*sic*] how Dinosaurs Died. I think that that mammals ate Babbies."

Figure 6.5 Death of the Dinosaurs

Now, how would we assess Jacqui's answers to her own questions? If we found them as part of a regular check on students' entries, we might wonder about her understanding of what we have taught. How do these answers communicate understanding of essential questions within the unit?

Depending on when these answers were written, we might consider them excellent results of the student's own research. But perhaps they were notes taken down during a classroom presentation. As such they would form a good summary of current knowledge.[8]

As Popham (2008) and others have noted, the purpose of formative assessments is to adjust instruction if necessary. What if Jacqui's classmates listed nothing or only one cause of dinosaur extinction, the meteor impact? How might we modify instruction in the middle or toward the end of a unit?

Popham (2008) and others have suggested an approach that will be useful here. That is, during our unit planning, we not only specify our unit goals, essential questions, and intended outcomes but also take key skills and understandings and break them down into manageable elements. "Identify all requisite precursory sub skills and bodies of enabling knowledge" (p. 36). This requires that we do a task analysis on the essential knowledge and skills within our units so we can identify students' mastery of them during the unit. This is not an easy task, but it is a really important one.

But let's take a specific example and see how this might work.

Writing a coherent paragraph will require the following skills and understandings, perhaps not in precisely this order:

word functions and relationships—nouns, verbs, adjectives, adverbs, conjunctions, and objects;

construction and nature of sentences (consider different kinds, e.g., declarative), questions, and complete thoughts;

rules of grammar;

use of punctuation to separate thoughts for expression;

relationships among ideas with connecting words (e.g., conjunctions and connecting adverbs: *and, but, for, or, therefore, nevertheless,* and *however*);

sequences of events and ideas and words that connect (e.g., *first* and *second, primarily* and *secondarily*);

nature of a paragraph containing one major idea; and

nature of topic sentences, their placement and importance.

This is not, I'm sure, a complete list, but for an English teacher (as I was for many years), it's a beginning that shows the idea of what a teacher walking about her classroom with an iPad listing all of these skills and understandings can be checking for.

In Appendix A I've listed a set of task analyses for problem solving, critical thinking, and creative thinking you might consider.

Another terrific resource will be the sets of 21st century rubrics created by exemplary districts like Catalina Foothills in Arizona. Under the leadership of Mary Jo Conery, this district has created rather detailed rubrics for Communications, Critical and Creative Thinking, Cultural Competence, Leadership, Self-Direction, Systems Thinking, and Teamwork (www.cfsd16.org/public/_century/centMain.aspx).

We will see in Chapter 10 how Pat Burrows, an eighth-grade language arts and writing teacher, used her rubrics for critical thinking.

What a listing of the important subskills will do for us and for our students is to provide a more precise array of what it will take to become better at writing a good paragraph, solving problems, thinking critically, or understanding the nature of the U.S. Constitution.

STUDENTS' ROLE IN FORMATIVE ASSESSMENTS

For a very long time, I have been an advocate of sharing more control with students in our classrooms. This means that they should have choices to make that involve what to learn, how to learn it, and how to demonstrate what they have learned and understood.

Why?

On the face of it, this is a very logical assertion based on human psychology. If we want people, at any age, to become intellectually and emotionally involved in something, they need to exercise their own choices, make their own decisions. Think of a recent project you undertook, and consider the level of interest and excitement and its relationship to the degree to which you had a choice in the decision.

> "When students make choices about their learning, their engagement and achievement increase" (Davies, 2007, p. 34).

> "Fairness means that students are partners in the assessment process" (Reeves, 2010, p. 208).

Consider school projects you completed wherein you did and did not have a choice. Consider life choices over which you did and did not have some control.

As noted researcher on assessment Anne Davies (2007) has written, "When students make choices about their learning, their engagement and achievement increase" (p. 34).

And Douglas Reeves (2010) has concluded, "Fairness means that students are partners in the assessment process" (p. 208).

What this means is that when we obtain information from formative assessments, we should be providing students with this feedback and engaging them in thinking how they can best learn the material at hand.

We can challenge students by examining results of formative assessments with questions such as these:

What does this information tell you?

What do you think we need to do? Differently? More of?

What have we done in the past that has been helpful? Why?

What are you/we going to do now?

We want students to be making decisions here, under our guidance.

One of my favorite teachers, Barbara M'Gonigle, taught math at Dumont High School (New Jersey). She regularly challenged students to examine their quiz and test results, to analyze same, and then to figure out what they needed to do to improve. At the end of a marking period her students would write letters home, explaining to parents how well they had done and what they were going to do to improve.

Recall at this chapter's opening we mentioned Harry, a third grader in Shauna Ullman's class. His growth was not automatic and resulted from Shauna's skillful use of formative assessment approaches, notably giving students a voice in how they were participating in the unit and the Primary Years Programme (PYP):

> As students became more familiar with an inquiry based approach to teaching, I found their questions deepened and became more connected to our objectives. Having discussions with my students about the key concepts, transdisciplinary skills, attitudes, and attributes of the PYP framework allowed them to see the bigger picture of what I was guiding them towards. Using the "analysing the inquiry process" sheet I created [see Figure 6.6] led to some *rich discussions about what we were learning and why we were learn-ing it. Students seemed motivated to think about which learning engagement activities they wanted to do next* [italics added] and some of the students expressed a sincere interest and enjoyment in con-necting our learning to the PYP vocabulary. (S. Ullman, personal communication, July 20, 2011)

Figure 6.6 I Am Learning to Inquire . . .

Central Idea: _____

Guiding question(s) Circle TEACHER or STUDENT: _____ _

Inquiry process: Tuning In, Finding Out, Sorting Out, Going Further, Taking Action, Reflecting, Drawing Conclusions

Name: Date:

Learning Engagements:

- KWL
- OTQ
- Journaling
- Experiment
- Web search
- Book/article research
- Video
- 3-2-1
- Interview
- Online discussion

- Book Browse
- Jigsaw
- Webquest
- PowerPoint presentations
- Guided reading
- Reading comprehension
- Art project
- Formal teacher test
- Ongoing learning journal
- Debate

[This is a shortened list from Shauna's original]

Briefly describe the learning engagement activity or activities completed:

Where are you in the inquiry process? Describe what you have learned:

What skills have you been working on: Research, Thinking, Self-Management, Communications

What new questions do you have?

What learning engagement could you do next to further your inquiry? (italics added)

Source: © Shauna Ullman (2011). Used with permission.

Teaching literature and writing to eighth graders in the Catalina Foothills District (near Tucson, Arizona), Pat Burrows is a teacher with a most interesting background. Not only has she experience in theater arts, but she also has a master's degree in organizational behavior. This field of study focuses on how organizations work to reach their goals and objectives. It often focuses on such key processes as problem solving, decision making, and leadership to make the organizations more effective and efficient.

Here's Pat's description of what impact these studies have had on her challenging students to think critically:

> Finally, there was one class/seminar that impacted me the most: Power in an Organization. As a matter of fact, what I learned caused me to leave the private sector and apply what I learned within our classroom. I give my students choices on a regular basis. Those choices range from choosing from menus to demonstrate their proficiency in a skill/knowledge to making decisions about using technology or other resources. Bottom line here: if my students do not feel that they have any power when it comes to what and how they learn, they don't "own" their learning and become "bystanders." (P. Burrows, personal communication, June 2011)

Pat has brought forth the most significant concepts related to learning: ownership and power.

Choices we regularly afford our students help to ensure engagement and motivation, both of which lead to higher achievement.

CONCLUSION

We have sampled a variety of formative assessments in the hopes of communicating the idea that there are many ways for students to share their thinking with us, ones that can lead to our taking some action to improve instruction.

One of the themes I articulated early on in this volume was that of students' assuming more control over their own learning. We have seen how formative assessments can serve a very useful purpose toward this end. When students know what's expected of them, are able to reflect on progress toward specific ends, then they can help their own learning by being involved in the decision-making process.

> "If my students do not feel that they have any power . . . they don't 'own' their learning."

As Pat Burrows summarized above, "If my students do not feel that they have any power . . . they don't 'own' their learning."

ENDNOTES

1. See Chapter 7 on this program and the guiding inquiry concepts: Form, Function, Change, Connection, Causality, Perspective, Responsibility, and Reflection.

2. The purpose of having common assessments is to "promote clarity, consistent priorities . . . common pacing. . . . [It promotes a] viable curriculum [and] creates ownership of the curriculum among those who are asked to teach it" (Dufour et al., 2006, p. 53).

3. There has been some research to substantiate this generalization.

4. These two are marvelous ways to challenge students to ask good and better questions to figure out what's in the Box. As I play these questioning games with adults I almost always notice that the questioners are initially not that facile with asking broad questions to eliminate whole categories—"Is this object man-made?" or "Is it found in the home, used for entertainment?" Some teachers have told me that the Magic Box—see Chapter 7—is their favorite way to help students with special needs ask more and better questions.

5. Anna's students also observed their own growth in inquiry. Kyle reflected, "I've grown in the level of questions that I ask using more of level three" (see Figure 2.2). RJ mentioned, "When I wrote level one questions I had to make more because those questions got little info while when I make level three I ask more but I get all the info that I need."

6. For an excellent report on using interactive whiteboards, iPads, and other media to record what "students *thought and learned* rather than what they *did*," see Burton, Krechevsky, and Rivard (2011). Authors stress what you see in Anna's and Kerry's uses of the Evidence of Inquiry form concerning students' growth in inquiry from Level I to Level III.

7. See http://thejournal.com/Articles/2011/07/11/Putting-the-iPad-to-Work-in-Elementary-Classrooms.aspx?p=1 for challenging applications for elementary school students. "Some of the most interesting applications are those that allow for student creativity and critical thinking. . . . First- and second-grade students in Arlington (VA) are creating their own online books, complete with student-generated text and images along with links to external sites, photos and videos. The students are then publishing their work online so that parents, fellow students and their peers around the world can see it too." Imagine the feedback possibilities here!

8. That is, dinosaurs died out not merely from the generally accepted impact of a meteor 65 million years ago but also from by-products of many volcanic eruptions at the same time. Jacqui has a broad view of this extinction, reflecting a contemporary understanding of that cataclysmic event.

REFERENCES

Barell, J. (1995). *Teaching for thoughtfulness: Classroom strategies to enhance intellectual development* (2nd ed.). White Plains, NY: Longman.

Burton, F., Krechevsky, M., & Rivard, M. (Eds.). (2011). *The Ohio Visible Learning Project: Stories from Wickliffe Progress Community School.* Dayton, OH: Greyden Press.

Davies, A. (2007). Involving students in the classroom assessment process. In D. Reeves (Ed.), *Ahead of the curve: The power of assessment to transform teaching and learning* (pp. 31–58). Bloomington, IN: Solution Tree Press.

de Bono, E. (1970). *Lateral thinking: Creativity step by step.* New York: Harper & Row.

Dufour, R., Dufour, R., Eaker, R., & Many, T. (2006). *Learning by doing—A handbook for professional learning communities at work.* Bloomington, IN: Solution Tree.

Dyer, J., Gregersen, H., & Christensen, C. (2011). *The innovator's DNA: Mastering the five skills of disruptive innovators.* Cambridge, MA: Harvard Business Review Press.

McPeck, J. (1981). *Critical thinking and education.* Oxford, UK: Martin Robertson.

Popham, W. J. (2008). *Transformative assessment.* Alexandria, VA: Association for Supervision and Curriculum Development.

Reeves, D. (2010). A framework for assessing 21st century skills. In J. Bellanca & R. Brandt (Eds.), *21st century skills—Rethinking how students learn* (pp. 305–326). Bloomington, IN: Solution Tree Press.

CHAPTER 6 APPENDIX

Here are what I consider to be important dimensions of problem solving, critical thinking, and creative thinking. These are meant only as a guide for the development of your own set of essential elements or skills within each process, taking into consideration your students' abilities, ages, and developmental levels. These are not necessarily listed in the order we might experience them.

Problem-Solving Elements

Analyze the Problem: Pose Questions[1]

represent graphically;

relate to similar problems encountered;

reduce to smaller parts;

reflect on assumptions and different points of view;

research for more information, causes;

reason toward acceptable causes, possible and viable solutions; and

recognize our feelings in dealing with complexity.

Identify Problems[2]

generate alternative solutions/perspectives;

identify criteria for good solutions;

run experiments/trials to test out possible solutions and assess results;

critique possible solutions/establish solution criteria;

decide and implement;

reflect on outcomes and thinking processes: "How well did we do?" and redesign as necessary.

Critical Thinking

Question to challenge

claims/conclusions;

authority of sources;

assumptions, preconceptions;

kinds/sources/reliability/validity of evidence;

potential slant and/or bias of sources;

definitions/clarity of terms; and

common understandings, status quo.

Consider/identify all relevant information/data[3]

Present different points of view (other side of the coin) and associated reasoning processes.

Make reasonable comparisons, identify logical links among them, and draw appropriate inferences:

- seeking causal reasons,
- projecting possible consequences and providing evidence, and
- drawing reasonable conclusions with supportive evidence, in accordance with criteria.

Continually reflect on thinking processes: "How well are we doing? What are we missing?"

Creative Thinking

Creative thinking is a problem-solving process—a way of redefining old problems and finding innovative solutions to new ones. It may involve some or all of these processes:

Clearly define a problem or redefine an old problem in a new way (from how to stay away from mosquitoes to how to keep them away from us):

seeking possible causes;

altering point of view, seeing it from different angles, perspectives;

reversing normal patterns of perception (de Bono, 1970), turning things around, inside out, upside down (normal: Columbus discovered America; reversal: America discovered Columbus);

searching for alternative solutions;

combining different aspects or elements (Einstein's "combinatory play with ideas");

thinking metaphorically, including use of similes and analogies (seeing "as if");

creating/removing artificial or perceived constraints;

thinking hypothetically about possibilities—Why not? What if? and

combining different ideas/solutions (scamper method, Dyer, Gregersen, & Christensen, 2011, p. 64).

Field-test, make decisions, implement, and assess.

Continually reflect on processes: How are we doing? How well did we do? What might we do differently next time?

ENDNOTES

1. Adapted from Barell (1995).
2. Adapted from Barell (1995).
3. This list is based on John McPeck's (1981) definition of critical thinking as a "certain skepticism, or suspension of assent" (p. 6) about what to believe and do.

From Stories to Powerful Questions

LITTLE LOBBYISTS TAKE COMMAND

April 14, 2011, saw two very different and dramatic events in Vancouver, British Columbia.

On that date it snowed in parts of the city, much to the amazement and amusement of some residents.[1] This means that for much of the city it was cloudy. But it was very sunny in West Vancouver, at least in one classroom at Mulgrave, an International Baccalaureate (IB) school, Grades PreK to 12.

On this very day, Thursday, there was a parade of five- and six-year-olds marching with much determination to the office of Karyn Mitchell, principal of the junior school. They were on a most important mission, one they had decided on themselves.

These children, with Jennifer and Maribel in the lead, had just concluded a six-week unit on life in the oceans and had become concerned about all the dirty stuff we now find there and call pollution.

"How can we prevent this?" Jennifer asked. "How do we tell people that we are killing animals living in the oceans?"

"How do we stop doing bad things to the coral reefs?" asked Maribel.

They had been learning all about the sea creatures that live in the ocean visible from their school. Their teacher had read them stories, they had visited the Vancouver Aquarium, and these adventures had included learning about how we are changing the habitats of wonderful creatures for the worse.

Lorraine Radford looked with pride on her students, all rightfully concerned about the destruction of our precious resource, the oceans. "What do you think we might do?" she asked.

> Jennifer suggested that we make posters to tell all the students in the school what should be done to keep the coral reefs and ocean healthy. This inspired her classmates to create posters during their choosing time [free play; see Figure 7.1]. The children organized themselves into partners spontaneously and set to work with great focus and commitment, drawing and writing about their ideas. Then they decided that they would like to display their posters on the walls around the school, so they went to show Ms. Mitchell and asked her permission to do this. They formed a procession as we walked down the hallway to her office, holding their posters proudly in the air (like a group of little lobbyists). When they returned to our classroom, several children decided to attach popsicle sticks to their posters so that they could hold them more easily to show others. The posters were displayed in the hallway outside the computer lab where they could be seen by all the Junior School students and teachers. (L. Radford, personal communication, May 2011)

Figure 7.1 Sea Poster

Source: Annabella Nowtash and Ava-Lillie Lee. Used with permission.

Needless to say, Principal Karyn Mitchell was surprised and delighted when Jennifer and her little band of lobbyists walked respectfully into her office, told her what they were concerned about, and suggested that they be allowed to display their posters where all members of the school could see them.

This little story amazed me because it shows how one teacher can help her students grow from being storytellers to being ardent questioners who freely choose to extend their learning by taking action.

"What do you want to do with the posters?" asked Karyn Mitchell.

"We want to take them down to the beach and show people how to be good to the ocean," said Jennifer.

Before they got to the Pacific Ocean, however, students agreed to display their messages outside the computer lab where there was a very large tree poster with this inscription to Mulgrave students who dare to take action: "Mighty oaks from little acorns grow."

Thus do we foster young entrepreneurs to strike off on their own pathways with new ideas.

TELLING STORIES, MAKING STATEMENTS

Like most kindergartners, Jennifer, Maribel, and their friends entered Lorraine Radford's all-day, full-year kindergarten class telling stories about their own experiences.

Little children are full of Why? questions (about weather, food, relationships, and the like), but when they get to kindergarten and you start talking about the local firehouse, they tell you stories about how their grandparents took them on a walk to see the big red engines and the black and white dog.[2]

This was the case in Lorraine Radford's classroom—until, that is, things changed dramatically because of how Lorraine taught her students how to ask good questions about objects, about the oceans, about food, about sharing, and about holidays.

How did Lorraine foster her students' growth from telling stories to asking questions such as one of Jennifer's first recorded questions about sharing during a unit titled Our Caring Classroom in October: "What if you want to play by yourself and somebody wants to play with you. You say, 'No thank you,' but they still play with you anyways. How can you solve the problem?"

How do we design a learning environment and fashion instructive experiences such that five- and six-year-olds get to feel that the questions they are asking are so important that they wish to share them with the entire school and, most likely, their parents as well?

In this chapter I wish to present what Lorraine Radford has so generously shared with me:

1. a description of the classroom experiences that foster inquiry;

2. an analysis of some of her students' questions, from October through May; and

3. the significance of some of her inquiry experiences (Observe, Think, and Question, KWHL, and choosing time) for students in all grades, K through 12.

MULGRAVE AND LORRAINE'S CLASSROOM

Tish Jolley, the IB coordinator, drove me up to Mulgrave School one day in February 2011. The school sits high on the side of a hill in West Vancouver, with its parking lots and playgrounds appearing as if carved out of igneous rock. Standing on the expansive front porch of the school you can look out over Vancouver Harbor (with several cargo ships from foreign lands anchored) and onto downtown Vancouver, at this time enshrouded in mist, low-hanging clouds, and perhaps the morning's fog, just as San Francisco is at this time of the morning.

The first day of my visit was a typical wintry gray day, but inside, the beautiful new and very contemporary school building was humming with students' excitement about seeing each other, seeing their teachers, and forthcoming field trips for which students in the upper school were excitedly raising money by selling all sorts of baked goodies.

After modeling various inquiry approaches in Grades 1, 4, and 6 (see videos at www.morecuriousminds.com/videos.htm), Tish introduced me to Lorraine Radford and her wonderful world of kindergarten explorations. Lorraine's walls were festooned with posters of students' thinking about intriguing subjects, such as Our Caring Classroom and Celebrate!

I saw much evidence of students' questions, some written in students' own handwriting. There were also KWHL charts with students' prior knowledge and wonderings filled in. These charts had been typed and displayed so all children could see and admire their classmates' wonderings about the world.

Here's what Lorraine told me subsequently about these charts:

As I type up each stage of the KWHL process, I paste these charts onto large sheets of differently coloured construction paper. This is done to highlight the steps of the inquiry process in order to help my students identify the different steps easily when referring to these charts during each unit e.g., the "What we think we know" step is always pasted onto blue background paper; "What we want to know" step is pasted on red background; "How can we find out what we want to learn?" is on purple; "What we have learned" is on brown. The words on the different charts for each step of the inquiry process are also always typed in the same colour. (L. Radford, personal communication, June 2011)

And Lorraine told me about her Wonder Book, a notebook she keeps on her desk, ready at hand, to record a student's question. Then, after school, she enters the question into her elaborate electronic data-preserving format called Development of Students' Questioning and Action (see Figure 7.2). Over the course of the entire school year, Lorraine jots down notes in her journal and then transcribes them to the computer for later sharing with parents, with students, and with observers such as me.

Lorraine explained how she communicates evidence of students' growth to them and to parents:

I don't have one "formal" sit down with my students to discuss how their questions have changed, but as they are sharing their questions for the current unit, I always try to comment on how well they are using the different question starter words and I positively reinforce how they are now asking questions which are more helpful, thoughtful (making us think), deeper, do not need just a "yes" or "no" answer etc. instead of just telling stories/making statements like they did at the beginning of the school year. Because I keep the inquiry process charts for all of the previous units (these are held together with rings and hang on hooks on the back of a cupboard next to the Wonder Wall), it is easy for me to refer back to the children's prior questions and point out how they have changed whenever it is relevant to do so during the year. I have also used their questions in my report card comments regarding the units of inquiry to indicate the development of their questioning/understanding to their parents. (L. Radford, personal communication, July 2011)

MAGIC BOX

Many teachers present students with something like a Magic Box. It might be a bag or a box with a mystery object in it. Usually, we place objects in the container so students can attempt to figure out what they are. I've used similar containers with teachers, challenging them to figure

Figure 7.2 Development of Students' Questioning and Action

Grade: Kindergarten 2010/2011   Teacher: Lorraine Radford

Student's Name:	Theme: *Who we are* Unit of Inquiry: *Our Caring Classroom*	Theme: *How we express ourselves* Unit of Inquiry: *Celebrate!*	Theme: *Where we are in place and time* Unit of Inquiry: *Home Sweet Home*
Jennifer	<u>Term 1 (and year-long)</u> <u>October</u> What if you want to play by yourself and somebody wants to play with you. You say, "No thank you," but they still play with you anyways. How can you solve the problem?	<u>Terms 1 and 2</u> <u>November</u> Why is Christmas called Christmas?	<u>Term 2</u> <u>January (Mini-inquiry into *Winter and Snow*)</u> Why does water turn into ice when it is too cold? <u>February</u> I wonder why some people can't find homes even though they are very rich and don't want to share their money with poor people?
	Theme: *Sharing the planet* Unit of Inquiry: *Under the Sea*	Theme: *How we organise ourselves* Unit of Inquiry: *From Field to Table*	Theme: *How the world works* Unit of Inquiry: *Up We Grow*
	<u>Term 2</u> <u>March and April</u> Why does the hermit crab hide from humans? Why does the mummy octopus die when her babies hatch? Why are turtles backbones attached to their shells? Do you think that anglerfish think humans are fish sometimes?	<u>Term 3</u> <u>May</u> How are bananas made? How is whipped cream made?	<u>Term 3</u>

Student's Name:	Theme: *Who we are* Unit of Inquiry: *Our Caring Classroom*	Theme: *How we express ourselves* Unit of Inquiry: *Celebrate!*	Theme: *Where we are in place and time* Unit of Inquiry: *Home Sweet Home*
	Why does the mummy turtle lay her eggs on the beach? Why doesn't she lay her eggs in the sand at the bottom of the ocean?	How does the coconut make milk inside it?	
	How come there are not many creatures down in the Midnight Zone?	How did the first seeds for fruits get made?	
	Questions asked after field trip to Vancouver Aquarium:	How do you make spaghetti noodles?	
	I wonder about how does the octopus stick on the window of the tank?	How do chickens lay eggs?	
	I wonder how do the sea stars stick on the rocks?	How are Yops (drinking yogurt) made?	
	April 14th – Action by Jennifer & Maribel:	How do lollipops get made?	
	During discussion about how we could help the marine animals and coral reefs from being harmed by different factors such as pollution, warming of ocean water, etc., Jennifer and Maribel both became very concerned about this issue and verbalized their desire to help prevent this. In response to my question about how they could do this, Jennifer suggested that we make posters to tell others in our school what should be done to keep the coral reefs and ocean healthy. This inpired her classmates to create posters during their choosing time. The children organised themselves into partners spontaneously and set to work with great focus and commitment, drawing and writing about their ideas. Then they decided that they would like to display their posters on the walls around the school, so they went to show Ms. Mitchell and asked her permission to do this. They formed a procession as we walked down the hallway to her office, holding their posters proudly in the air (like a group of little lobbyists). When they returned to our classroom, several children decided to attach popsicle sticks to their posters so that they could hold them more easily to show others. The posters were displayed in the hallway outside the computer lab where they could be seen by all the Junior School students and teachers.	How come worms like to eat apples?	

Key Concepts: Form (What is it like?)   Function (How does it work?)   Causation (Why is it like this?)   Connection (How is it connected to other things?) Change (How does it change?)   Perspective (What are the points of view?)   Reflection (How do we know?)   Responsibility (What should we do about it?)

Source: © L. Radford (2010).

out what's inside using a form of the old quiz show game, Twenty Questions. It's sort of like the Black Box problem at upper grades wherein we show students an input and an output and they need to figure out what's inside.[3]

Lorraine used the Magic Box (see Figure 7.3) as a form of preassessment for students' questions. Let's put an object inside and try to determine what it is.

In her classroom each student plays the role of VIP for the day. One of the student's responsibilities is to bring to school a mystery object. The student places it in the Mystery Box, and classmates try to figure out what it is.

As you will note from Figure 7.3, Lorraine has pasted many starter question words on the outside of the box: *What, Who, Why, When, Where, How, If, Is, Do, Does, Can, Will?*

Whenever a student uses one of these starter question words, Lorraine places it on her Question Ladder. By the time all of the words have been used as questions, students have usually figured out what's inside the box.

Figure 7.3 Magic Box

Lorraine continued with her description of these first few weeks of kindergarten: "The children love to see whether they can use all the question starter words and get right to the top of the ladder. Within a few weeks of being in Kindergarten, most of the students are using these words to pose questions instead of making statements when the V.I.P. student for the day is doing his/her 'show and share' time. As the weeks progress, those children who are ready, also begin to read these words for themselves and the V.I.P. student places each word on the ladder as he/she hears his classmates using them" (L. Radford, personal communication, June 2011).

Notice that these starter question words help students begin to read words. They also help differentiate between statements and questions, as do the hand signals Lorraine uses:

> I introduce the different hand signals for the children to use when they are indicating whether they are asking a question (one raised hand) or sharing a statement/connection (thumb and index fingers on both hands form a chain). If they have a new or interesting idea while the teacher or a classmate is sharing, they indicate this by putting a hand on the top of their head. These visual signals are modeled by the teacher to help them differentiate between a question, a statement/connection or a new idea as the class observes and discusses the mystery object when it has been taken out of the box after the students have asked questions using the ladder and starter words, and guessed what the object is. (L. Radford, personal communication, June 2011)

The box and the ladder help students learn to ask good questions, provide ample material for discussions about the mystery object, and often, according to Lorraine, lead to even more questions (using the relevant hand signals).

Let us also note the alternative form of communicating, not with words but with hand signals. A combination of verbal and visual communications is obviously working here at Mulgrave. It seems logical to say that the more modes of communication we employ (verbal, visual, physical/nonverbal, mathematical, artistic, emotional), the more learning opportunities students will have.[4]

> "I introduce the different hand signals for the children to use when they are indicating whether they are asking a question (one raised hand) or sharing a statement/connection (thumb and index fingers on both hands form a chain)."

A "SIMPLE INQUIRY PROCESS"

With this introduction, Lorraine launches her units of inquiry on caring and sharing, celebrations, homes, oceans, and food production as well as a comparison between the life cycle of humans and that of butterflies. Students' new awareness of the difference between a statement, such as "I know where tomatoes come from," and a wondering about how they are grown leads to a four-step inquiry process, building on the hand signals:

> I think that the following steps of the simple inquiry process model, which I use with the children during each unit of inquiry, also help to make them aware that their questions, statements/ connections, suggestions for finding the answers, and sharing of their newfound knowledge are all valuable contributions towards helping us construct our understanding of the central idea:
>
> 1. What we think we know (statements)
>
> 2. What we want to know (questions)
>
> 3. Finding out (suggestions for how to find out the answers)
>
> 4. What we have learned (sharing newfound knowledge and understanding) (L. Radford, personal communication, June 2011)

Lorraine uses a form of inquiry directed by these questions:

K What do I *think* I know about the subject?

W What do I want/*need* to know more about?

H How will I/we go about finding answers to our questions?

L What are we learning (during and after our inquiries)?

A How can we apply what we are learning?

Q What are our new questions as we inquire?

Notice we are initially asking students what they *think* they know. They might have misconceptions, and that's fine. One kindergarten teacher told me that using this word–*think*–liberated her students from being overly cautious about mistakes. And also note that we ask, What do want and *need* to find out? Students might not want to know much of anything initially, but if we treat them as junior investigators, scientists, and professionals, they will have questions they need to ask to figure out solutions to problems (Barell, 2007).

It is at these very early stages of learning more about questioning that we see the power of inquiry. We take children who are naturally curious but who come to school telling stories and help them learn to use our language to figure things out, to go out exploring on their own. All through the power of questioning.

AN INQUIRY INTO SHARING THE PLANET: LIFE UNDER THE SEA

Living close to a harbor leading to a vast ocean has many benefits for students, among which are becoming familiar as they grow up with what an ocean is, what changes it might go through (e.g., tides), which creatures live there, and how we can use and protect it for fun and sport.

Lorraine commenced her unit of inquiry with a variety of learning experiences, including the following:

1. Read illustrated books such as *Ocean* (Sheila Rivera) and *Where Am I?* (Moira Butterfield) and ask, "Where is our home? Is the ocean a home for something? What do you think lives in the ocean? Where do you think these animals or plants live in the ocean—near the surface, in the middle, at the bottom?"

2. Commence KWHL chart with students' statements in response to, "What we think we know." Use a globe for Observe, Think, and Question about the earth, landmasses, and oceans. Students illustrate their answers. Lorraine noted, "When I have recorded the children's prior knowledge statements on the 'What we think we know' chart, they also always work together on creating large group posters to illustrate their thinking because I find that this generates more discussion about their prior knowledge and ideas/suggested answers than when they are working on their own separate sheets of paper" (L. Radford, personal communication, June 2011). Elicit students' initial questions and post (preassessment).

3. Teacher direct questions (using resources), "What kinds of different marine animals and plants are found in our part of the Pacific Ocean? (form) How do the depth and temperature of the ocean affect animal and plant life? (form, connection, causation, change—IB inquiry concepts; see below; pre-assessment).

4. Learn about sea animals and plants with classifying activities: by habitat, by physical characteristics—animals with holes, animals

with stingers, soft-bodied creatures, creatures with legs, creatures with one or two shells (preassessments and formative assessments).

5. Prepare for the class's visit to Vancouver Aquarium: Observe, Think, and Question with sea stars. How are they alike and different? What questions do you want to ask about them at the aquarium? Teacher points out differences among questions: those with "straightforward answers and those that are more complex." Create research groups for sea stars at the aquarium.

6. Visit Vancouver Aquarium, where students observe some of the 70,000 sea creatures, including sea stars; visit the white-sided Pacific dolphins and beluga whale live encounters; and learn about the ongoing Clean Up the Beaches campaigns (preassessment and formative assessment).

7. After the visit, students write in journals: "What did you inquire about and become knowledgeable about at the Aquarium?" (formative assessment).

8. Research students' questions. Illustrate creatures that live in different ocean zones. View *IMAX Deep Sea,* among other videos. Follow with discussions (formative assessments).

9. Introduce *The Adventures of Gary & Harry—A Tale of Two Turtles* by Lisa Matsumoto and *Coral Reefs in Danger* by Samantha Brooke (All Aboard Science Reader). "Draw or write about how you think the ocean gets dirty" (formative assessment).

10. Each student selects an individual question to research (Jennifer: "Why does the mommy octopus die after babies hatch?"). Teacher sends individual worksheet home with the child's question. Share learnings with class.

11. For creative writing in journals, each child selects a marine animal that she has learned about:

    "I would be a _____ because. . . . I would live in the _____ zone because . . ." (formative/summative assessments).

12. Various summative assessments include drawing pictures of different creatures, writing a story (with a beginning, middle, end, and problem to solve), having a personal interview that includes the teacher's and student's self-assessment.

One of the more colorful learning experiences (see Figure 7.4) involved students' drawing what they thought they already knew about

Figure 7.4 What We Know Group Illustration

oceans and the creatures that live therein. We can see that the extent of their prior knowledge would lead to a wide variety of inquiries about this most complex ecosystem. As you can see, Lorraine places strong emphasis on students' drawing—using art to express themselves—since this is easier for them than using a written language. We use art, pictures, and other visual means of communications in our everyday lives, and art helps children develop this means of representing their world. "It is useful to be able to receive and process information through a diversity of representational modes" (Copple, Sigel, & Saunders, 1984, p. 67).[5]

Here are some of the students' initial questions:

Esther: Why can't the marine animals that live at the top of the ocean go to the bottom where the anglerfish live?

Mark: Why do fish and whales have to stay in the water?

Jennifer: Why does the mommy octopus die when her babies hatch?

Maribel: What is the slowest creature in the ocean?

Bill: How come anglerfish can live in the Midnight zone?

Sophia: I wonder why the ocean is blue?

So many questions!

I can imagine all Lorraine's children sitting on the carpet with pictures and stories wondering about various sea creatures living within different zones of the ocean, listening to their friends' ideas and then, as adults do in similar circumstances, finding new questions to ask.

Some of these questions led to individual research projects for each student.

How could they find answers?

Jennifer: My Dad suggested a book, but I wanted to use the computer because it gives you more information.

Maribel: I used the encyclopedia and the computer. You can also ask a friend or older people like parents.

Nat: I called my grandpa because he knows a lot about fish.

Quite resourceful, wouldn't you say?
And what did each find out?

Jennifer: I learned that the mommy octopus dies of exhaustion because she has not eaten in 11 months. She could not leave her cave, not even to eat because she needed to keep caressing her babies to give them oxygen and also to protect them from predators. [Mrs. R. asked, "What does 'exhausted' mean, Jennifer?" "It means so, so tired!" "What does caressing mean?" "It means stroking her babies."]

Maribel: First, I thought the fastest animal was the barracuda, but the slowest I did not know. I thought it could be the fish that walks on its fins [tripod fish] or sea worms. I thought it may live on or near the bottom of the ocean, near the mud, near the abyss. I learned that the slowest fish is the dwarf seahorse and the fastest is the sailfish. Mrs. Walsh [teacher's assistant] read a book to me about it, and my Mom helped me look in the encyclopedia and on the computer.

> Students were fascinated by creatures' living in different zones of the ocean: the sunlit, twilight, and midnight zones.
>
> Esther: The sperm whale can dive from the Sunlit Zone to the Midnight Zone. My brother helped me to find out on *Mad Science.* There are different kinds of animals in the Midnight Zone, and Twilight and Sunlit Zones because of the pressure of the water, and the coldness and the darkness.
>
> Jennifer: In the Midnight Zone, it's so dark that the fish need lights and they have soft bones so they don't get crushed by the pressure of the water.
>
> Mark: Anglerfish are bioluminescent. [Mrs. R. asked, "What does that mean, Mark?" Mark's response was, "They make their own lights."]

Perhaps there were such intriguing questions because of how Lorraine organized her students during the inquiry process. Not only were there many large-group discussions about readings, pictures, and questions, but each child had her own research question, as we've just seen. Each child was included in a small-group investigative team and, while at the aquarium, these teams conducted their studies of various sea stars (the bat, sand, rose, and sunflower sea stars) with the help of parent volunteers.

By all these various means, Lorraine has provided her young oceanographers with many and varied opportunities to observe objects and artifacts close at hand, to reflect on what they already might know about them, and then to wonder, to pose meaningful questions. Observe, Think, and Question is one of our most productive inquiry approaches (see Figure 2.1 on page 31). And because of Lorraine's varied research projects, we understand the importance of how we phrase the *W* of the KWHL: "What do we want and *need* to find out if we are, as young oceanographers, to understand deep sea creatures and how they survive in the ocean? How they might be threatened?"

HOW DO WE KNOW STUDENTS HAVE IMPROVED?

Because Lorraine has kept such precise and complete records, we can examine her students' growth from October through May of the year 2010–2011 (see Figure 7.2). Mulgrave is an IB school, and it reflects certain educational principles and practices at all three levels of schooling. Within the Primary

Years Programme (ages three to twelve), there are guidelines for students' inquiry that structure and provide meaning for what we are asking about and learning. The PYP framework, that is, the inquiry framework that Lorraine uses to teach concepts that have "universal significance . . . each of which has major significance, regardless of time or place, within and across disciplines" (International Baccalaureate Organization, 2007, p. 16), includes the following key concepts:

form,

function,

connection,

change,

causation,

perspective,

responsibility, and

reflection.

The International Baccalaureate inquiry concepts are the following:

Form—What is it like?
Function—How does it work?
Causation—Why is it like this?
Change—How is it changing?
Connection—How is it connected to other things?
Perspective—What are the points of view?
Responsibility—What is our responsibility? and
Reflection—How do we know?

Consider a unit of inquiry you are currently (or were recently) engaged in. How do these concepts reflect your major, guiding, essential questions? How do they reflect what students want and need to find out?

"The key concepts, also expressed as key questions, help teachers and students to consider ways of thinking and learning about the world, and act as a provocation to extend and deepen student inquiries. . . . They . . . provide a key—a way into a body of knowledge through structured inquiry" (International Baccalaureate Organization, 2007, pp. 16–17).

Figure 7.2 presents the electronic data format Lorraine used to record each child's questions, and what is not evident here is that she not only recorded the questions but also classified them in accordance with the inquiry concepts by color: red for causation (Why is it like this?), green for function (How does it work?), and so on.

For example, Lorraine recorded no questions for Mark during the first two units (Our Caring Classroom and Celebrate!) in October and November. Then, during the Under the Sea unit, he burst on the scene with these questions about causation:

Why do fish and whales have to stay in the water?

Why do whales have to blow air out of their blowholes?

Why do fish have fins?

Why do waves come onto the beach?

Yes, it may be true that Mark had questions he didn't articulate or that Lorraine did not hear. It might have been the case that Mark didn't voice his wonderings early on because his ability to maintain focus on the topic under discussion during class was somewhat immature and he was easily distracted. But after spending time with caring, encouraging adults, he became a more engaged, verbal inquirer who then made valuable contributions to discussions regularly. It may also have been the March 4 visit to the Vancouver Aquarium that opened his eyes wide to the mysteries and fascinations of nature! Here was stuff to look at, touch, and hear, whereas the Our Caring Classroom and Celebrate! units may have been more abstract for him. Let's consider another example, Linda:

October (Our Caring Classroom): no questions

November (Celebrate!): Why do we have to have turkey on Thanksgiving?

March and April (Under the Sea): Why is the whale heavier than an elephant? How do dolphins make their sounds?

So in what two ways has Linda grown?

CLASSIFYING QUESTIONS

How would you classify Linda's questions? What, if anything, do the numbers of questions suggest? For some students the numbers tell an interesting story. Consider, for example, John: In October, he asked no questions; in November, he asked one question; and in March/April, he asked seven questions, all seeking to understand why (causation). Examples are, "Why are anglerfish called 'anglerfish'?" and "Why is the Equator always warm?"

So we can observe students' growth in these simple fashions:

1. the number of questions and

2. the concepts they reflect.

Most of Lorraine's kindergartners, quite logically, learned how to ask *Why?* questions to come to understand how a strange phenomenon came to be, like the equator's being warm. So Linda has grown in these ways:

1. moving from making statements to asking questions,

2. asking an increased number of questions, and

3. asking questions reflecting the different concepts (causation and function).

Here we can also refer to E. P. Torrance's (www.ststesting.com/ngifted .html) ways of classifying responses to questions that call for creative thinking. For example, his tests would ask questions such as, "What would happen if a fog covered us except for two inches from the ground?" and "How many different uses can you think of for a spare/used tire?"[6]

He classified answers by

Fluency—the number of answers;

Flexibility—the different points of view expressed;

Originality—how creative, novel the answers were; and

Elaboration—the amount of detail in the response. (Torrance Test of Creative Thinking, www.indiana.edu/~bobweb/Handout/cretv_6.html)

We can see from early data in Lorraine's class that some students certainly became adept at asking more questions—fluency. And most of these questions related to causation; they reflected one concept, one point of view. There were a few questions asking, How does it work? ("How do dolphins make their sound?") And there were one or two reflecting different perspectives ("What if you want to play by yourself and somebody wants to play with you . . . ?"). There were no questions about connections, responsibility, or reflection.

Lorraine's students were not, at this young age, very flexible in their thinking, meaning they did not ask different kinds of questions (form, causation, function, connection).

But these are generalizations and our data may be incomplete.

OTHER ASSESSMENT CRITERIA— JENNIFER'S TURNING OUTWARD

Look at Jennifer's very first question: "What if you want to play by yourself and somebody wants to play with you. You say, 'No thank you,' but they still play with you anyways. How can you solve the problem?"

What do we see here? What PYP inquiry concept would you use to identify her question? Form? Function? Causation? Reflection?

Lorraine identified Jennifer's question as one of perspective taking: What are the points of view? Do you agree with her assessment?

There's more here. She's asking a hypothetical question: "What if?" I don't find many examples in all the data I've examined of this kind of What if? question. We know how important these kinds of questions are, especially in science, where they lead to hypotheses and experiments.[7]

Jennifer senses a problem she wants to solve and isn't quite sure about how to go about solving. So there's problem posing, one of the most important intellectual skills at any age. This is the ability to sense that there might be something wrong, something out of kilter, a discrepancy that will need to be remedied.

In February, Jennifer asked, "I wonder why some people can't find homes even though they are very rich and don't want to share their money with poor people?"

This seems like a complicated comparison of rich and poor people and their money. This might also be a reflection of a growing social consciousness, a concern for others and for nature, reflected in her march on Mitchell.

In April, Jennifer returned to an earlier theme: "Do you think that anglerfish think humans are fish sometimes?"

Her ability to think of different points of view is striking and sets her apart from her classmates. This might be one reason she was the leader of the pack marching like little lobbyists down to Principal Karyn Mitchell's office that day in April.

When I presented Jennifer's sequence of questions here at a workshop, a participant pointed out that her early question about playing a game was all about her, very egocentric. She grew to be able to ask questions about the conditions faced by other people and the points of view of anglerfish. A most interesting transformation.

Here is Lorraine's year-end assessment of Jennifer as e-mailed to me: "She is an astute thinker who has generated many original ideas, and has progressed very well academically throughout the year. She is an articulate, confident communicator, who shares insightful ideas enthusiastically during class discussions. She has far exceeded expectations in reading and creative writing. She has a strong, outgoing character, and is often determined to do things in her own timeframe. As far as her play goes, she is imaginative and creative, and can be a cooperative, caring classmate. Overall, she is a very perceptive, creative and talented child" (L. Radford, personal communication, June 2011).

EVIDENCE OF REPRESENTATIONAL COMPETENCE

The questions in Figure 7.5 are quite amazing to me.

For example, in Linda's and Mary Ann's first questions, they are imagining situations contrary to the factual: Why can't animals live in places where they do not? And why can't we humans do what fish can do?

These questions seem to challenge conventional thinking about what Piaget called "concrete operations," that is, that children reason primarily from what they can see, touch, taste, and hear. But there might be something else here, and that is what developmental psychologists call "representational competence."

Figure 7.5   Analyzing Students' Questions

Here are some Spring 2011 questions from Lorraine's students. See what processes and concepts you find within them:

1. Linda: Why can't animals that live at the top of the ocean live at the bottom like the anglerfish? If the food helps our bodies, does the food we eat help other animals? At the beginning of world, was there food?

2. Mary Ann: Why can't we live under water, but fish can?

3. William: When dinosaurs lived on earth, were there giant apples?

What concepts do you see in these questions? Comparisons, originality, time travel and relationships, situations contrary to fact, imagination?

We understand the world by means of the internal and external ways we have of representing, drawing, re-creating, and fabricating it. We create internal pictures when we think, and we communicate among each other by means of various "representational systems or modes" (Copple et al., 1984, p. 22): linguistic, musical, pictorial, mathematical, nonverbal, and the like.

Perhaps Linda and Mary Ann are two advanced students who can transcend the immediate—the top layer of the ocean where fish swim—to consider its alternatives—the lower layers and those of us who do not live in the ocean. (Of course, having a picture right in front of you makes it easier!)[8]

Challenging students to deal with what is not present has been called by researchers "distancing strategies," and Lorraine has been able to elicit from these two students curiosities wherein they are going beyond the immediate, the present, to the senses and the concrete. Why would we engage in such approaches? To enhance students' "representational competence," their abilities to interpret and make the world meaningful using a wide variety of concepts. To enhance their cognitive development (see Copple et al., 1984).[9]

WHY NOT?

Of course, another element within these questions of Linda and Mary Ann is asking, "Why not?" Think of what this demands. This demands not only holding two different and nonpresent-to-the-eye concepts in mind but considering a counterfactual possibility. "Why can't we live under water" the way fish do, not in a submersible habitat? I asked Lorraine if this question had come from the title of or a line in a book. Lorraine told me that it was only after Mary Ann asked her question that they read such books as *What's It Like to Be a Fish?* (by Wendy Pfeffer).

I have always associated this ability with George Bernard Shaw, who famously noted, "You see things; and you say 'Why?' But I dream things that never were; and I say 'Why not?'" (www.bartleby.com/73/465 .html).

These questions that ask, Why not? may reflect a more complex way of thinking about sea creatures and the problems they face. We should listen for them and, where and when appropriate, encourage students to engage in these kinds of comparisons and contrasts because they develop our abilities to think, compare/contrast, and draw logical conclusions.

We can analyze Lorraine's students' growth in questioning in the following ways:

1. Using International Baccalaureate inquiry concepts: form, function, causation, connection, change, perspective, responsibility, and reflection. Which do they ask more/less of? Who asks which kinds of questions and not others?

2. Using E. P. Torrance's creative thinking criteria: fluency (number of responses), flexibility (different points of view), originality, and elaboration (providing details).

3. Using other evident criteria, such as time travel ("When there were dinosaurs, were there giant apples?"), asking Why not? questions and considering situations contrary to fact ("Why can't we live under water?"), and asking What if? hypothetical questions that may present alternative ways of looking at the world and/or a playing with variables in a situation ("What if I were a fish?").

4. Asking about problems to solve, decisions to be made, hypotheses to be tested, and creative works to be designed.

5. Others:

These are some criteria we can use to observe students' growth and development over time.

I have been privileged to observe the following in Lorraine's classroom:

1. students' growing in ability to ask questions and making fewer statements;

2. students' asking more questions than they did previously;

3. students' asking a few questions that reflect their own flexibility—posing questions from different points of view; most questions concern causation (Why is it like this?), a few illustrate connections (comparing rich and poor, upper and lower zones), and a very few demonstrate perspective taking ("Do you think anglerfish think humans are fish?"); and

4. students' asking questions that transcend the IB and Torrance criteria to include time travel, Why not? questions, and situations contrary to facts.

The time travel, comparison, Why not? and perspective questions may reflect more complex thinking on students' part. We would want to continue monitoring these students' progress perhaps with travel journals in the future.

QUESTIONS FOR LORRAINE RADFORD

While working with the first graders in Lorraine's school, I brought in pictures of my mother at different stages of her life—from a teenager to a woman in her eighties. The students were studying changes between generations. At the end of their examining the photos and arranging them chronologically, I said, "What questions would you ask my mother were she sitting right next to me?" and I held up one of the more recent photos. They had very good questions, one of which was, "What was your life about?" (see video of this episode at www.morecuriousminds .com/videos.htm).

So at the end of these case studies I want to afford you the opportunity to ask each of these teachers a question or two. If you wish to e-mail them to me, I'll pass them on—jbarell@nyc.rr.com.

CONCLUSION

Questioning is empowering, and the assessment of our abilities in this miraculous human capacity is one that puts us in control of our own learning and development into responsible citizens.

Lorraine has deeply challenged her students in so many ways, using wondrous approaches that benefit not only kindergarten students but those in all grades.

Let us review what can be done in all grades:

1. Keeping Wonder Books of students' curiosities from October through May. This is, perhaps, the most comprehensive way to observe and monitor students' growth. "I do this because I find that most of my Kindergartners are not ready to attempt to write down their questions during the first term. It takes them a long time because they are still learning how to form the letters and they need help with spelling most of the

words, and then they tend to lose their train of thought. I also find that writing their ideas on a chart while they are watching me, can also take too long for those children who have difficulty with sitting in one spot for a length of time" (L. Radford, personal communication, July 6, 2011).

2. Tracking students' questions during the year. We've seen how Shauna Ullman, also at Mulgrave, has developed her own system of recording and monitoring students' questions. I asked the IB coordinator, Tish Jolley, for her assessment of what in Lorraine's classroom was transferable to other, higher grades. She e-mailed me the following:

> We hope to develop this [method of tracking students' questions] in the next year in all grades as it is proving to be really interesting and quite exciting. (Shauna and I think, anyway!) The process is telling quite a story in terms of seeing what students are learning, how their knowledge and understandings are developing, as well as where their interests lie. In their unit dealing with plants as a life-sustaining resource for all living things, Shauna tracked their questions and we have seen different students focusing on different areas that obviously caught their interests e.g., pollen and flowers, seed germination, and photosynthesis, to name a few. (T. Jolley, personal communication, July 7, 2011)

3. Extensive use of inquiry approaches such as Observe, Think, and Question (using wide varieties of artifacts—the sea stars—and media—books, videotapes, and IMAX movies) and KWHL as a guiding structure for inquiry. Recall that Piaget said that "to understand is to invent," meaning we actively construct meanings from the stuff before us (Piaget, 1973). Lorraine has provided rich content both in her classroom and at the aquarium.

4. Providing students with many and varied experiences to enhance their abilities to think about the world through classification, comparison, contrast, and drawing conclusions. The benefits of being able to classify objects, experiences, and people in multiple ways include having more control over our own environments, understanding the world more clearly, and being able to communicate such understandings to others (Copple et al., 1984). It is not surprising to me, therefore, that some of Lorraine's students are able to handle multiple representations (lower/upper zones) and ask questions contrary to fact.

5. The use of children's blocks for free play in kindergarten (I once asked Lorraine about this, one of my favorite subjects). Such free play has been an issue for many years because some adults wish to squeeze so much "content" into kindergarten to prepare students for the upper

grades. I'm glad to say that children in Lorraine's kindergarten enjoy daily, designated periods of what she calls "choosing time," time for independent and/or sociodramatic play. Here, she said, students often continued to think through what they had been learning about sea stars and various other creatures living or being threatened in the Pacific Ocean. Play is an activity wherein students are in control, and this is important because here they learn how to master many realities, pose and solve problems, and be creative. Thus, play is one educative experience that combines three elements of control:

a. internal reality—We can make a block into an oceangoing Greenpeace rescue craft,

b. internal motivation—We play because it is fun in and of itself, and

c. internal command—We are in charge, commencing and ceasing at our own will.

6. Distancing experiences. Because students seem to be creating multiple representations of reality through their questions ("When the dinosaurs lived, were there giant apples?"), we would be encouraged to engage them in "distancing" experiences as suggested by Copple et al. (1984). Challenge students to think of the "non-present" (p. 25). "Involve children in planning, anticipating future events, reconstructing the past, translating ideas from one mode to another" (p. 25).

What Lorraine was doing, and what all of us can and should do, is to provide mind-expanding experiences for our students involving the immediate present, the past, and the future: compare objects in the present with those experienced in the past, for example. We need to "encourage children's tendency to actively reconstruct what they've experienced, thus adding to the richness, as well as the accuracy of their mental representations" (Copple et al., 1984, p. 234).

7. Extensive use of art in the classroom. This is not just an experience for young students. Drawing a representation of a fish, of a mathematical word problem, or of Iago in Shakespeare's *Othello* can be a very rich learning experience. Students' drawings can communicate to us how they are understanding the content we are teaching, how they understand their world. And of course, some students will be more adept at drawing their understandings than in using oral language. Recall Michael's picture of the sun's core in Chapter 6.

Thus, at this very early age, we are witnessing how children gain control over their experiences and environments through the use of language development, artifact observations, and deep and intense investigations of their own curiosities.

When Karyn Mitchell asked the little lobbyists what they wanted to do with their posters, they responded, "Take them to the beach and show people!"

Tish Jolley noted, in conclusion, "We are beginning to see more authentic action and independent learning in the higher grades. By using a common language and developing these concepts right from the start, we are paving the way for deeper investigation. In Grades 3 and 4, students understand about their responsibility towards the planet and the importance of action, no matter how small the deed." Mighty oaks from little acorns grow.

Indeed, maybe we see here the beginnings of an entrepreneurial spirit—not in the commercial sense of inventing products for sale but in the sense of charting our own courses toward new and unexplored territories or making new statements and gaining new perspectives on life.

ENDNOTES

1. One resident posted her amazement on YouTube. (Unfortunately, the photographer has taken down the post.)

2. My first experience with this phenomenon came while I was doing research on childhood play in New York City during my doctoral studies. I'm still intrigued by students' being so curious outside of school while, inside, their inquisitiveness requires nurturing to manifest itself.

3. The Black Box also serves as a metaphor for companies like the former Enron, where nobody could figure out what went on inside, how it made its money.

4. However, recent research indicates that there are scant if any data to connect "learning styles" with achievement.

5. Such representational competence is, of course, just as important in the upper grades of elementary, middle, and high school. We interpret the world through visual means, and we communicate our understandings of people, events, and abstractions through all the visual arts—hence their vital importance for the curriculum! Note the use of visual language: "I see the problem clearly. Let's see if we can work this out. What is your school's vision? Look at the problem from this perspective."

6. During qualitative research on imaginativeness in high school, I once asked this question: "What if all the snow and ice in Antarctica melted?" (This was prior to awareness of climate change!) One student replied, "Venice would no longer be unique."

7. One of the most famous What if? questions came from Einstein, who, perhaps while daydreaming in school, asked, "What if I were to ride along a ray of light and turned around. What would I observe?" His answer to this question led to a revolution in our thinking about the universe, to the Special and General Theories of Relativity, first published in 1905.

8. Lorraine recalled, "My students and I were observing the large ocean zones chart displayed on the Wonder Wall at the time, and they were pointing out

and naming the marine animals which each of them had drawn for this chart. They were also explaining their reasons for placing them in a particular zone" (L. Radford, personal communication, July 8, 2011).

9. One strategy taught to me by Irving Sigel challenges students at this age to think beyond what actually happened. "What did you do over the weekend?" "We went to Grandma's house." "How did you go?" "We rode in Daddy's car." "I see. What if you had no car or it didn't work? How could you then get to see Grandma?" We challenge students to think beyond what did occur to imagine alternative possibilities, thereby strengthening their cognitive abilities to deal with the world.

REFERENCES

Barell, J. (2007). *Why are school buses always yellow? Teaching inquiry preK–5.* Thousand Oaks, CA: Corwin.

Copple, C., Sigel, I., & Saunders, R. (1984). *Educating the young thinker—Classroom strategies for cognitive growth.* Hillsdale, NJ: Lawrence Erlbaum.

International Baccalaureate Organization. (2007). *Making the PYP happen: A curriculum framework for international primary education.* Cardiff, Wales: Author.

Piaget, J. (1973). *To understand is to invent.* New York: Viking.

"My Inquiry Skills Shot Through the Roof!"

Kerry Faber's sixth-grade classroom in Edmonton (Ekota School) is set up in a U-shaped configuration with an open area right in the middle.

It is in this magical square that so many adventuresome learning experiences have taken place over the years:

exploring the continent of Antarctica,

constructing an aboriginal village,

re-creating a fur trading fort,

building a medieval castle, and

reconstructing—perhaps for the first time in Canada!—a replica of Leonardo da Vinci's ideal city.

This is not your normal classroom, because Kerry Faber is an extraordinary educator who always challenges her students to exceed their own high expectations, to become the developers of their own learning and understanding through a wide variety of projects like those listed above.

After a one-day visit to Ekota, the father of one of the students, Shannon, told me that being in such a project-oriented classroom has made all the difference for his daughter. Prior to working with Kerry, when she was in a more traditional setting, Shannon had been a somewhat listless student.

Since Shannon began working with Mrs. Faber, she has blossomed academically. It has been amazing to watch Shannon complete her assignments and projects. While she will still come to us with some questions, most of the time she is able to complete her assignments by finding the proper information on her own and the quality of her work has increased dramatically.

As Shannon's ability to complete her assignments has improved, her comprehension of the material has increased. This also helps Shannon create better and more complete study notes for exams which translates into better grades. Shannon is also much more confident in school. (N. & K. Routier, personal communication, March 5, 2010)

What this letter and the list of very challenging projects do not reflect is the primary role of inquiry within Kerry's classroom. She has used, and provided the model for, several of the inquiry strategies mentioned in this book and others (see Barell's [2007] *Why Are School Buses Always Yellow?*) and has formatted the Evidence of Inquiry form introduced in Chapter 6 (see Figure 6.4 on page 113).

Now, how did Sydney come to reflect on a unit called Evidence and Investigation by concluding, "My inquiry skills shot through the roof"?

This unit involved solving a mystery that Kerry set up right in that magical square.

There was a body outline and various pieces of evidence scattered around it. I revealed this scene when I pulled back a blanket that had been covering it before science class. I posed this question: "What do you think happened here and what observations of evidence lead you to think this?" Then I used this scene to teach them how to conduct different tests. About once a week we would discuss our hypotheses as to what likely happened based on new information gathered from the tests. Children were encouraged to build on the ideas of others as well as question and debate ideas shared. People sometimes commented on walking by our room and seeing us engaged in some very active discussions while sitting around the scene on the floor. I would sit with the kids and facilitate the discussion—paraphrasing and guiding through questioning. The kids often went back to their desks afterwards and did some reflective writing based on these discussions. (K. Faber, personal communication, March 2010)

So students had to examine the scene and the available clues and, with the help of additional lessons on fingerprinting, chromatography, and graphology, create a logical scenario to explain what had occurred. They were, in effect, playing the roles of detectives and investigators like those seen on TV shows such as *NCIS*, *Law & Order*, and *Cold Case*.

Kerry used the Evidence form to help her assess students' levels of inquiry at the beginning of the unit and throughout. I have copies of all of these forms, commenced in early November 2009. Here are some of their initial wonderings:

Jessica: What tools would you use [to solve the mystery]?

Max: What is the crime? Who are the suspects?

Sarah: When did this crime happen?

Danielle: What facts should one have to be a suspect?

Initially, we can see some students focusing on gathering information about the alleged crime scene: time, kinds of evidence available, and suspects.

But some students asked questions at a more general or higher level (perhaps Level II of the Three-Story Intellect; see Figure 2.2 on page 33):

Carter: Why are some crimes left unsolved?

Reid: What is the most common thing found at a crime scene?

Jessica: How would you prove if your suspect was guilty?

Interestingly, a number of students in Kerry's class wondered about our inability to solve a crime, as Carter did. This speculation runs counter to our experiences with television programs where all of the crimes are solved within sixty minutes or less.

Kerry noted in a recent e-mail (April 2010): "We actually discussed this a few times. The kids understood that much of what was on those shows was not real or even accurate. They suggested reasons for why the crime had to be solved in one episode."

These students, like the adults who examine seashells and reflect on their own thinking, often begin at the most logical level—gathering information. We can see these young sleuths asking lots of What, Where, Who, and How questions to learn as much as they can before they begin hypothesizing about suspects and possible motives.

Here Level I questions are most appropriate. Kerry noted, "I want the kids to know that this level of questioning definitely has its place in our inquiry process. These are the questions that we build on."

How to account for the more general questions—What if a crime isn't solved? What are elements common to all crime scenes? I'd bet these reflect the strong emphasis in this class on inquiry across the board, in all subjects. Some students, obviously, are able to abstract from the crime scene details questions of a more general nature.

GROWTH IN QUALITY OF QUESTIONS

Now, how did students and teacher observe growth of students' inquiry skills? Let me share with you the reflections of only a representative sample of Kerry's students to exemplify their observed growth.

Here is Carter's summary at the end of the unit: "I think I have grown during this unit. I have learned to ask questions more in depth. . . . At first I was asking questions like, 'Who is lying on the ground?' By the end I asked questions more in depth like 'Did the fibre on the ground come from a jacket or was a blanket unraveling? Did someone put it there on purpose?' I have enjoyed this unit."

Rebecca Lee noted, "[This unit on investigations] got my brain really working. It got me asking process to apply questions" (see Three-Story Intellect, Figure 2.2).

Kerry further noted that Rebecca "is reflecting more on what an activity taught her than recording just the details and procedures. She is thinking about the application of her knowledge in other situations." In other words, Rebecca is becoming more complex in her thinking, growing from noting details to how they might, in general, be applied elsewhere.

And about Jessica's thinking and questioning, Kerry noted, "Questions are becoming deeper, more complex. Showing processing of experiments conducted [for example], 'I wonder if you took a piece of someone's hair and analyzed it but it didn't show the DNA?' . . . and 'What if it was fake hair like a wig?'"

Here Jessica is comfortable with entertaining outcomes contrary to those desired—not finding any DNA. As we shall note below, this question suggests an ability to see multiple sides of an issue, an indicator of cognitive development beyond a focus on the more immediate and the concrete.

We can see that Carter has moved from a simple, "Who's that?" kind of question to searching for causes, for alternative sources of clues—from a jacket or a blanket. He's grown, perhaps, from focusing on what's before him to considering alternative sources of information. As we shall see, searching for alternative possibilities can be a sign of growth in cognitive complexity as well as good problem-solving tendencies.

So we have students who represent growth from Level I (gathering) to Level II (processing) kinds of questions. Of course, we would need to check their thinking within other units to see if they exhibit the same facility for asking "deeper, more complex" questions. Have these skills been transferred, for example, to literature and math or social studies? Kerry advises me that she does, indeed, have evidence from units in social studies, language arts, and math that corroborate the reliability of these observations.

COGNITIVE DEVELOPMENT

One of my surprises in examining the data from Kerry Faber's class was the evidence that suggested growth in cognitive development. This means that some students seemed to reflect growth from a comfort primarily with data—"just the facts, ma'am," as Sergeant Joe Friday used to say on *Dragnet*, a show from the early days of black-and-white television.

As Kerry noted about one student, she "likes to work with facts and record details." This focus on what Piaget called the "concrete" is, of course, important. Concrete operations characterize young children's reasoning during the early years of elementary school.

But investigators need to do something with these facts, to sort them, relate them, find patterns, and search for solutions to the puzzle. At about the age of Kerry's students, eleven and twelve, some students grow into a more mature way of thinking known as formal operations, wherein they can think more abstractly and consider multiple possibilities not immediately evident in the immediate data or evidence.

We can look at a body lying on the ground and think of many possible causes that led to this situation; we can imagine a variety of suspects with different motivations and formulate an explanation that considers all factors and not only those immediately evident to sight, sound, and touch.

Formal operations has always suggested to me the ability to transcend the concrete to imagine the impossible, the contrary to reality, the myriad possibilities that come from a lively imagination. What if? is a question I often hear on *Law & Order* when the detective is asking about something directly contradicted by the evidence before him or her. This is sort of like Copernicus's asking, "What if the sun is the center of the solar system and not the earth?" a question that defies the evidence of our immediate perceptions of the sun's "rising" and "setting" daily.

Let's see how this growth may be in evidence in Kerry's classroom. I say "may be" because I am keenly aware that we are dealing with a limited set of data within two separate classes over a two-year period, but with the same inquiry-oriented teacher. I think it's worth using these samples to key our thinking toward the intellectual development that she is definitely working to foster.

About Shannon, Kerry wrote, "[She] is developing in her ability to process information based on hands on activities and pose questions. These are mostly 'What if' and not related to the purpose of the activity. Looking at a situation from a different perspective and using a wider variety of questions will be a good goal to work on" (Evidence of Inquiry form, January 2010).

The ability to take a different point of view is one important element within cognitive growth. In the last chapter, we noticed how Jennifer's questions seemed to develop in this fashion from October to May of her year in kindergarten.

Here I think Kerry is urging Shannon to broaden the scope of her investigations with her What if? questions, to see the situation from multiple perspectives, definitely a characteristic of more formal, abstract thinking. Shannon did ask many What if? questions, for example, "What if two different inks show the same color?" This suggests she's able to see the possibility, however remote and removed from immediate experience, that this could happen.

Not Knowing the Exact Answer

By contrast, another student, Chintan, "didn't like not knowing the 'exact answer,' but now [two months later] he likes to share his perspective and listen to others to consider a situation from different angles" (Evidence of Inquiry form, January 2010). Here is quite direct evidence of change over time spurred on by the critical thinking Chintan has been challenged to engage in during this unit on investigations.

Kerry noted, "When Chintan listens to others' ideas he often challenges them to prove their reasoning by asking them questions like, 'How do you know that?' or 'Are you sure that's really the way it is?' to 'What background information do you have to prove that?' He'll also comment that, 'Maybe it's actually . . . instead of what you are thinking'" (Evidence of Inquiry form, January 2010).

During this year's (2011) unit on the Iroquois consensus approach to decision making, students worked through problematic situations (see Figure 8.1). I interviewed several of the students on Skype shortly after

Figure 8.1   Iroquois Consensus Decision Making

For this project, you will imagine that you are a member of an Iroquois clan in the 1600s that is facing a number of problems. Your clan must come to a consensus about how to address these problems and explain why you made your decisions. (See Figure 8.2.)

Each member of your group will need to choose a role to play in your clan and will bring an important point of view to the consensus decision-making process. As a clan, you will work together to create a poster that you will present to the Grand Council that describes and defends your decisions.

It is very important that every single member of your clan agree to each of your four solutions to the problems you are facing. Ever since the Peacemaker introduced the Great Law of Peace, the Iroquois have only made decisions that every representative in the Grand Council agreed upon, and you will need to use this model to make choices in this project. True consensus is built through talking, listening, and considering different ideas until a common understanding is reached.

this enriching experience. It was evident from students' comments that they were good at projecting consequences:

"Wait, does that [approach] make sense?!"

"Is that realistic?"

Kerry noted the differences she's seen in some of these students' behavior between fifth and sixth grades: "Last year you would have said, 'That's *dumb!*' But this year you ask questions" to get people to think of the consequences, for example, of mounting a raid on another group of Iroquois and stealing their grain.

"Why ask questions?" Kerry asked her students during this video interview:

Mann: You can get the person to be more curious. And you become more independent yourself. You learn more by thinking of questions and considering others' ideas.

Obviously, one goal for Kerry during this simulation was for students to consider all points of view before making a decision, not to get stuck in what we call their own "confirmation bias," finding and using only evidence that confirms their own points of view.

But on the other side of the coin, Ayan wrote in one of her summary reflection entries on the Evidence of Inquiry form, "The consensus model

Figure 8.2 Iroquois Consensus Decision Making Problem 1

Problem 1: Land Dispute

The crops of the neighbouring Snipe Clan from the Cayuga Nation have slowly been creeping onto the edge of your clan's farmland. Recently, they have been harvesting crops from this part of your farmland. This means that your clan has less food to harvest. Many clan members are worried that the clan will run out of food in the winter if the Snipe Clan is not stopped from using your fertile land.

- Some members of your clan think that the best response to this problem would be to start stealing mature crops from the Snipe Clan's land to make up for the lost food. They argue that this solution is only fair.
- Other people feel that your clan should simply move its farmland to a different area away from the Snipe Clan. They point out that the farmland will become unfertile in a few years anyway and are afraid to challenge the Snipe Clan, which is powerful and can be violent.
- Another group in your clan wants to send the Snipe Clan a wampum belt to declare war on the Snipe Clan. They think that the actions of the Snipe Clan must be confronted directly and forcefully.

sounds nice but I don't think everybody could get along in one." To which Kerry responded in writing, "You are taking a more realistic approach than some of your classmates." Ayan was one who often raised questions when somebody proposed a solution "that [she] didn't think was entirely workable."

SEEKING OTHER EVIDENCE OF COGNITIVE GROWTH

Now, here we're dealing with only a few students. But my purpose is to illustrate (or disclose) the kind of data that might become evident once we begin examining students' use of inquiry within a structured framework.

What other evidence might we seek? We might look for students' engaging in the following:

1. Considering multiple motives to explain perpetrators' actions. This would involve considering their lives, the multiple factors of their relationships with the victim.

2. Searching for more clues than are immediately evident, as has been done (see above).

3. Creating an explanatory framework/explanation that takes all clues into account, especially clues not immediately evident, as well as motives not immediately evident. Such a framework, or scenario, will explain the facts but might also, like a good scientific theory, predict where we might find more conclusive evidence.

4. Projecting consequences of actions into the future, perhaps the distant future.

5. Being comfortable with drawing key abstract concepts from an investigation, such as freedom, responsibility, civil rights, and the like.

6. Dealing with if-then propositions that are by nature abstract: "If all criminals make mistakes, and this person is our leading suspect, then we should be able to find him or her having made a serious mistake somewhere along the line." You've no doubt heard this reasoning on *Law & Order* or *CSI* at one time or another. Kerry advised me, "The kids will often ask questions framed like this but they often don't have the background knowledge to process the question to a logical conclusion or the perseverance to investigate on their own."

There are no doubt other indicators. Consider how we use our imaginations to create fantasy friends the way many children do. At a more advanced age, we should be able to reason in the world of fantasy, perhaps the way James Cameron did in creating his blockbuster movie *Avatar*. This is seeing what's possible in the future and being able to construct characters that act out of recognizable human motivations.

> How does a teacher foster good problem solving?
>
> Kerry Faber: I left the problem solving to the kids....I got better at keeping my mouth shut, just asking them how they were thinking things through....They feel so empowered. I'm having a great time watching them.

FOSTERING PROBLEM-SOLVING SKILLS

It is evident by now that some of Kerry's students are thinking like good problem solvers—identifying the crime, seeking causes and motivations, and considering a wide range of alternative solutions or explanations.

Considering alternative points of view and perspectives is not only a sign of cognitive growth but also an indication of good problem-solving skills. Maybe your colleague sees the situation differently. Maybe she can imagine how one or two as-yet-unnamed persons might be suspects.

Jack Bauer, the fictional hero of *24*, a very intense, well-plotted national security drama, was often thinking one or two steps ahead of the alleged terrorists as well as those in command of CTU. Good problem solvers imagine alternative perpetrators, motives, means, and causal factors not evident to others.

Of course, the essence of being a good problem solver is to generate a solution that actually solves a problem. So often we hear in the national press about legislative proposals—currently about the employment, health care, and debt situations, for example—that don't deal with the real issues—in this example, those leading to the 2008 near disaster and subsequent financial crisis.

Part of being a good problem solver is to identify the problem correctly. This entails asking lots of question to get to the core or the heart of the matter. Of course, with a dead body in front of you, the problem is rather plain—who did it? But with complex social, psychological, and economic/political situations—like health care—getting to the heart of the matter is often very, very complex, requiring the skills Chintan has exhibited above.

Recall what Carter said about his problem-solving abilities in this crime scene investigation: "I think I have grown during this unit. I have learned to ask questions more in depth. . . . At first I was asking questions like, 'Who is lying on the ground?' By the end I asked questions more in depth like 'Did the fibre on the ground come from a jacket or was a blanket unraveling? Did someone put it there on purpose?' I have enjoyed this unit."

What do you see here that relates to problem solving?

Perhaps it's Carter's initial problem definition—"Who's this lying on the ground?"—a logical initial information-gathering (Level I) question.

What do his higher, Level II questions contribute to his being a good problem solver?

What do the latter questions say about his concern for evidence, something every good crime stopper should pay meticulous attention to? Remember Sherlock Holmes's legendary ability to spot evidence on somebody's clothing with an initial glance.

Kerry's comment about Carter's self-reflection will lead us into considering critical thinking: "Carter's strength with inquiry is in his ability to listen to what has been said and think critically about it. He will rephrase, make analogies and ask further probing questions. He has strong background knowledge to draw from to make comparisons" (Evidence of Inquiry Form, January 2010).

How do we foster making good choices?

Kerry Faber: One of the reasons I use the non-directive approach is to give some choice back to the student. If I just direct, they are expected to do what they are told. They don't have to think for themselves or decide what choice they could make—of perhaps a variety when faced with an open ended question (What could you choose to be doing right now with this time you have?). I usually add "What APPROPRIATE thing could you choose to do . . . ?" This also makes them think of what is socially or academically acceptable. This is after they have been prepped on what choices they could possibly make.

DEVELOPMENT OF CRITICAL THINKING

Related to becoming better questioners and developing a more mature style of thinking (formal operations), we can expect in a unit like this that students would claim that they've become better critical thinkers. And, indeed, they did.

For example, Sarah said at the end of the unit, "I think I have grown in my critical thinking a lot because of all this. We had to use it throughout the whole unit."

Aaron concluded, "I think I have grown my critical thinking skills a lot because I've been asking great questions and my inquiry skills have gone up, up, up!"

Shannon reflected, "I think I have improved in critical thinking because of being able to be a forensic scientist and do many hands on activities. . . . We got to do online finger printing and I found out how to do teeth impressions."

When I visited this classroom in February 2010, I spent some time listening to students tell me all about their investigations and how they solved the mystery. I also challenged them to define for me what they meant by *critical thinking* as they had been practicing it.

We all agreed that what they had been doing was gathering evidence, analyzing it, and using it to draw reasonable conclusions about what had happened in the problematic scenario. They had learned a lot about fingerprinting, chromatography, and other related processes we can see weekly on *CSI*.

Here are some examples I've selected to illustrate students' growth in their ability to think logically, using available evidence, toward a reasoned conclusion:

> "[Sarah] is able to give proof behind some of her logical reasoning, but it needs to be more detailed. Sarah states 'You can get a better mental picture of what happened (when critically thinking).'"

> Jessica wrote, "I think I have become a much better critical thinker during this [crime scene] unit. We have done many tests. I think the most important skill an investigator needs is to have critical thinking [like doing various tests]. . . . When you're an investigator you can't just use one piece of evidence to know who the suspect is. You have to find many."

> Marilee noted about her own thinking, "I think I have grown because when we first started the unit I was very excited. I didn't know how to use my background knowledge. [Later, this] background knowledge helped me make better inferences and it helped me ask better questions." Kerry noted that Marilee "is trying to show her own reasoning, but is sometimes challenged to demonstrate it in a thoroughly logical manner. She is unable to clearly write her ideas because she hasn't thought everything through carefully. She often won't persevere with her ideas to complete a logical conclusion. She is still at the stage in which she needs me to encourage her and ask questions to guide her through the process. Sometimes I have to make suggestions to keep this process going. It often has to do with level of maturity and confidence."

Also consider what Kerry means by "a thoroughly logical manner." When we deal with evidence, we should be asking these kinds of questions:

1. Is it relevant and related to the scenario at hand? When we find a corpse with a knife through his chest slumped over his own desk, it may or may not be relevant that there is a set of golf clubs in the corner. It may or may not be relevant that there is a half-consumed cup of coffee on his desk or that the window is partly open.

2. Is it verifiable? Can everybody agree that there was that cup of coffee and that it, indeed, had the victim's prints on it as well as one other unidentified set?

3. How can all the relevant clues be related? Here's the challenge, of course, that calls for the creative mind to imagine a scenario that explains all the clues and points to a perpetrator. Agatha Christie was elegant in her ability to imagine explanations unconceived by others involved in the case.

Marilee is also using a key critical thinking word, *inference.* An inference is a conclusion we draw based on relating different pieces of evidence. For example, consider this scenario: "John crossed the lake and tied up at the dock."

Now, how did John cross the lake?

We might initially conclude that John was in a boat. How? We use the clues "lake," "crossed," and "tied up." We relate them to our prior knowledge and realize we've done that before in a boat or at least seen films in which this occurs.

But we could use the same context clues to logically arrive at a different mental picture to explain the little vignette: John rode in a seaplane, on a surfboard, or, James Bond–style, in a waterborne automobile that has wheels as well as a propeller and rudder.

In addition to gathering pieces of evidence and using logic to relate them and draw reasonable conclusions, we can say that some of the other skills noted above relate to critical thinking:

questioning assumptions, common wisdom, evidence, and generalizations;

defining and clarifying terms;

taking another, alternative point of view;

considering evidence contrary to assumptions, beliefs, and initial conclusions; and

asking What if? questions.

As we can see, all these intellectual processes are related when it comes to solving a problem and/or critiquing a claim made by somebody.

CREATIVE THINKING

We are creative when we are solving problems. This is how some psychologists define creativity. During the Apollo 13 mission, NASA had to become very creative in the uses of onboard equipment to keep astronaut Jim Lovell and his companions (Swigert and Haise) alive. You might remember that a crisis of survival was caused when one of the liquid oxygen tanks in the service module exploded, causing an aborted moon landing and the crew's having to move to the return module, Aquarius. You might also remember that dramatic scene in the film *Apollo 13* when Ed Harris (Gene Kranz) comes into a room with a bunch of onboard equipment and declares, "Failure is not an option. We have to find a way to solve the problem [of too much build up of carbon dioxide] with this equipment."

It was the equivalent of trying to find a way to make a square peg fit into a round hole.

But they did it, and of course the crew of Apollo 13 survived with some creative problem solving.

Creativity is what Kerry's students have been practicing when they

1. look at a situation from a new and different point of view;

2. reframe the problem with a new question;

3. make analogies, metaphors, and models; and

4. think of alternative, unusual, novel solutions to the problem.

Recall Chintan's challenging "others to consider a situation from different angles."

Recall what Kerry noted about Carter's thinking: "Carter's strength with inquiry is in his ability to listen to what has been said and think critically about it. He will rephrase, make analogies and ask further probing questions." Being able to see similarities enhances our ability to solve problems because we can draw from one experience and apply it to another. Analogies lead to metaphor, one of the hallmarks of the creative mind: "If music be the food of love, play on."

Many problems can be successfully and creatively solved just by reframing the question we ask. For example, years ago we would ask, "How do we stay away from biting mosquitoes?"

Then somebody reframed the question to be, "How do we keep mosquitoes from biting us?" This question led to many varieties of bug spray that we use today.

"MY INQUIRY SKILLS SHOT THROUGH THE ROOF!"

And now let's return to Sydney—"My inquiry skills shot through the roof!"

At the end of her Evidence of Inquiry form she wrote, "Inquiry is very important [because] I wouldn't have been able to have an inference at the end, but to me this unit has been a wake-up call in the world of critical thinking and inquiry."

Figure 8.3 Kanupriya's Model Aeroplane

One of Kerry Faber's challenges is to build a flying craft that can travel at least three meters in the air.

Kanupriya's first attempts led to planes that did midair flips, made nosedives, and landed belly-up. She modified the wings several times. Her patient reflections after so many failed trials told her she needed a new fuselage. At the dollar store she found a foam sword that had to be modified and that became her fuselage. Swords into fuselage. Creative thinking spurred by the questions, What if? and Why not? After further modifications, she produced a model that flew more than three meters and landed body up! One of the characteristics of a good problem solver and creative thinker is persistence in pursuit of a goal. Kanupriya certainly exhibited this quality.

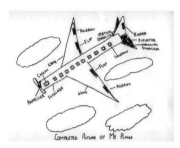

And she ended her lengthy journal reflections recording all of the four or five mistrials and the successful trial with these creative questions:

Will it be possible for "aeroplanes to run on water or hydrogen in the near future?"

In the future will it be possible for man to travel "faster than the speed of sound (mach 2, mach 3) . . . without spending much money?"

We'll see, Kanupriya. Good questions.

I think Sydney is here using *inference* synonymously with *conclusion, claim,* or *judgment.* We can infer that John crossed the lake in a boat, but with some critical questioning we can logically arrive at alternative and logical conclusions.

Why has it been a "wake-up call" for Sydney?

Perhaps she is referring to the solving of crimes. Critical thinking is the basis of our entire judicial system. We are all, if indicted, presumed to be innocent until proven guilty or until proven guilty beyond a reasonable doubt. This means that in a court of law the evidence must lead to the overwhelming conclusion that someone has, indeed, committed a deed or action that goes against the laws and customs of society.

Critical thinking is also concerned with having a healthy skepticism about what to believe and accept. I'm sure Kerry's students raised many good questions about somebody's tentative conclusion about guilt or involvement. These questions about what to believe are the heart of critical inquiry according to John McPeck (1981): "Critical thinking involves a certain skepticism about what to believe or do" (p. 6). Remember these same students' questions in Chapter 6 about flying penguins. Not real! they said emphatically.

Sydney might also be referring to another aspect of critical thinking: considering evidence that contradicts our favored points of view, looking at the other side of the coin or issue. This isn't easy because of our own preferences for our ways of thinking and believing. There are many kinds of bias—political bias wherein we favor one point of view over another, selection (or confirmation) bias wherein we choose only those samples/pieces of evidence that confirm our own point of view or create a certain image or conclusion (as in propaganda).

I imagine on several occasions somebody raised a question that challenged the selection of evidence: But what about this or that? You're overlooking a key piece of evidence. Kerry notes that during discussions she heard these comments: "Don't forget we learned or figured out [this piece of evidence] that doesn't fit with what you are saying." "That doesn't sound logical based on. . . ."

So some of Kerry's students have excelled at drawing reasonable conclusions by bringing together evidence in a logical fashion. In her notes, she has indicated where there has been growth and where there needs to be more work: "Looking at a situation from a different perspective and using a wider variety of questions would be a goal to work on."

And about one student Kerry wrote, "[He] needed to be more thorough in clearly stating the proof to back up his choice of the culprit." We cannot make unfounded accusations and expect them to withstand the scrutiny of the kind of critical thought Kerry's students have been engaged in.

IMPROVING THE DEPTH AND QUALITY OF OUR UNDERSTANDING

One primary goal of conducting various inquiries and investigations is to come to deeper understandings about the subjects we are learning. In this unit, Kerry's students have certainly deepened their understandings of the following:

1. how to conduct a forensic (evidentiary) investigation,

2. the nature and importance of critical inquiry and thinking, and

3. the importance of being keen observers and collectors of evidence and knowing how to use it appropriately. For example, what if two pieces of evidence seem to contradict each other? What can we do? "I think I have grown during this unit. I have learned to ask questions more in depth. . . . At first I was asking questions like, 'Who is lying on the ground?' By the end I asked questions more in depth like 'Did the fibre on the ground come from a jacket or was a blanket unraveling? Did someone put it there on purpose?' I have enjoyed this unit."

QUESTIONS FOR KERRY FABER

What questions would you now like to ask Kerry Faber based on what you know of how she fosters and assesses inquiry? Send them to me, and I'll forward them on: jbarell@nyc.rr.com.

CONCLUSION

We can see from this—albeit very limited—sample that inquiring into complex situations like the one Kerry presented to her sixth-grade students involves asking lots of questions, considering alternative points of view, and drawing reasonable conclusions. As in life, not all students' final conclusions were the same. They saw the evidence and final inferences differently.

What I hope has become evident is that this kind of learning experience can provide a wealth of information about what we call 21st century skills—inquiry, problem solving, critical thinking, and the dispositions that accompany them—openness, cooperation with others, risk taking, and tolerance for ambiguity.

Again, let us review what can be done in all grades:

1. Challenge students with puzzles, mysteries, and problems to solve that might involve extensive investigations and gathering of evidence to arrive at sound conclusions.

2. Provide them with a means similar to the Evidence of Inquiry form or the travel journal (or wikis, Google Docs, and the like) in which to record initial questions, how they conducted their purposeful investigations, and reflections on their own growth in inquiry, problem solving, and critical thinking.

3. Give students feedback on their thinking as often as possible. These formative assessments, given early and often, will help them achieve unit goals.

4. Continuously model inquiry and how you wish students to apply it. This year Kerry told me that she was surprised and delighted to see something she's never noticed before, how students had brought inquiry into their writing on the district writing exams. For example, one writing prompt concerned time: "Time is a peculiar thing . . . we cannot stop it . . . time changes things . . . there is nothing we can do about it." But Rickey paused and asked these questions: "But what if we could change that? What if a hundred years between one man's birth and a huge event in history didn't mean that that man would never see the event? What if a species dying out didn't mean that species would never walk the earth again?" Sounds like H. G. Wells or, more recently, theories of time travel perhaps made possible by Einstein's general theory of relativity, stating that spacetime is curved and that this warping is called "gravity."

POSTSCRIPT

One of the benefits of having students keep records of their thinking and especially of their development over time is that we will continually be surprised by the conclusions they draw at the end of the year. The curriculum is not what's written down in a textbook, nor is it solely what we as teachers seek to enact in our classrooms. The curriculum also comprises those unintended learnings that students acquire while being in our room, being with their classmates, and working through what we, together, have worked on for these nine months.

I mentioned Shannon's dad at the beginning of this chapter. Come to find out her brother, Rickey, was in Kerry Faber's classroom this year as well. What he wrote at the end of his Evidence of Inquiry form relating to the study of the Iroquois consensus model and working through a simulation thereof bears sharing with you:

I think that using inquiry was a big help in understanding the Iroquois. It's just so much more efficient than staring blankly at a textbook and reading chapter after chapter of humourless, uninteresting and just plain lame text that is trying to convince you that this subject is interesting via the least interesting methods possible without defying some law of physics while you scream about how bland it is. . . . The text method just pours some knowledge into your head and leaves you to forget it.

The inquiry method refuses to do that. It makes sure you think about the knowledge it gives you and makes things more entertaining for you. The text method's most entertaining activity is a worksheet with an animal picture in the corner. The inquiry method's most interesting activities are: [Here he lists several] Build Your Own Glider; Mock Legislature; Grand Council, Problem Solving, 20 Questions, Smart Board Games (all Iroquois); Creative Projects, Interesting Homework, Candles and Alka Seltzer, Reflection and Many More.

The emphasis, according to Rickey, is on inquiry's challenging us to think, build, solve, create, and reflect—essential capacities for the 21st century.

REFERENCES

Barell, J. (2007). *Why are school buses always yellow? Teaching inquiry preK–5.* Thousand Oaks, CA: Corwin.

McPeck, J. (1981). *Critical thinking and education.* Oxford, UK: Martin Robertson.

"STEM Changed My Life!"

Karla is an eighth grader at Perkins Middle School in Sandusky, Ohio. The science, technology, engineering, and math (STEM) project I describe below is one that changed her life. She transformed herself from a person who accepted what others told her to do to someone who took much greater control of her own life.

STEM projects are problem-based experiences that focus on developing students' abilities in science, technology, engineering, and math. Many schools across the country have adopted such innovative approaches, some in an effort to qualify for Race to the Top federal funding. These projects seek to enhance students' interests and capabilities in subjects in which our citizens have not performed as well as students in other countries.

But more importantly, projects such as the ones Karla and her classmates engaged in reflect the idea that learning should be problem oriented. John Bransford and his colleagues (Bransford, Brown, & Cocking, 2000) compiled a most useful summary of what we know about learning in *How People Learn*, and they drew this conclusion: "There are many appealing strengths to the idea that learning should be organized around authentic problems and projects that are frequently encountered in non-school settings" (p. 77).

> "There are many appealing strengths to the idea that learning should be organized around authentic problems and projects that are frequently encountered in non-school settings" (Bransford, Brown, & Cocking, 2000, p. 77).

The STEM projects described below reflect this focus on authentic, ill-structured problems that adults might face in their world of work. This project differed from other national efforts to enhance teaching in science, math, and technology in these separate subjects. This was a project undertaken by the entire sixth, seventh, and eighth grades, commencing with the latter. Some might observe that the content is STEM and the approach is inquiry (C. VanVooren, personal communication, September 2011). I would note that in science and math, at least, the process of inquiry should be considered content.

This was the very first STEM project for Karla and her classmates. But these kinds of projects are not new to many schools in Ohio where there is currently a thriving network of STEM schools (www.osln.org/).

Here's the background for Karla's story, and this experience, I submit, will present us with other ways of determining whether students are improving at problem solving and creative thinking. But in addition, I think you will see how this very challenging experience will provide evidence that for some students STEM projects can provide us with evidence of students' becoming more self-reliant, more confident, and more resourceful as leaders and decision makers, outcomes they hadn't developed while sitting in more traditional classrooms.

THE CHALLENGE

In the fall of 2010, Karla and her classmates were challenged to design a roller coaster for an amusement park:

> To continue its domination as the "World's Roller Coast," Cedar Point design engineers need your help. They want to bring a new coaster to the park, one that will generate much publicity and many riders. What is your vision for Cedar Point's new roller coaster? Where should it be built? What will it look like, and what will it be named? Who should be its target audience? How will the park finance it? How far can designers go with the ride and still keep it safe for riders? If you build it, what will make them come?

And Cedar Point is well known to any resident of Sandusky. This amazing park sits on a spit of land between Sandusky and Lake Erie. Its existing roller coaster rides have names such as Millennium Force, Maverick, Corkscrew, and the Raptor (www.cedarpoint.com/). You can imagine riding slowly to the top of one of these coasters, chugging along (as they used to years ago), reaching the high point, looking out at the beautiful blue waters of Lake Erie, and then beginning your plunge down over 100 feet, going ninety miles per hour with your gut up around your voice box and your heart pounding away like mad—that is, if you're over fifteen.

Karla worked on a team with several other students acting as lawyers (Legal Eagles), architects, financiers, and marketing experts. Each team was led by a teacher-selected CEO. During their weekly two-hour meetings, students had to solve many problems of design, safety, publicity, and finance. No easy task, especially if you were new to the roller coaster improvement business.

But they had the benefit of experts in engineering, marketing, architecture, and financial planning, all of whom visited their schools to present information and respond to probing questions. Imagine hearing about design principles from someone who actually designs buildings, not from a textbook!

Students followed a simple problem-solving approach during which they learned of the problem each team faced: "Learn all that you can about the problem before beginning. You might start by brainstorming everything that comes into your head when you think about the problem. Try to observe objects and things related to the problem. Then discuss what you know about the problem with others. Perhaps you should interview or survey others . . . to see how others view the issue. You may need to do some research on the Internet to better understand the problem. Be a detective! Find facts! Leave nothing unexplored!" (Perkins Local Schools, 2010).

Following this initial exploration students were encouraged to write a "challenge statement":

"In what ways might we _____ so that _____?"

PROBLEM SOLVING

Once they understood the problem, students were encouraged to generate solutions. Initially, each CEO had to figure out how to organize the team, how to approach the problems.

One of the leaders, Brandon, told me (in a telephone interview with several of his classmates): "I let the people in charge of each area decide

Figure 9.1 Tackling a Problem

The steps in the Sandusky model include the following:
    learn all you can about the problem,
    brainstorm ideas,
    observe objects related to the problem,
    discuss what you know,
    interview/survey important persons,
    conduct research to gather needed information, and
    write a challenge statement.

what to do to solve the problem. (See Figure 9.1.) We used a lot of trial and error in building the coaster. We originally started building it out of K'Nex, but then we switched to cardboard because we didn't have enough K'Nex"[1] (M. Darr, faculty advisor, personal communication, May 18, 2011).

You can see that Brandon delegated responsibility, and now I wonder where he ever had experience with this kind of leadership.

During November each team posted its comments on wikis (see Figure 9.2). (Unfortunately, this site is longer live, but many schools use this resource, or Google Docs, to enable students to communicate with each other.) Here you can see the CEOs organizing their subgroups and keeping them on task: "I will be around on Tuesday to make sure you are on task."

To create a viable design, CEO Natalie challenged her team: "Architects, you need to find out a lot of information for our financial and marketing officers. They need to know an estimated time and how much land you will be using for the roller coaster. I know this can be stressful but if one person doesn't do their work in this project we all will not get a very good grade."

Marketing involved creating an appealing brochure. Once again, here is Natalie's comment: "The marketing officers were supposed to get their brochures done soon but our groups brochure is hardly done. They are doing good work by taking very good notes. I believe they could work a little harder."

Financing this operation involved hands-on math problem solving, according to CEO Carlee: "In financing we decided how many people would be able to ride per hour. If our ride holds 16 people and has 3 carts running at a time, and runs at 75 mph we can get 1,440 people through the ride per hour. We were talking about a rational(e). Shannon and I still need to finish that. If we have any special things about our roller coaster then I could use those!"

Figure 9.2 Problem Solving Groups on Wiki

Financing this operation involved hands-on math problem solving according to CEO Carlee:

In financing we decided how many people would be able to ride per hour. If our ride holds 16 people and has 3 carts running at a time, and runs at 75 mph we can get 1,440 people through the ride per hour. We were talking about a rational(e). Shannon and I still need to finish that. If we have any special things about our roller coaster then I could use those!

Figuring out legal permits for building on or near a beach:

Ohio Department of Natural Resources. They deal with submerged lands and in Ohio which means at a certain point of the beach that goes to the water and the land under it is they own it and you need a submerged land permit." (Notes from Legal Eagles, 11/11)

I recall eighth grade math problems from a textbook that were neither this authentic nor exciting.

One student asked, "How much g force can a person bear during a coaster ride?" Consider the variables in this problem, speed, acceleration, potential/kinetic energy, height of ride, age/weight of rider, centrifugal/centripetal forces acting on the body. . . These are the kinds of problems that expand our thinking, that help us develop from concrete operational thinking (Piaget) to more formal, abstract reasoning where we can deal with multiple variables.

Some students were figuring out legal permits for building on or near a beach: "Ohio Department of Natural Resources. They deal with submerged lands and in Ohio which means at a certain point of the beach that goes to the water and the land under it is they own it and you need a submerged land permit" (Legal Eagles, November 2011).

I recall eighth-grade math problems from a textbook that were neither this authentic nor this exciting.

One student asked, "How much g force can a person bear during a coaster ride?" Consider the variables in this problem: speed, acceleration, potential/kinetic energy, height of ride, age/weight of rider, and centrifugal/centripetal forces acting on the body. These are the kinds of problems that expand our thinking, that help us develop from Piaget's concrete operational thinking to more formal, abstract reasoning where we can deal with

multiple variables. (I wonder how many eighth graders were in on figuring out this very complex problem.)

A week later, Carlee had to make hard decisions about financing: "Today we decided how long we would take our loans out for and I decided on having a ten year loan so we had enough time to pay everything back. I still need costs of legal fees, permits, insurance, and marketing so I can find the total cost of construction for our coaster."

Designing the actual roller coaster involved, according to Mary Darr, using software called Roller Coaster Tycoon. You can download a demo and take a ride (www.rollercoastertycoon.com/us/downloads). See how your digestive system responds to these heights, severe hairpin turns, and stomach-in-the-throat plunges down, down, down toward the ground! Then use all of your senses to imagine what All Coaster Construction did with these models.

At midcourse another CEO, Shannon, made this observation: "I think that we are close to half way point. We still need to accomplish listening and following directions. I am most proud of keeping everyone in line of what they are supposed to be doing."

REFLECTIVE PAUSE

What strikes you about all of these wiki comments from the CEOs? What are they learning in this project? And how valuable are these experiences for them as young people?

Imagine having this kind of responsibility as an eighth grader. Shannon's comments remind me about what they used to tell me during Naval Reserve Officers Training Corps education at Harvard, that being a naval officer and division leader at sea requires that you achieve the organization's goals and objectives through the work of your men. You are responsible for their work.

At the end of twelve weeks of hard work, there came the day of reckoning, the presentations to peers and professionals. Shannon made these wiki notes: "I am exited about presenting the whole project. I cannot wait for the professionals to see the hard work we put into this. I am also nervous because I will be talking about the whole project along with Carlee."

I get the sense that this presentation was different from what many have had to do, that is, do a panel presentation about our research project. Natalie, Shannon, Carlee, and other members of their teams were presenting their models and commercials to representatives from Cedar Point, the adult experts on roller coaster design, marketing, financing, and legal issues.

Mary Darr noted that "students were able to come up with ideas that we are too old to think of ourselves because we are not fourteen-years-old. One group had the idea of painting a coaster with glow-in-the-dark paint, and another group suggested that the handlebars be made of mood-ring material, so that friends could see how each other was feeling when they touched the bars. Acting cool in front of friends would be difficult if the lap bar turned a color that showed nervousness. Those were both ingenious ideas."

The representatives from Cedar Point asked these kinds of questions:

"Why did you consider a device to disinfect the ride before new riders get on it?"

"How did you come up the numbers you used for your financial plan?"

"How did you come up with the concept for the name of your coaster?"

"What can Cedar Point do to attract more people your age?"

Responding to these kinds of questions is exactly what Grant Wiggins (1998) means when he speaks of students' engaging in authentic tasks and, in the process, receiving feedback from discerning listeners, classmates, or experts in a specific field. This is how the world works, and these students are learning that a product often goes through many iterations before it is presented. We therefore ought to provide students with authentic work wherein they have to make trials, tests, experiments, and near-final presentations to receive a continuous flow of feedback. For some it's this feedback that encompasses the most important learning along the pathways toward achievement of deep understanding.

INTERVIEWS WITH STUDENTS

I had the pleasure of interviewing these CEOs shortly after they completed their models and presented them to an audience of peers as well as folks from Cedar Point. I asked them what they enjoyed about the roller coaster project, what they learned about themselves.

> Brandon: You learned more ways to get things done. This was more challenging, [especially when] others were not willing to cooperate. This was different from previous experiences [in the regular classroom] . . . More applied to the real world.

> Laura: Creativity came out. . . . I loved doing things differently. . . . We learned how to respond to others' opinions. . . . CEO was involved in all the tasks and saw it all come together.

> Kayla: Brainstorming ideas from all . . . [trying to get] all to agree. Tried to incorporate others' ideas. . . . If we disagreed, we voted. . . . [Another CEO made executive decisions when disagreements occurred]. This stuff was more complex.

What do you see here in these comments?

IMPORTANCE OF TEAMWORK

According to many team members, the most valuable aspect of this STEM project was an important 21st century skill, learning how to solve problems collaboratively. Here are excerpts from the end-of-project written reflections:

> Emmy said, "Working together is most important because you all have to be on the same page and if you're not, you get off task."

> Nicholas commented, "The most important thing about STEM is TEAMWORK!!!!"

> Sydney observed that "you have to learn how to deal with arguments" and those who do not participate.

> Carlee noted, "I like my team because we are able to bounce ideas off each other and work well to get everything done."

Jalen said, "The thing that I thought was most valuable about the STEM project was the problem solving because I know that there will be tons of times in my life where I will have to solve problems quickly."

So what was most significant after all was completed was the struggle they all experienced, the difficulties of learning how to listen to each other's different ideas, how to incorporate different ideas into a consensus decision.

In telephone interviews, several of the CEOs told me that they found the problem solving most challenging—finding solutions to problems required them to "think differently," as Karla said, to be imaginative, to be creative, and to think out of the box.

This involved a lot of hard work at figuring out problems, searching Google for ideas, and narrowing ten ideas down to two or one.

And then the CEOs would have to arrive at a consensus, not an easy task by any means. They had to learn, for example, "how to incorporate other peoples' ideas" into an agreed-on solution. Some CEOs worked for compromise, and others made a final decision themselves.

Note Jalen's thinking ahead to occasions when he will be able to use these kinds of problem-solving processes. Here is one test of students' understanding what we are teaching—their ability to transfer concepts and skills to new situations. Researcher John Bransford and his colleagues (2000) have concluded that "the ultimate goal of learning is to have access to information for a wide set of purposes—that the learning will in some way transfer to other circumstances. In this sense, then the ultimate goal of schooling is to help students transfer what they have learned in school to every day settings of home, community, and workplace" (p. 73).

Transfer, or in Bloom's terminology, application, is one of the true assessments of understanding. So when students respond to a test item with "We never studied this," it may be a reflection of our challenging them to use concepts and principles in a novel context when they are not able to make such applications of knowledge.

DRESS REHEARSALS AND FEEDBACK

Before the final presentations, each team ran a dress rehearsal to get feedback from other students. Mary told me that "Most students made 'junk models' first to test out their ideas before creating their final models. They had to solve problems when the materials they were using did not work as they wanted them to work and the models did not look like the images they had created in their heads."

Kids saw others' ideas; responded, "That's pretty neat"; and changed some of their plans. Here students had an opportunity to rehearse their ideas, to put them out in public, to throw them up against the wall and see which ones stuck.

This, as Wiggins (1998) so appropriately has pointed out, is what we do in life. Just look at any episode of *House*, starring Hugh Laurie as a cantankerous but sometimes brilliant doctor leading a team of interns attempting to figure out what's wrong with one patient. All the young doctors throw out ideas, possible causes. Sometimes Dr. House agrees and says, "Do the test"; other times he or another member of the young team shoots down the idea for various stated reasons, all examples of good critical thinking. ("But that cause doesn't explain these symptoms.") On other occasions Dr. House diagrams on a flip chart parts of a KWHL chart: What do we already know? and What do we want to find out?

STEM CHANGED MY LIFE!

> "STEM made me actually start to do better in school and to start thinking about what I wanted to do with the rest of my life. . . . I started to think differently because I realized it was time to become a better person and to grow up and to reach the expectations that my parents have for me and I have for myself."

And now Karla. At first she was bored. "I thought there was no purpose to STEM," she said, but she persisted and made the project her own. "I wanted to find some purpose for the project." And she did. "STEM made me actually start to do better in school and to start thinking about what I wanted to do with the rest of my life. . . . I started to think differently because I realized it was time to become a better person and to grow up and to reach the expectations that my parents have for me and I have for myself."

How did this occur? Karla learned that to not be totally bored, she had to sit up and take some responsibility for her own behavior. "I had to ask a lot of questions," she told me in a phone interview. And this led to her first evaluation of the roller coaster project wherein she mentioned that it made her "think differently," that is, given the opportunity to identify and resolve real problems (personal and professional with the coaster), to think outside the box and learn how to come up with good solutions.

STEM AND TRADITIONAL CLASSES

So how did STEM projects compare with regular classes?

What pleased some students was learning "more ways to get things done, rather than just [sitting in class and] answering specific questions."

Brandon said there were "more variables" you had to work with, more points of view (others' ideas) you had to reconcile. Figuring out how long a roller coaster ride could and should be and how much gravitational force (g-force) would act on the body were complex problems without textbook answers at the end of the chapter.

NASA is asking you "to imagine, and design, a community on the planet Mars.

Our area is Arabia Terra and the reason we chose it was because it's a flat surface, it's like a valley."

NASA has created this contest: www.nasa.gov/exploration/analogs/hdu_project.html

During a subsequent challenge—building a colony on Mars—you had to "project consequences" of building this or that kind of structure and responding to a variety of What if? scenarios—you find a camera, somebody gets killed, someone starts stealing from the group, a piece of exercise equipment breaks down and cannot be fixed, someone becomes ill and cannot do his job, space is found to add an extra crew member.

Other students mentioned the difference between sitting and responding to worksheets and having to figure out a very complex problem—for example, the g-force on a human body, the legal rules for coaster placement—with very few guidelines. There were no answers in the back of the textbook to the dilemmas they faced.

And that, said John Dewey (1933), is when thinking begins, when we face some "doubt, difficulty or uncertainty" (p. 12). These projects were fraught with uncertainties, both for students and for their teachers.

BENEFITS OF STEM

What are the benefits of this kind of project?

Some teachers noticed a transfer effect into their regular classrooms—students' becoming more self-reliant, resourceful, and focused on the tasks at hand. With projects such as designing a restaurant menu complete with prices and portion sizes, after the STEM experience students didn't have to keep running to the teacher, Mr. Phil Graber, to ask a lot of clarifying questions. Sometimes these questions serve the purpose of minimizing whatever ambiguities there are in an ill-structured problem so students don't have to think! They want to be told exactly what to do. But Phil noticed his students had learned how to solve some problems on their own or within the group.

"We had to teach ourselves!" said one student.

Recall from Chapter 3 what Samantha told Mrs. Faber's class after just four days of the teacher's modeling inquiry: "She's not answering us, guys. We have to ask her the right questions to get her to ask some questions so we can figure out the answers to our questions."

Either way works.

NEW PERSPECTIVES ON STUDENTS AND TEACHERS

During a seventh-grade STEM project, planning an advertising campaign for teens and tweens for the Cleveland Indians, one teacher, JoAnna, felt it very frustrating: "It was the blind leading the blind! We worked through this with the students."

Imagine being a seventh grader used to the teacher standing up in front of the room, asking questions, receiving answers, writing stuff on the whiteboard, all the while exuding this air of authority. You know she knows everything about her subject, be it algebra, literature, or science. She's the authority.

Now, in having to figure out how to attract kids to a baseball park, she's right there with you asking, "How do we do this? I don't know. What do you think?"

> "The teachers were out of their comfort zone. This was a super learning experience—to work outside of our own comfort zones."

A sixth-grade teacher, Candi, noted about their project of creating original musical instruments, "The teachers were out of their comfort zone. This was a super learning experience—to work outside of our own comfort zones." How often do we see a teacher in a very structured classroom being stretched well beyond his knowledge base, wrestling with a problem he's never encountered before? Recall in Chapter 2 where we focused on teachers' modeling their own inquisitiveness and how significant this is.

Candi continued, "I couldn't control [the learning environment] as well and had to let them make their own mistakes." (Consider the benefits here.)

Another seventh-grade teacher, Bob, noted that the experiences of working with students in this fashion—around a table, on the floor, at the computer, interviewing experts—"gave us different points of view on their intelligence." In other words, we saw them assuming responsibilities as general managers, not merely sitting at desks responding to our questions.

Maureen noted that one "low performing" student made excellent suggestions about how their presentation could be better. Dawn noted that one shy, retiring girl became, as the result of the STEM group work, far more "outgoing. It was a difference of night and day!" she told me excitedly over the telephone.[2]

This is what we can expect when challenging students to do what one seventh grader, Adam, called "solving tougher problems . . . using grown-up ways of thinking." STEM was a taste of the "real world," as students so often told me. Indeed, they know the difference between doing seatwork in a classroom and tackling tough problems adults face all the time.

And perhaps most significant of all, as Adam continued, the Indians project "Gave us a big objective and we could make it our own." What I think Adam is referring to here is that for once in their young lives teachers had presented him and his friends with a meaningful challenge that afforded them maximum control over their own learning. They had to make hard choices—who was to be in charge, how to define the problem, how to figure out solutions. There was no right answer as in "Yes, that's the correct answer, Adam. Good for you!"

Here we see the benefits of any problem-based approach to education— affording students meaningful opportunities to take more control of their own learning and to make decisions, some of which will lead down blind alleys, some of which might have regrettable consequences, others of which will be more profitable. But students are living lives of people in the world who are charged with taking actions and living with consequences.

Mary Darr, the faculty leader of these STEM projects, observed, "Unlike standardized tests, these challenges encourage students to work together in an authentic environment to generate something new, to fig- ure out what to do when answers aren't obvious. Here they have to pull everything together," meaning apply knowledge from all subjects they've studied: English—create polished keynote presentations free of spelling, capitalization, and grammar errors; art, music, and technology—make the graphics, sound, and color schemes clear and visually appealing; math—compose financial plans and create 2-D and 3-D models; physics— create their roller coaster models while considering the impact on the human body, an area studied in health class; social studies—contact gov- ernment agencies for building and zoning permits; and speech—during the final presentations, as well as during research, students make tele- phone calls to experts to gather information needed for the project.

And Paul Daugherty, director of curriculum, noted that life for middle school students today is very "individualistic" and "social only within a cocoon." STEM provides them with opportunities to create a product and persuade an authentic audience using logical arguments and good reasons.

No wonder Karla transformed her life.

"You have to ask a lot of questions," she concluded.

Very entrepreneurial, I would say.

Science, technology, engineering, and math projects at Perkins Middle School were assessed in accordance with these 21st century skills:

collaboration in group problem solving;

cooperation in small groups;

communications, presenting solutions in a "clear/effective manner";

problem solving/creativity, generating ideas to solve problems;

organize, manipulating data in an "orderly, structured, and clear format";

self-direction and social responsibility; and

technology fluency.

Subject matter standards included the following:

English—write arguments to "support claims with reasons and relevant evidence,"

Science—understand "forces between objects act when objects are in direct contact or when they are not touching,"

Math—equations and expressions, and

Social studies—understand that "choices made by individuals, businesses and governments have both present and future consequences."

Source: STEM 8 Roller Coaster Project, Sandusky, Ohio (2010).

HOW DO WE KNOW THEY'RE GETTING BETTER?

This question was always front and center during my conversations with not just the eighth-grade students but their teachers and the sixth- and seventh-grade students and teachers.

STEM challenges were so novel and complex that they were dramatically different from anything these students had ever worked on, in or out of school. I asked Mary Darr if students felt they had ever experienced anything like designing and publicizing a new roller coaster, and the students' response was "a resounding NO." What does this answer tell us about their lives in schools up to the point of embarking on these STEM projects?

I asked her to ask the students if they thought they had improved in their problem solving:

> They were quite vocal with a huge "YES." They explained that they used the exact same problem solving process that they had been taught in the first STEM project to complete the second one [establishing a colony on Mars complete with a constitution],[3] even though the teachers did not explicitly instruct them to do so. They made a challenge statement first. They said making a challenge statement helped them to organize the problem and their ideas, making it easier for them to come up with a wider variety of solutions to the problem. They also said the quality of their work improved from the first project to the second project because they were able to better understand, apply, and use the problem solving steps they had learned from the first project in completing the second project.

Here's what some of the students said in another phone interview about their ability to "apply and use the problem solving steps they had learned from the first project":

> Carlee: We used our Problem Solving Journals to write out the problem and solutions. . . . We wrote a Challenge statement and then figured out all of the problems to be included.

> Darcy: Our Challenge statement was like the main idea—"How to create a stable colony" [on Mars]. . . . The Creative Problem Solving packet helped us organize information and visually see it.

> Kayla: We brainstormed solutions . . . bounced ideas off each other. . . . The roller coasters looked pretty similar, but our Mars habitats all looked different.

Toward the end of our phone conversation, Carlee added, "With the Mars project we had total freedom. . . . [This experience] gave us a creative outlet instead of doing worksheets."

Carlee's last statement will always resonate with me because STEM projects as conducted in Sandusky are an antidote, a timely and productive one, to primarily doing worksheets in our classrooms. Students of most ages know when they are being challenged to do authentic work and not being asked merely to find the correct answer and fill in the blanks.

I was impressed to hear students make these statements. But do their statements constitute good, reliable data for growth? And how do we know if students are becoming better at problem solving from such projects as those experienced by the students at Perkins Middle School?

HOW TO ASSESS PROBLEM SOLVING

Here are several ways to assess problem solving:

1. Teach students a problem-solving process (see Chapter 6, Appendix A), and observe how they use it. Mary refers here to the students, without adult prompting, writing a challenge statement: "Now that you have completed your exploration of the problem [getting all the facts], write your problem into a challenge statement. This helps you to narrow down the focus of the problem so you can begin brainstorming ways to solve it." For example, "In what ways might we _____, so that _____."

In the case of the Mars habitat problem, students spontaneously and without direction applied what they had used. This is a good indication that they had learned a problem-solving process, and therefore, we might conclude they had improved. When Carlee told me she could "see" the problem after writing her challenge statement, I took this to mean she had clearly identified the key problem—to construct a viable habitat.

What we also see here is students' becoming adept at using the language of problem solving—challenge statements, seeing the problem, brainstorming solutions. This can be a key indicator of improvement—using the language of problem solving, critical thinking, and the like. (I generally prefer to challenge students with a variety of problematic situations and then ask them to reflect on how they figured things out to identify important steps. This is what we did with second graders who said, "Make the problem littler and littler." In this fashion students are generating their own problem-solving protocols, ones that can be developed during the course of an entire year. But the STEM approach described in this chapter served their purposes very well because it saved valuable time and was easily understood [Barell, 1995, p. 168.])

2. Compare students' products—in this case the earlier roller coaster models with the later Mars habitats. The students Mary interviewed following these projects judged the second one to be of better quality because they knew something about problem solving. Perhaps they were better at "analyz[ing] ideas and choos[ing] the best way to solve the problem" (M. Darr, personal communication, June 2011) or at testing and evaluating solutions. You might also see if there is evidence of some advanced problem-solving strategies (see Figure 9.3), such as breaking problems down into manageable parts, drawing pictures to understand, challenging assumptions, and the like.

As part of their culminating experience for the Mars project, students created videos of their habitats. On viewing several of these,

Figure 9.3 A Different Way to Visualize Problem Solving

Research/Identify
Essential Facts
"What is the evidence/data?"

Identify Causes/
Assumptions
"Why?"

Problematic

Project Consequences
of Alternate Solutions
"What if we do this. . .?"

Relate to Similar Problems
"What can we compare
this with?"
Draw Tentative
Conclusions

Steps:

Analyze the problem: pose questions.

Represent graphically.

Relate to similar problems encountered.

Reduce to smaller parts.

Reflect on assumptions and different points of view.

Research for more information, causes.

Reason toward acceptable causes, possible and viable solutions.

Recognize our feelings in dealing with complexity.

Identify problems.

Generate alternative solutions/perspectives.

Critique possible solutions/establish solution criteria.

Decide and implement.

Reflect on outcomes.

Source: Based on Barell (1995).

I thought that we could use a rubric or self-assessment guide that includes these criteria:

   a. Technical proficiency—Has the student mastered the film medium, exhibiting the ability to create and separate scenes with smooth transitions, mix sound effects, and use introductions and credits?

b. Knowledge of Mars represented—Is it significant, representative, and comprehensive?

c. Reasoning process—Does relevant information lead to logical conclusions?

d. Organization—Are the different parts clearly demarcated/separated/labeled? How are they linked? Do they add up to a logical whole?

e. Aesthetics—Is the work pleasing visually? How does it use color, transitions, and sound to create a smoothly integrated montage that is consistent, gives the sense of a whole product (and not a bunch of disparate, jarring parts)? This criterion is, for me at least, a real challenge to break down into parts. Perhaps you can do better!

3. Have students keep logs/journals during the process, as students at Perkins did using wikis. They might have used Google Docs or any other electronic form of journaling. The point is that students and teachers can review these problem-solving process journals to discover how students went about solving problems. Did they analyze, test out, and evaluate ideas before suggesting them? How often do they pose important questions during the problem/challenge process? And if we are engaged in projects over long periods of time or in each of several years in school, we can use the travel journal model described in Chapter 6.

4. Engage students in end-of-project assessments as Mary Darr has done here. These included formal written assessments and interviews with faculty as well as outside observers. Ask questions such as, How would you describe how you went about solving this problem/meeting this challenge? What did you do when you reached an obstacle? What have you learned from this project? Then ask, How might you have solved similar problems in the past? Give examples. What might you do differently in the future? What have you learned about problem solving?

5. Look for transfer from a project such as one of those described above to other educational settings such as the "regular" classroom. As we have noted above, one of the eighth-grade teachers, Phil Graber, mentioned that he saw students' work on a subsequent class project reflected more self-reliance on the part of students. They were better organized.

When I asked several of the eighth graders the transfer question, "How might you use these problem-solving processes in other subjects as well as outside of school?" Darcy responded, "This process can be helpful in real life." "How?" I asked. She said, "For example, yesterday we went on a field trip to a mission control simulation for the space shuttle. I was in charge of communications with the astronauts and my main communications instrument was out. 'What am I going to do?' I asked. 'Use PostIt notes' is how I solved the problem."

Yes, she might have done this anyway, without the benefit of STEM, but it may be significant that she related this incident as an example of creative problem solving, something she didn't do that much of in her regular classrooms.

You might also ask the question Jalen brought up: "How might you use any of these problem solving processes in the future?" When will you write out a challenge statement, brainstorm solutions, and think creatively?

6. Give preassessments and postassessments. Mary Darr and her staff did not do this during their first, experimental year, at least not with problem-solving tasks. How might you do this? One way is to give a challenge similar to designing a roller coaster or a Martian habitat and just ask students how they would approach it. See how they analyze the situation, what kinds of questions they might ask. See if they break it down into smaller parts, attempt to represent it visually, relate it to prior problems, challenge assumptions, ask for more information, and the like. Figure 9.3 is drawn from previous work on problem solving (Barell, 1995) and lists problem-solving steps used by good problem solvers. We can compare before-and-after analyses to see if students have become better in their thinking. Use these as preassessments, formative assessments, and summative assessments. For these kinds of analyses it helps to have students record their thought processes, just as we do in paired problem solving, an effective process first pioneered by Benjamin Bloom at the University of Chicago in the 1950s.[4] Here initial, intermediary, and final concept maps could be helpful, just like Michael's concept map of space could be (see Figure 4.3).

7. Conduct a preassessment and postassessment of cognitive development similar to that mentioned in Chapter 5: Peel's (1966) courageous airman problem where we are assessing the degree to which students can see beyond the given facts and imagine an array of possible causes and contingencies. We administered this scenario to several of the eighth graders, but only after the final STEM project. Here are some of their answers:

a. "I think the pilot was not a careful airman because he flew into the sky ride cable."

b. "The pilot was not a careful airman. . . . He needed more work training for a situation like this."

c. "No supporting evidence was stated to why he flew into the 'aerial' sky ride cable. Anything could have caused this event such as the wind blowing the cable into plane's course of motion."

d. "'Only courageous pilots are allowed to fly over high mountains.' . . . Is the quoted sentence a rule? Just because I am courageous does not mean I am suited to fly over high, dangerous mountains. So this pilot may have been brave and courageous but left out the most important part, *safety*. So that's not to say that weather, wind, radios or anything of that sort did not play a role in the crash."

What differences do you see among these four eighth graders' responses?

Can we say that STEM played a role in the thinking of these students?

No, we have no preassessment measures of their cognitive abilities. Remember from Chapter 5, Peel's (1966) test helps us make some, perhaps tentative, conclusions about students' contingency thinking, their ability to imagine possibilities, as the students who wrote c and d have done.

Notice also that the last student asks whether there is a rule that only courageous pilots can fly over high mountains. Invoking the concept of a generalization seems to me to be rather complex, higher order, abstract reasoning. What do you think?

We do not know enough about students' prior educational experiences, in school or at home, to assert that the last two students grew as a result of STEM. Mary Darr reported that they were close friends and happened to be on the same roller coaster team:

I worked with both Allison and Angela on the first STEM project. In the first few brainstorming sessions, both girls took on leadership roles in the discussion, even though neither one was the CEO. They were more apt to feed off of each other's ideas, as they were already friends with each other. Allison was an architect, as she is very artistically creative, and Angela was involved in marketing. . . . Their behavior did differ from others in the group in terms of leadership and creativity and in wanting all aspects of the final product to be perfect. Allison tweaked and re-tweaked the coaster model multiple times until presentation day, and then she still wasn't satisfied with it. I did not see that level of intensity and passion in others in the group.

Perhaps what we learn from this assessment of cognitive abilities is that assuming leadership responsibilities might reflect one's ability to think of possibilities beyond the immediate, concrete, and obvious. Maybe students' being good friends who enjoy bouncing ideas off each other also helps develop their abilities to think outside the box, to consider alternative possibilities? At least they might get different points of view.

Maybe encouraging other students to play leadership roles will enhance their intellectual abilities to look into the future, to consider workable alternatives. That's what leaders have to do: plan for the future, anticipate unexpected consequences, and think through all possibilities thoroughly.

> When we're engaged in a large-scale project like these STEM undertakings, we can foster students' contingency thinking with these kinds of questions:
>
> What if...?
>
> Suppose this happens...? Suppose you couldn't use this material, if there were no permits available, if the topography, weather, or public opinion obtruded into your plans?
>
> What might happen here, today, tomorrow, next week, next month...?

My friend and former colleague, Irving Sigel of Educational Testing Service at Princeton, taught me the benefit of what he called a "distancing strategy" to enhance cognitive development. Ask students to describe an event—say, going to Grandmother's over the weekend. How did you go? Now, what if your car wouldn't start? What if it had rained? Suppose somebody had taken sick? Sigel and Saunders (1979) used this distancing strategy with young children and concluded that this was one way to enhance their cognitive development—by placing little road blocks in their way and challenging them to think of alternatives.

AGAIN, TEAMWORK

This brings us to another one of the 21st century skills or capacities, learning to work in a group. We've seen the importance many of the students placed on "TEAMWORK!" Doug Reeves (2010), founder of the Leadership and Learning Network, has stated that "performance will be measured not by the success of the individual, but by the success of the team, perhaps a multinational team with members spanning the globe" (p. 310).

For years we have been encouraging students to work in small groups, in teams, going back well before the surge in cooperative learning approaches. When we consider how many businesses and industries depend on teamwork today—information/communications technology, military/defense, medical care, sports/recreation, and so many more— it's no wonder that we are stressing the vital importance of knowing how to work well with others, how to bounce ideas off each other and work toward a mutually agreed-on product. In Chapter 12 we will discuss how After Action Reviews can help structure such reflective small-group analyses.

What are some criteria we might use to assess participation in a cooperative group? We presented some criteria in Chapter 6, and here's another list based on students' comments from their STEM experiences:

a. all members' participating productively and accepting responsibility for specific roles;
b. listening and responding to each other;
c. as Carlee said of her group, "bouncing ideas off each other";
d. playing roles of gatekeeper, on tracker, timer, recorder, and so forth—keeping everybody on the same page;
e. helping to build from others' ideas toward better questions/ solutions ("I like what Darcy said, and what if we add this . . . ?");
f. helping team members understand concepts (explaining, diagramming, making analogies: "You might think of it/visualize it this way.");
g. presenting different points of view ("What if? Here's another way of looking at what we're doing.");
h. challenging assumptions ("What if this isn't true?");
i. working toward consensus and incorporating others' ideas into group thinking;
j. reflecting on process and feeding back to group what it has and has not focused on and accomplished; and
k. helping group set new directions as necessary.

While touring one of the High Tech High Schools in Rensselaer, New York (on the other side of the Hudson River from the capital, Albany), I spoke with a young man about the projects students were working on, for example, "Is the Hudson River Nasty?" He spoke of the authenticity of the projects, all relating to what we do in the world beyond school. But of equal importance had been his role in working on teams, on one in particular where he felt good to have helped other students understand the problem and find solutions.

It was significant to me that he mentioned his role in teamwork. He quickly mentioned that he'd applied to several colleges and that they, too, placed a strong emphasis on students' working in groups to solve authentic problems.

As Thomas, a seventh grader, told me, "No business is successful with one person. Need lots of people. Can't just do it alone. If we work together, we can do anything."

Did he learn this during STEM? We cannot tell.

ASK MARY DARR

Now, after experiencing, if only vicariously, the thrills of climbing the highest roller coasters at Cedar Point, what questions would you like to discuss with Mary Darr and your colleagues? You can send your best to jbarell@nyc.rr.com, and I will forward them to her.

CONCLUSION

At the conclusion of the seventh-grade campaign to attract more teens and tweens to the Cleveland Indians stadium, one executive with the ball club, Mr. Jason Kidik, noted that the presentations were "pretty impressive. . . . They thought outside the box. . . . We saw presentations not put together by a marketing team." And most impressive of all? "Seeing their thought processes was unique. It was fun to see how they came up with their ideas."

This is the kind of helpful feedback we can have with any authentic problem-based learning experience. It need not be as all-encompassing as a STEM project.

What is also meaningful here is "seeing their thought processes." Here's one valid way of determining if students over time are improving in their thinking—how they think through complex, ill-structured problems. We want to know how well students can articulate their problem-solving processes as one guide toward observing their improvement.

Having this kind of experience may change your life. It may force you out of your comfort zone, especially if you are a teacher used to the high structure of teaching from a textbook or a state-designed curriculum.

That's the value and the challenge of projects such as those faced by the sixth, seventh, and eighth graders in Sandusky. As Mary Darr noted, here students had "to put it all together" using all of their life and school experiences to solve a real problem. This is not something easily measured by a high-stakes standardized test.

ENDNOTES

1. K'Nex is the brand name for toy construction equipment of rods and connectors.

2. Marla worked with a group of gifted students and noticed their struggle with this more authentic, open-ended, ill-structured problem. "They wanted it perfect. They need to be right." And that's not the way this kind of problem solving works. Authentic problems in life are messy, are often complicated, and do not lend themselves to one-answer, right-wrong thinking.

3. NASA has recently (2011) created a project called Imagine Mars wherein it challenges students to design a habitat for life on Mars complete with architecturally sound structures appropriate for that environment: www.nasa.gov/multimedia/podcasting/jpl-mars-pod20110606–1.html. View the video of students working through this challenge.

4. To assess students' abilities to work collaboratively in an alternative high school setting, I once filmed their response to a simple challenge: "Please rearrange the room so that all these kinds of chairs are located here and all of the others are arranged by height, color [or whatever criteria you choose]." We looked at the film and analyzed our behaviors. Then we could compare this preassessment with how students acted cooperatively out on our various field trips.

REFERENCES

Barell, J. (1995). *Teaching for thoughtfulness—Classroom strategies to enhance intellectual development* (2nd ed.). New York: Longman.

Bransford, J. D., Brown, A. L., & Cocking, R. R. (Eds.). (2000). *How people learn: Brain, mind, experience, and school.* Washington, DC: National Academy Press.

Dewey, J. (1933). *How we think.* Lexington, MA: D. C. Heath.

Peel, E. A. (1966). A study of differences in the judgments of adolescent pupils. *British Journal of Educational Psychology, 36*(1), 77–86.

Perkins Local Schools. (2010). *Creative problem solving.* Sandusky, OH: Author.

Reeves, D. (2010). A framework for assessing 21st century skills. In J. Bellanca & R. Brandt (Eds.), *21st century skills: Rethinking how students learn* (pp. 305–326). Bloomington, IN: Solution Tree Press.

Sigel, I., & Saunders, R. (1979). An inquiry into inquiry: Question asking as an instructional model. In L. Katz (Ed.), *Current topics in early childhood education* (Vol. 2). Norwood, NJ: Abex.

Wiggins, G. (1998). *Educative assessment: Designing assessments to inform and improve student performance.* San Francisco, CA: Jossey-Bass.

10

"Cookie-Cutter A" Becomes Self-Directed Student

Rachel was an eighth-grade student in Pat Burrows's writing and literature class in Catalina Foothills School District (CFSD). She grew from what Pat called a "cookie-cutter A student" to one who exemplified a "hallmark of critical thinking," that is, the ability to "ask further questions."

Pat observed her students all year, and Rachel stood out because by year's end her "responses were of a superior quality and generally included questions she created while thinking about the scenario or issue" at hand.

How do you suppose Pat accomplished this feat? We all know the students who just want to play the game they've learned so well: figure out what's going to be on the test, study for that, and get their well-deserved gold stars. So what do you suppose this teacher in a district near Tucson, Arizona, did?

Let's find out.

Pat used the district's 21st Century Learning Rubric for critical thinking, and this included the specific skills of abstracting, analyzing perspectives, constructing support, and using deductive and inductive reasoning (see Figure 10.1 on page 214).

Catalina Foothills School District's 21st Century Learning Rubric—Skill: Critical and Creative Thinking

1. Identifies "another situation or information that contains a similar general or abstract form": abstracting/proficient

2. Articulates "a detailed opposing position and the reasoning behind it": analyzing perspectives/advanced

3. Presents "a clear and accurate treatment of all available evidence that addresses the central point of the claim": constructing support/advanced

4. Accurately "identifies logical conclusions implied by the generalizations or principles": deductive reasoning/advanced

5. Draws "conclusions that reflect clear and logical links between the information or observations and the interpretations made from them": inductive reasoning/advanced

---

Source: Catalina Foothills School District (2006, 2011; www.cfsd16.org/public/_century/pdf/Rubrics/CFSDCritical&CreativeThinkingRubrics.pdf); adapted from Marzano, Pickering, and McTighe (1993).

These were Pat's general guidelines promulgated throughout the school district. Mary Jo Conery, the assistant superintendent for 21st century learning, had done a masterful job of working with teachers to craft these guidelines, and at this writing (2011) she was still leading her district in revising and extending them based on teachers' observations of their viability (see www.cfsd16.org/public/_century/pdf/Rubrics/CFSD Critical&CreativeThinkingRubrics.pdf).

What Pat Burrows did was to cull from all of these guidelines a scoring rubric for all of her 155 students.

At the end of the school year, after students had read and analyzed books such as *To Kill a Mockingbird* and *Animal Farm* and engaged in extensive experiences with the arts and strategies of persuasion, Pat concluded that Rachel had excelled in all critical thinking categories:

Rachel "consistently provided examples and created analogies to clarify [her] thinking for the reader" (abstracting).

She identified "opposing views in her persuasive letter . . . consistently supported her ideas with specific and relevant examples . . . [and] did articulate different perspectives by creating examples and analogies."

Rachel "identified and analyzed a host of critical details in order to reach a significant conclusion about why and how Orwell wrote *Animal Farm*" (inductive reasoning).

REASONING USING EXAMPLES, ANALOGIES

You can see the importance for Pat Burrows of the good critical thinker's being able to reason by using examples, data, analogies, and comparisons.

What this involves is finding similar circumstances, events, personalities, and the like with which to make comparisons. And what does this entail?

Let me illustrate with my experience with a high school student I observed once while doing qualitative research that resulted in my first publication, *Playgrounds of Our Minds* (Barell, 1980).

Betsy sat in her senior-year history class while learning about World War I. She loved her teacher and was always asking questions that took the subject to a different level. For example, one day she asked, "Was Kaiser Wilhelm the Hitler of World War I?"

Now, just consider what Betsy might have been thinking leading up to this question: Both were leaders of Germany during crisis periods, both had specific leadership qualities, both were motivated by different historical events, and so forth. In other words, Betsy and anybody responding to this question would have to be analyzing these leaders to make a comparison between them. Such comparison would, of course, involve similarities, differences, and most importantly, drawing a conclusion. But it was Betsy's creative insight to bring these two leaders into juxtaposition, creating the metaphorical comparison.

IMPORTANCE OF MAKING COMPARISONS

Engaging in these kinds of analyses is a vital element in critical thinking—we are identifying the important characteristics (elements, variables) within one leader and relating them to another (family, schooling, military service, nationality, view of Germany's role in the world). At the same time we are discarding those that are not significant (dress, hair color, and the like). This process of comparing and contrasting has been found to be a key element in advancing students' intellectual growth and achievement (Marzano, 2003, p. 80). What we are doing here is classifying, identifying, and sorting, in accordance with the degree of relevance and importance, the attributes of an experience or object.[1]

Pat Burrows knows that what is important for Rachel and her friends is to be seeking out and making their own comparisons, not to be memorizing teachers' examples. What happens when Rachel extends her thinking to find examples with which to make a point is that she is creating linkages within her own mind, fashioning, if you will, new and significant connections among all of the experiences she can recall.

Creating these networks of associations and connections is what we do to enhance meaningfulness of any concept, topic, or fact (Johnson, 1975). Yes, it is like creating a concept map for a word such as *pioneer* or *run.*[2]

So what Pat Burrows was encouraging her eighth graders in her writing and literature class to do all along was to seek out relationships, to make connections, to fashion meaningful bridges from the new subjects to older ones, from recent experiences to those of the past. This act of identifying, fashioning, creating, and designing is a most important one at any level of schooling because of its core challenges—to observe, to analyze, to break apart, to differentiate characteristics of an experience or object, and then to draw a conclusion that yes, Kaiser Wilhelm was like Hitler or no, he was not. And to give good reasons for this conclusion.[3]

Ellen Langer (quoted in Lambert, 2007), a psychologist from Harvard, has observed that "the process of actively drawing new distinctions produces that feeling of engagement we all seek. . . . Research has shown that mindfulness is . . . enlivening. It's the way you feel when you're feeling passionate" (p. 94).

> "The process of actively drawing new distinctions produces that feeling of engagement we all seek. . . . Research has shown that mindfulness is . . . enlivening. It's the way you feel when you're feeling passionate" (Ellen Langer, quoted in Lambert, 2007, p. 94).

Imagine, a mental activity we've been engaged in almost since the dawning of our conscious minds ("Hey, her present is bigger than mine!") is so valuable in learning stuff! Time was when educational researchers spent many an hour investigating what they called "time on task." It turns out that when we challenge students to make distinctions between different objects and experiences, we are enlivening their emotional selves and contributing to their successes in schools.

For an excellent discussion of the value of challenging students with classification activities from a very early age, see *Educating the Young Thinker—Classroom Strategies for Cognitive Growth* by Carol Copple, Irving E. Sigel, and Ruth Saunders (1984, pp. 118–120). It makes sense to assert that the more we engage students of all ages in analyzing simple to complex objects and phenomena, the more general and meaningful categories of experience they will develop.

CFSD

Mary Jo Conery, assistant superintendent at Catalina Foothills, is the leader of the 21st Century Learning initiative in this district. You will find CFSD in most lists of current school districts (known as P21) that have adopted this approach to preparing our students for the new century.

What this has meant is devising the rubrics mentioned above. You will find at www.cfsd16.org not only rubrics for critical thinking but guidelines for assessment of students' growth in the following areas:

problem solving,

decision making,

experimental inquiry,

error analysis,

investigation,

invention,

scientific inquiry,

cultural competence, and

leadership.

As you might imagine, it is no easy task to identify what we want students to be able to do, for example, within the categories of problem solving and scientific inquiry.

This involved a two-year process of curriculum development, aligning these objectives with local, state subject matter standards. And then the district worked on the performance-based standards illustrated above. Concepts that were critical during this process were what we call "authentic" work, achievement, and assessment, that is, observing how students think within situations we find in life, not merely in school.[4]

And as I mentioned above, Mary Jo Conery was in the process of challenging teachers to field test all these rubric descriptions against what their students were actually doing. In some cases they were refining and clarifying the language used so that we can observe within our classrooms what it means to compare by selecting "characteristics that encompass the most essential characteristics of the items and present a unique challenge or provide an unusual thought." What does this look like for any student's written work or discussion in class? Can it also apply to works of art?

From the Catalina Foothills School District's 21st Century Skill Rubrics

Cultural Competence

Worldview (Advanced): Asks complex questions about other cultures; seeks out and articulates answers to these questions through both research and contact with natives of the target culture.

Leadership

Decision Making (Advanced):
   Makes sound decisions and judgments based on all relevant sources of information (internal and external).
   Makes decisions considering intended and unintended consequences.
   Efficiently makes decisions that support the entire perspective and scope of a situation or issue.

Source: Catalina Foothills School District (2011).

We all say we want students to be critical and creative thinkers, but what does it actually look and sound like in the classroom? Defining this is the significant challenge CFSD has undertaken and met.

RACHEL, THE COOKIE-CUTTER A STUDENT

When I asked Pat Burrows to describe Rachel (not her real name), she told me that Rachel came from a home with highly educated parents, where discussions around the dinner table or at leisure were common. She was a good athlete, starring in track and always being the one who would encourage her teammates along toward achievement.

Rachel was also a student who would help her fellow students. When a young girl who was very shy gave Pat the answer, "I don't know," to almost any question, Rachel would gently nudge her, saying, "You know the answer to that question. Go ahead!"

Pat Burrows said about her, "Rachel enjoys science fiction and fantasy novels. Tested by our gifted coordinator and designated as a 'gifted student,' she is a rather serious person who doesn't take issues or life lightly. Rachel was focused in class and consistently handed in her work; she is perceived by her peers as a responsible person" (personal communications, May 2011).

When I asked what it meant to be a "cookie-cutter A student," Pat said, "They're students who take no risks. Get all As."

We also know these students as ones who ask so many questions about what they're studying or how to do something because they wish to reduce the challenge of ambiguity, of figuring things out for themselves, down to almost zero. No doubts or difficulties. No really hard work of thinking through the problem.

Rachel was, like so many of her friends, a student who couldn't really support her conclusions with examples, analogies, or experiences. She probably just said, "That's my opinion," and was comfortable leaving it at that. Pat noted that a good way to describe Rachel and some of her friends early on was "reluctance fueled by a hesitation to reflect on 'why' she held certain opinions. That reflection process does, at some point, require a paradigm shift which I often referred to in class as 'upsetting the apple cart': all of the apples have to be rearranged and that takes effort and a willingness to embrace change—a scary proposition for a young adult in the throes of adolescence."

"Are they the ones who are also good at guessing what's on the teacher's mind?" I asked.

"Yes!" Pat responded emphatically.

Well, we all know these students. Ones bent on achieving an A per-haps to the point of memorizing just about anything and everything to please the teacher, not to understand the subject more thoroughly. That's the kind of student I was in some classes.

But Rachel became a different student in Pat's classroom. She slowly moved away from not taking risks and toward asking a lot of questions, one of the key elements in critical thinking.[5]

How Rachel Grew

At the end of the 2011 school year, Pat reflected on her progress with Rachel and her classmates:

Reflecting on the instructional practices and strategies I used to guide my students through the process of thinking critically has led me to several significant conclusions:

1. A safe environment is critical to developing critical thinking.

2. The process must begin with developing the art of questioning.

3. This skill is best taught through modeling and scaffolding.

4. Discussions, both in small groups and whole class settings, empower students to develop their critical thinking skills. (P. Burrows, personal communication, June 2011)

Notice how Pat identifies perhaps the single most important element in teaching thinking at any level, a "safe environment," one I've called the "invitational environment" (Barell, 1995, 2007). What does this entail? We discussed this at length in Chapter 3.

Then she focuses on two elements of equal importance, modeling and scaffolding.

MODELING

> Pat's framework of critical thinking questions: "What are the basic facts? What is the key issue/ problem? What are our assumptions? What are the likely consequences of our actions? What predictions can we logically make?"

To model good questioning, Pat used a questioning framework from the beginning of class. Here you can see crucial questions that can be applied to almost any situation, issue, or problem: "What are the basic facts? What is the key issue/problem? What are our assumptions? What are the likely consequences of our actions? What predictions can we logically make?"

By constantly referring to asking these kinds of questions, Pat was able to help students understand their meaning and value when analyzing a situation, for example, after reading the novel *Whirligig* (Fleischman, 2010). Here a young man makes a terrible decision that results in his killing a young and talented woman.

What are the consequences of his action? What predictions can we make?

What were his motivations?

What assumptions was he making?

And so on. Pat modeled these kinds of questions for a more thorough understanding of the character and his actions.

This, of course, led to encouraging students to apply such questions to their own lives:

What are the consequences in your own life if you don't give your best effort in this and other classes?

What assumptions do we make about our relationships on any given day?

Do you consider the ripple effect of the decisions you make in life? Or do you simply assume that there will be a safety net provided by friends and parents? (P. Burrows, personal communication, July 2011)

Another form of modeling, of course, is to think aloud, to share our own questions and thoughts with students. Pat did this during the reading of *Animal Farm*, telling students that at first she used to blame the pigs for not being informed. "Every citizen has a responsibility to know what's going on," she told me. "There's no excuse for not knowing what's going on."

"But now, I tell students I'm less critical of the animals. I now understand the use of fear in controlling masses of the population." Pat was sharing with her students how her own thinking has changed about important issues of power and control in this book.

SCAFFOLDING

During a unit on the elements of persuasion, Pat drew from students their definitions, some of which included notions of trickery. Indeed, Rachel wrote, "Before we started our unit on persuasion, I thought to persuade was to deceive . . . telling small lies or exaggeration."

She asked how students would persuade somebody to take an action. They analyzed commercials for the ASPCA and concluded that all those pictures of cute animals were "overload."

She used, among several persuasive speeches, George Vest's summation to the jury speech given in a Missouri courtroom in 1870, the one that led to our calling dogs "man's best friend."[6]

Man's Best Friend

"A man's dog stands by him in prosperity and in poverty, in health and in sickness. He will sleep on the cold ground, where the wintry winds blow and the snow drives fiercely, if only he may be near his master's side."

All of these experiences helped Pat introduce important elements of persuasion: logos (logical reasons), pathos (use of emotions), ethos (the trustworthiness of the persuader), and mythos (cultural beliefs). Because of the emphasis on the skills and art of persuasion established by Mary Jo Conery for the whole district, some of these processes had been taught to Rachel and her classmates in seventh grade.

Another way of scaffolding, or arranging learning experiences for students' success in reaching a goal or objective, is for the teacher to model a set of questions as students think through a problem.

For Rachel it was in writing a persuasive essay to the CFSD bus company to argue a point about discharging passengers. Its practice of letting students off the bus at specific places did not make sense to her (not always the most convenient for students). She argued against their current practice "to maintain maximum equality and convenience among the students."

Here's part of the teacher-student interaction as conveyed to me by Pat Burrows (personal communication, June 2011):

Rachel: I'm getting ready to write a letter to the bus company. I've done my homework. They may not value my point of view. They may totally disregard it.

Pat: And then? What will you do?

Rachel: [After some reflection] I might get parents involved. Their point of view might be more influential.

Pat: How serious is the situation?

Rachel: When I think of it, it's unfair. [Then, considering the possible consequences of her action] There's no way they'll kick me off the bus.

What do you think of this exchange? What elements of critical thinking do you see here? What has Pat done and not done in posing her questions?

SMALL-GROUP INTERACTIONS

Another way in which Pat helped Rachel grow perhaps stems from her studies in organizational behavior. She obtained a master's degree in this subject, and I wondered how this might have influenced her work in the classroom. Organizational behavior and development focuses on many ways of helping organizations reach their goals and develop their human potential and capacity to their maximums. Goal setting, developing internal communications, conducting action research, and analyzing problem solving, decision making, and conflict resolution processes are some of the elements of this field of study.

What Pat did with her students was to set them up in heterogeneous groups to consider problem scenarios (e.g., regarding *Animal Farm,* "What if Boxer had learned to read?" or "If you were one of the animals . . . ?"). But there was a rule that she enforced: If you had been the leader of the group last time, you couldn't be this time.

This meant that Rachel, having been a leader once, had to sit and listen to others' points of view and, if she disagreed, to persuade them using all the experiences and information she had at her disposal. Rachel had to learn how to convince, how to persuade. "This frustrated her," Pat said. "She had to be led, and when the group didn't agree, she had to summon her best arguments."

"Sometimes I prompted with analogies," Pat concluded. "What is this like? What can we compare this to?"

Stretching our students' thinking in this way is superior to just giving them the analogies to memorize or the models to regurgitate. It's the analogies and comparisons that each of us makes that we will remember, not necessarily those we have mastered from a textbook. (Of course, each model, metaphor, analogy, and comparison needs to be tested or analyzed for its fit, its congruency with the object or experience to which it is being compared.)

HOW DO WE KNOW RACHEL IMPROVED?

Now, given all Pat Burrows has done with all of her students, what is the evidence that at least one, Rachel, has grown "the most in her critical and creative thinking skills"?

Let's commence with a synthesis Rachel wrote on completion of the unit on persuasion. After identifying her early misconceptions, that persuasion involved "telling small lies or exaggerations," she listed the different elements: logos, pathos, ethos, and mythos.

ARGUING WITH RELATIONSHIPS
AND CONNECTIONS

Then she proceeds to identify what she calls "subtle persuaders," like "mind filters, mind framing, placebos (labels we give), context, and social influence": "Mind filtering is when you interpret what you see based on

Figure 10.1 Critical and Creative Thinking: Student Evaluation

Critical and creative thinking: Student Evaluations
Ms. Burrows
8th grade Writing and Literature

Student: Rachel

Skill	Rubric Score	Comments
Abstracting	4	Student spared no effort in identifying key pieces of information to include in assessments, and these pieces of information were at the literal as well as interpretive levels of thinking. Student consistently provided examples and created analogies to clarify thinking for the reader.
Analyzing Perspective	3	While the student did identify opposing view in persuasive letter, she did not identify the cause/source of that view; however, in all other assessments, the student did articulate different perspectives by creating examples and analogies.
Constructing Support	4	This student consistently supported her ideas with specific and relevant examples which clarified and strengthened her perspective and points.
Deductive Reasoning	4	In the propaganda assessment, this student analyzed how propaganda affected various groups and began that analysis by identifying the benefits reaped by the controlling group.
Inductive Reasoning	4	In the author/text relationship analysis, student identified and analyzed a host of critical details in order to reach a significant conclusion about why and how Orwell wrote *Animal Farm*.

Overall assessment:
   This student improved the most in her critical and creative thinking skills. This improvement is marked by the student's ability to expand upon a single idea/issue/topic and utilize examples and analogies to extend her thinking and to clarify that thinking for the reader. Additionally, the breadth and depth of such articulations is enhanced by the use of vocabulary and word choice that clearly demonstrates an internalization of the concepts and elements in persuasion.

what you believe. If you believe that obesity is a common problem, you will think of it when you see a family indulge. If you don't, you will just see a hungry group of people. Framing is using positive or negative aspects of things to create an image. 80% lean beef will sell faster than 20% fat, because although they are the same thing, lean is positive and fat is negative" (personal essay, April 2011).

Mind filtering is something we do normally, perhaps to interpret the myriad experiences we have on a daily basis. It helps us make sense of experience, but as Rachel has demonstrated, it can condition how we interpret certain events.

Pat Burrows pointed to this excerpt as one example of Rachel's being able to make those comparisons, to find analogies and relationships that help her draw reasonable conclusions, the essence of critical thinking. She has found "specific and relevant examples which clarified and strengthened her perspective and points" (Scoring Rubric, "Constructing Support," see Figure 10.1).

Rachel used her own background knowledge to make a convincing point. But beyond that she has demonstrated deep understanding of the concept. She "clearly demonstrates an internalization of the concepts and elements of persuasion" (Pat Burrows's overall assessment).

Another excellent example of Rachel's growing from September of eighth grade, when she seldom gave reasoned arguments, to April of that year comes from her analysis of George Orwell's *Animal Farm*. After briefly summarizing Napoleon's rise to power and his subjugation of all animals except pigs and dogs, Rachel connected the story to what she'd learned in world history:

> Orwell had a strong loathing of Josef Stalin, who was represented by the pig Napoleon in *Animal Farm*. Napoleon's key trait was of being a ruthless and coldhearted leader and of manipulating and using the people living in poverty. . . . Orwell blamed Stalin for the death and destruction of hundreds of thousands of Russians throughout the Russian Revolution and could never forgive him for consorting with Nazi leader, Hitler. . . . Napoleon begins his rise to power soon after the revolt has been completed. In an undignified attempt to seize absolute power, he eventually eradicates his only competitor, Snowball, from the farm by chasing him out with trained dogs. His attempt succeeds and Snowball (representing Leon Trotsky [a challenger to Stalin's predecessor, Lenin]) is successfully exiled, leaving Napoleon to command the farm with an iron fist and a pack of trained dogs (representing the secret police). These events coincide with the reality of what was happening in Russia, and through *Animal Farm*, Orwell exposed the blatant cruelty and corruption Stalin was consumed by.

On completing my first reading of Rachel's essay, "Author, Subject and Audience," my first question to Pat Burrows was, "Did Rachel make all of these historical comparisons on her own? Was she repeating what you had said in class, comparing *Animal Farm* with Stalin's policy of collectivizing the peasantry in the Soviet Union?"

"No," said Pat emphatically, thus emphasizing that for Rachel these were original connections. We who long ago studied Orwell's masterpiece might see the relationships Rachel has elaborated as well known, but for her they were original.[7]

Thus, at the conclusion of the summative essay, Pat wrote, "You spared no effort in making critical connections between the allegory and historical events/figures. I will truly miss reading your ideas and insights next year."

TAKING THE OTHER POINT OF VIEW

I mentioned above Rachel's dissatisfaction with how the CFSD bus company discharged passengers. Rachel and her friends were taught not to tear down somebody's else's argument but to "prove how you are right."

So in creating her letter to the bus company Rachel made certain to acknowledge the position of the bus company: "It is quite possible for you to argue that students using your bus company should be restricted to their designated bus stops. . . . Another argument likely to be brought up is that there would be very little reason to exit a bus on a stop other than your own. While it is true that the bus would leave residents closer to their homes if they were to exit at the final stop [as is done now], it is actually inefficient for both the students and the driver."

Here you see Rachel being aware of the argument counter to her own, knowing what the other side of the issue is. Many adults have difficulty with looking at a point of view that opposes their own. Research by David Perkins (1985) confirms this challenge that we all face. Here is where our confirmation bias enters in. We are far more comfortable with our own conclusions and ideas. The result is that we seek information to confirm what we already believe rather than consider counterarguments.[8]

Pat Burrows's summary comment is the following: "While Rachel did identify opposing views in her persuasive letter, she did not identify the cause/source of that view." The CFSD rubric for analyzing perspectives calls for the advanced student to "articulate a detailed opposing position and the reasoning behind it. If a strong line of reasoning does not underlie the position, [the student] articulates the errors or holes in the reasoning" (CFSD 21st Century Learning Rubric).

CONCLUSION

I think we have ample evidence of Pat Burrows's summary comments on Rachel's work during this school year: "This student has improved the most in her critical and creative thinking skills. This improvement is marked by the student's ability to expand upon a single idea/issue/topic and utilize examples and analogies to extend her thinking and to clarify that thinking for the reader. Additionally, the breadth and depth of such articulations is enhanced by the use of vocabulary and word choice that clearly demonstrates an internalization of the concepts and elements in persuasion."

What is also of importance here is the various ways in which she helped her students grow. Many made progress, but no one else achieved at Rachel's level, and this is why I have focused on her growth as a disclosure model case for Pat Burrows's writing and literature class.

Her modeling her own thinking, structuring units and lessons around questioning, and critical reading of and thinking about classics such as *To Kill a Mockingbird* and *Animal Farm* all led to Rachel's transcending the label "cookie-cutter A student."

Pat Burrows has a major in theater arts, and I can imagine her acting out various parts during the teaching of her novels, being Scout or Napoleon, asking other characters question after question to model inquisitiveness for her students. I can hear her playing the What if? game, presenting various scenarios to characters to stretch her students' imaginative thinking into the world of the possible.

She also has a master's degree in organizational behavior, and her experience has helped her conceptualize all that she is doing with 21st century capacities: "Perhaps the greatest impact that OB [organization behavior] has had on me is that I 'see' how all of the discreet benchmarks are interwoven with each other and, in turn, that recognition has influenced me to focus on a handful of really important skills: critical thinking, reading for a purpose and using appropriate skills therein, writing that empowers students to boldly explain their perspectives/opinions, and asking questions that lead to more questions. With that overview in mind, I have found that my teaching makes sense to me and my students."

And recall from Chapter 6 how she applied significant lessons from her master's degree course in power in organizations: "I give my students choices on a regular basis. Those choices range from choosing from menus to demonstrate their proficiency in a skill/knowledge to making decisions about using technology or other resources. Bottom line here: if my students do not feel that they have any power when it comes to what and how they learn, they don't 'own' their learning and become 'bystanders'" (P. Burrows, personal communication, June 2011).

The gift of enabling students to own their own work, their progress, and their choices has contributed significantly to the growth of Rachel and her friends. All people want to feel as if they are in control of their own lives and not merely following the orders of others. This applies in business as well as in our classrooms. The more choices our students have, K through 12, the more they will feel as if they own their own learning and are standing at the wheel directing their own ships, not merely following what the captain tells them to do. And we know that having choices in the classroom directly relates to achievement: "When students make choices about their learning, their engagement and achievement increase. When they have no choices, their engagement and learning decrease" (Davies, 2007, p. 34).

> "When students make choices about their learning, their engagement and achievement increase. When they have no choices, their engagement and learning decrease" (Davies, 2007, p. 34).

I'm certain Rachel and her classmates loved this class because their teacher was somebody who believed in the value and meaningfulness of what she was teaching.

She performed her magic, however, within quite explicitly outlined and detailed guidelines established through collaboration with Mary Jo Conery.

QUESTIONS FOR PAT BURROWS

Based on her story of upsetting Rachel's apple cart, what questions would you ask Pat Burrows? Discuss these with colleagues, and send them to me: jbarell@nyc.rr.com.

APPLICATION IN THE CLASSROOM

1. Have a clear definition of what we mean by critical thinking. There are many definitions, but to make it observable in the classroom we need to know what it sounds and looks like. John McPeck (1981, p. 6) has a definition I like: "a certain skepticism" about what to believe and do. Others call it thinking moved by good reasoning. Matt Lipman, my former colleague at Montclair State University, called it thinking affected by context, criteria, and self-correcting. For Lipman, critical thinking involves making judgments using criteria or standards about art, politics, sports, education, business, and any human endeavor.

2. Work with your own rubric or—better yet, as with CFSD—a district set of 21st Century Learning Rubrics, guidelines for instruction. This means developing your own or modifying what already exists. The development process has taken a long time in CFSD, and under Mary Jo Conery's leadership the district is seeing the results. Pat Burrows is one teacher working successfully with all her colleagues in what appears from the outside to be a very forward-looking and acting district.

3. Create what Pat Burrows calls a "safe environment" where students like Rachel and her friends are encouraged to move out of their comfort zone, to take certain risks for learning. We all learn by stretching our minds, and this might have been difficult for students like Rachel. She was often "frustrated," according to Pat, during some of those small-group sessions where she had to be led and had to reason by logic and not by power of personality.

4. Create problematic scenarios within various units of instruction that challenge students to do what Rachel did. Remember Mary Jo Conery's use of Neumann and Associates' (1996) ideas of "authentic achievement" involving work performed by adults (and students as well!).

   a. Analyze complex situations by asking good questions, considering assumptions, taking alternative points of view, projecting consequences, and arguing from the positive, not negative.
   b. Provide multiple ways for students to interact with each other. This might be in small groups or be by using iPhones, iPads, iPods, Google Docs, Google Cloud Connect, and other convenient media with which to share and critique ideas.
   c. Foster an environment wherein students are responsible not only for their own thoughts but for listening to, adding onto, and/or critiquing others' ideas. We grow not by listening solely to our own points of view but by considering what others think and how they have arrived at their positions. (Remember the rubric: "Articulates a detailed opposing position and the reasoning behind it," CFSD 21st Century Learning Rubric, Analyzing Perspectives.)

5. Implement the practice of all students' and teachers' keeping inquiry journals within which—weekly, at least—they record the questions and comments they have about various issues/topics/problematic situations. This way we will have a record of students' growth over time. All students can replicate the practice currently in place at Normal Park Museum Magnet School, where students from kindergarten through eighth grade keep what principal Jill Levine calls travel journals. Each student's journal travels from unit to unit and from grade to grade. See Chapter 6 on formative assessment.

6. Collaborate with colleagues on best practices, on aligning the curriculum, and on common assessments. These collaborations might also focus, as with Pat Burrows's class, on how we are teaching our students to think critically for the 21st century. All the elements within the CFSD 21st Century Learning Rubrics are actually curricular threads woven through all grades, woven through all subjects, and especially, for all students.

ENDNOTES

1. The Catalina Foothills School District's rubric for classifying lists these processes for a "proficient" student: "Creates categories that focus on the significant characteristics of the items." For the skill of comparing, an advanced student must select "characteristics that encompass the most essential aspects of the items and present a unique challenge or provide an unusual thought." It is not enough, therefore, to identify key characteristics. We want them to lead to an unusual or unique conclusion.

2. *Run* happens to have more definitions than any other word in the English language according to the new Oxford English Dictionary (http://simonwin chester.com/2011/05/run/).

3. And this is what all comparisons and contrasts should result in: not drawing a Venn Diagram but drawing a conclusion based on the items/experiences we compare and contrast.

4. Mary Jo relied heavily on the work of Fred Neumann and Associates (1996) as described in *Authentic Achievement—Restructuring Schools for Intellectual Quality.* Here the term *authentic achievement* "stands for intellectual accomplishments that are worthwhile, significant, and meaningful, such as those undertaken by successful adults: scientists, musicians, business entrepreneurs, politicians, crafts people, attorneys, novelists, physicians, designers, and so on" (p. 21).

5. One of my favorite definitions of critical thinking comes from John McPeck (1981) in *Critical Thinking and Education.* Critical thinking is "a certain skepticism or suspension of assent toward a given statement, established norm, or mode of doing things" (p. 6). Obviously, Pat Burrows was doing an excellent job of challenging her students to ask good questions.

6. "The one absolutely unselfish friend that a man can have in this selfish world, the one that never deserts him and the one that never proves ungrateful or treacherous is his dog. Gentlemen of the jury: A man's dog stands by him in prosperity and in poverty, in health and in sickness. He will sleep on the cold ground, where the wintry winds blow and the snow drives fiercely, if only he may be near his master's side" (http://en.wikipedia.org/wiki/George_Graham_Vest).

7. As pointed out to me by another observer, what would have been a further and perhaps deeper demonstration of understanding is whether Rachel could compare Napoleon and his actions to any contemporary events that had not yet been analyzed by others.

8. "The typical argument in our sample [of high school, college, and graduate students] concentrates on one side of the case, does not develop that side very fully, and neglects relevant counterarguments and appropriate hedges" (Perkins, 1985, pp. 14–16).

REFERENCES

Barell, J. (1980). *Playgrounds of our minds.* New York: Teachers College Press.

Barell, J. (1995). *Teaching for thoughtfulness: Classroom strategies to enhance intellectual development.* New York: Longman.

Barell, J. (2007). *Why are school buses always yellow? Teaching inquiry preK–5.* Thousand Oaks, CA: Corwin.

Catalina Foothills School District. (2011). *CFSD 21st Century Skill Rubric— Critical & creative thinking.* Retrieved from www.cfsd16.org/public/_century/pdf/Rubrics/CFSDCritical&CreativeThinkingRubrics.pdf

Copple, C., Sigel, I., & Saunders, R. (1984). *Educating the young thinker—Classroom strategies for cognitive growth.* Hillsdale, NJ: Lawrence Erlbaum.

Davies, A. (2007). Involving students in the classroom assessment process. In D. Reeves (Ed.), *Ahead of the curve: The power of assessment to transform teaching and learning* (pp. 31–58). Bloomington, IN: Solution Tree Press.

Fleischman, P. (2010). *Whirligig.* New York: Laurel-Leaf.

Johnson, R. (1975). Meaning in complex learning. *Review of Educational Research, 45,* 425–460.

Lambert, C. (2007, January–February). The science of happiness. *Harvard Magazine,* p. 94.

Marzano, R. (2003). *What works in schools—Translating research into action.* Alexandria, VA: Association for Supervision and Curriculum Development.

Marzano, R., Pickering, D., & McTighe, J. (1993) *Assessing student outcomes: Performance assessment using the Dimensions of Learning Model.* Arlington, VA: Association for Supervision and Curriculum Development.

McPeck, J. (1981). *Critical thinking and education.* Oxford, UK: Martin Robertson.

Neumann, F., & Associates. (1996). *Authentic achievement—Restructuring schools for intellectual quality.* San Francisco, CA: Jossey-Bass.

Perkins, D. N. (1985). Reasoning as imagination. *Interchange, 16*(1), 14–16.

11
Inquiry Begins at Home

Once upon a time, there lived a mother who not only bore a baby boy who grew up to be very famous in America but also became almost as famous because of the way she raised him.

The mother was Sheindel Rabi, and she lived in what is now southeastern Poland. Her son was Isidore I. Rabi, and he grew up to be a very famous nuclear physicist who did pioneering work on the characteristics of the electron. This research led to his receiving the Nobel Prize in Physics in 1944.

His research also meant that he was a very prominent player in a massive scientific undertaking to win World War II, the development of radar. The Brits had, by the time of the Battle of Britain in 1941, rudimentary radars able to spot German bombers headed their way in daylight.

Rabi, working at the radiation laboratory at MIT, helped develop radars for nighttime spotting as well as air-to-surface and height-finding radars (Conant, 2002, p. 256).

Rabi was also in close communications with J. Robert Oppenheimer out at Los Alamos where the super-secret Manhattan Project was under way.

Rabi was, indeed, a most successful individual, and after the war, President Harry S. Truman selected him as the chair of the newly created Atomic Energy Commission.

RABI'S SUCCESS

We aren't too sure of what contributes to the success of very famous men and women unless we ask them.

One of Rabi's colleagues did just that shortly before Rabi died in 1988. The family was poor and emigrated to the United States. Rabi's father first lived down on the lower east side of Manhattan, and then mother and son came over. They moved to Brooklyn and lived not far from where I eventually taught at Thomas Jefferson High School on Pennsylvania Avenue in East New York.

What made him a successful scientist?

"My mother made me a scientist without ever intending it. Every other Jewish mother in Brooklyn would ask their child upon coming home from school, 'So, did you learn anything today?' But not my mother. She always asked me a different question. 'Izzy,' she would say, 'did you ask a good question today?' That difference—asking good questions—made me become a scientist" (Sheff, 1988, p. A26).

> "Izzy, did you ask a good question today?" (Sheindel Rabi to her son, Izzy).

And that difference could revolutionize education around the world without costing one thin dime!

SHEINDEL RABI

I have often wondered what in her background led Sheindel Rabi to challenge her son in this way. Rabi himself says she was not highly schooled. Growing up, probably on a farm in Silesia, she learned somehow that asking good questions was a very important thing for the education of a young boy (and presumably a young girl).

I wonder what she meant by a "good question." This is up to each of us to decide.

Notice that she asked him not "Did the teacher ask?" but "Did *you* ask," putting the responsibility squarely on him to pay attention, to observe, to note what he might not understand, to be aware of those doubts, difficulties, uncertainties, perplexities, mysteries, and intriguing situations he encountered that would cause him to wonder, Why? How? What if?

"Did you ask a good question *today?*" Not yesterday or last week, but every day!

In other words, did you disturb the universe of what you knew and what your teachers were trying to teach you to say, There's something that's not clear, that is puzzling, that needs attention!

PARENTS

When I tell that story, I am usually addressing teachers, many of whom are parents.

Occasionally, I have the good fortune to tell my Antarctica story to parents because of its potential power to influence how they encourage their children to find a topic they can become passionate about, leading to a life of inquiry (Barell, 2011).

Recently, while at the Sarah Rawson International Baccalaureate Elementary School in Atlanta, I met two parents, Randy and Jennifer Gragg. Their son Spencer was in kindergarten in the school, and they said he was most curious.

I asked if they'd be interested in keeping a journal about his questions during the year. They both agreed, and what appears below is a list of the questions they jotted down in their journal during Spencer's year in kindergarten:

Sarah Rawson Smith Elementary

11/10/10—How much blood do we need to survive?

(Class was discussing school blood drive.)

Why do my toes go from big to small?

Why do I have ten toes and ten fingers?

Why can't we feel the earth moving?

Why can't we feel the continents moving?

1/4—Do the continents touch on the ocean floor? (discussing continental shifting during the time of dinosaurs)

1/6—How deep is the ocean? (watching a video about the ocean)

1/15—Was Apollo 11 the first space craft to leave the earth?
   How did the Earth form?
   When was space made?
   How big will space be when it stops growing and when will it stop growing?
   (reading a book about space flight)

1/17—Why is the equator so hot? (discussing different regions of the earth)

3/15—How many smoke detectors in my school? (discussing safety with fireman at school)

March—Why does food in the cracks of your teeth cause cavities? (after visiting the dentist)

March—What is the state with the most volcanoes? Are they all active? (after reading a book about dinosaurs)

March—What was the size of the Japan tsunami? (after seeing a news report)

May—Why does it get colder the higher you get in the sky? It should get warmer the closer you get to the sun. (talking about flying)

May—Why does your body need sleep? (getting ready for bed)

May—How do potholes on the road form? (seeing a pothole on our street during a walk)

I asked Randy what his analysis of Spencer's questions was after submitting this list. He said,

> We can't say that the depth or breadth of his questions increased over time. (His first question was . . . How much blood do we need to survive?) However, it appears as though there was a direct correlation between asking a question and his interest in the subject. We asked him virtually every day what questions he asked in school, and it was apparent that he didn't think of a question every day. Mostly when the subject piqued his interest. It's important to note that not all of the questions were asked in school. Some were asked while walking, playing, or reading.

I also found two more questions on my desk that didn't make the list. They were written down on January 28.

1. How many countries are in the world? (don't have the context) and

2. How many trees are in the world? (while on a walk in our neighborhood)

FROM NUMBERS TO DEEP CAUSATION

I must say that I'm intrigued by a number of Spencer's questions:

> Why can't we feel the earth moving?

> Do the continents touch on the ocean floor? and

> Why does it get colder the higher you get in the sky?

These questions manifest what seems to be a significant difference between asking about how many countries there are in the world and why it's hot at the equator. As Randy says, it may just be the subject he was studying at the time. But notice the thinking required to answer some of these Why? questions.

I've wondered about each of these, often about rising in the atmosphere. When we're flying along from coast to coast at 35,000 feet, we know it's freezing cold outside. But why? I bet that many a college graduate would struggle with the answer to that question.

And I've often wanted to see exactly where the Pacific plate subducts beneath the Asian. Can you, indeed, see the trench and where the two plates meet? (Assuming you had sufficient light and a safe diving bell.)

We can see, using the International Baccalaureate concepts (form, function, causation, etc.), that some questions are definitely asking for causation and others address form.

As with Lorraine's students (see Chapter 7), I am intrigued by this time comparison: "How big will space be when it stops growing and when will it stop growing?" What is Spencer imagining here?

I wonder, if we probed his thinking a bit, what might he say? How big is space? What does it mean for space to grow? Why do you think it grows? How big it will grow?

I wonder what is Spencer's concept of space and its growing. I assume these were topics mentioned in the book his father read to him. The question projects into the future, and it would be interesting to know if the same or similar questions were asked in the book.

> "How big will space be when it stops growing and when will it stop growing?" (Spencer Gragg).

Spencer's dad notices that Spencer asks questions when he is interested. Yes, we ask more questions when we are as interested as Spencer is in these topics or as I was with Antarctic exploration as a seventh grader.

MODELING OUR INQUISITIVENESS— "DID YOU EVER WONDER?"

Here is another opportunity for me to focus on what we model for our children. If we want them to grow up to be inquisitive, we will do as my grandfather continually did, that is, ask, "Did you ever wonder . . . ?" For example, Did you ever wonder why the sun setting on the horizon appears larger than when it is at its zenith? Ever wonder how we know the earth spins on its axis?

Modeling Inquiry at Home

"Did you ever wonder?"

"What if?"

"Have you seen them all?"

"Can you take the other side of the argument?"

How do we as parents and grandparents model our inquisitiveness?

"HAVE YOU SEEN THEM ALL?"

We will model questions my mother taught me. When she was sixteen, her father pointed to the snow falling in LeRoy, New York. "Look, Betty," he said, "each one of those flakes is unique."

"I don't believe it," she said directly to her scientist father, the inventor in 1925 of the nonsugar dessert, D-Zerta.

"What do you mean?" he asked incredulously.

"Well, how do you know each is unique? Have you seen them all?"

What a model of good critical thinking! I stepped into the same trap when, while taking her on a tour of the American Museum of Natural History, I happened to mention that "all grains of sand are unique."

What did she say? You guessed it! "How do you know? Have you seen them all?"

"WHAT IF?"

And another question my grandfather, Llewellyn Ray Ferguson, used to ask is, "What if we took these two substances and mixed them together?" Well, I was too young to have any idea, but between my grandfather and me this was an enormously enjoyable game wherein the prize was learning, enjoyment, and building trust between grandfather and grandson.

He used the same approach every scientist does when puzzled by perplexing phenomena, asking, "What if we could create a nonsugar dessert?" The result? D-Zerta.

"CAN YOU TAKE THE OTHER SIDE OF THE ARGUMENT?"

My mother tells me that my father and grandfather used to get into furious debates when I was child about the efficacy of Franklin Delano Roosevelt's social programs, such as Social Security, and some of his work construction projects, such as the Tennessee Valley Authority (a program that had many lawsuits filed against it, according to Jennet Conant, 2002).

My grandfather would lay out his arguments—and I've heard them in my own life—about how Social Security was a terrible program. "We should be allowed to invest our own money!"

And then, said my mother, "Your father would ask, 'Now, Ray, can you take the other side of the argument?'"

Ray would say adamantly, "Why would I want to do a damn fool thing like that!"

THE CHALLENGE

People, some of them educators, who have learned of Izzy's amazing story have brought it home and made it an expectation at dinnertime. "I want to know if you have asked a good question today."

This can make a significant difference in the lives of all students.

Especially if their teachers set the same expectation.

In addition to issuing this challenge, follow Randy and Jennifer's lead and note your child's growth with inquiry during a year and through the years. We all make videos of our kids; why not record some of their curiosities on film? It would make an interesting record for later years. And we'd be able to foster more growth as some of the splendid teachers in this volume have.

Best wishes.

AT HOME

1. Continuously model our own curiosities about anything of interest: stars, animals, plants, characters in stories/the news:

   I wonder . . . I'm curious about . . .

   What surprises/amazes/fascinates me is . . .

What if we did this . . . ? Let's pretend/suppose . . .

What's the other side of the issue?

How did we figure this out? What are we learning here?

2. Keep a running journal/video record as Randy and Jennifer did.

3. Explore nature, take trips to museums and aquariums, watch and wonder. Find answers to some questions and record in journals.

4. Watch and question *Nova*, the Discovery Channel, and news programs.

5. Invite children to watch and work along with you.

6. Keep your own journal of wonderings. Share with family.

7. Play "What if?" games: car didn't start, computer went blue.

REFERENCES

Barell, J. (2011). *Quest for Antarctica: A journey of wonder and discovery* (2nd ed.). Lincoln, NE: iUniverse.

Conant, J. (2002). *Tuxedo park—A Wall Street tycoon and the secret palace of science that changed the course of World War II.* New York: Simon & Schuster.

Sheff, D. (1988, January 19). Izzy, did you ask a good question today? (Letter to the Editor). *The New York Times*, p. A26.

After Action Reviews

Following these marvelous stories from teachers who are pioneers of 21st century teaching and learning, what more is left to do?
We should once again ask how we can use our results.
For this let us turn to the world of military operations and business.

AFTER ACTION REVIEWS (AARs)

Following the Vietnam War, there were those in the military leadership who felt we needed to examine the practices and procedures we followed in combat. The U.S. Army developed a process known as an AAR.

An AAR is a three-step reflective process that provides any organization with a planning and reflection framework for all significant undertakings. It includes the following questions asked immediately following a planned operation:

1. What was supposed to happen?

2. What did happen? and

3. What accounts for the difference? (Fullan, 2001, p. 89)[1]

An AAR is designed to take place as an open forum of inquiry where the army tolerates no sugarcoating and strives to discover the truth about the

"The After Action Review has democratized the Army. *It has instilled a discipline of relentlessly questioning everything we do* [italics added]. Above all, it has re-socialized many generations of officers to move away from a command-and-control style of leadership to one that takes advantage of distributed intelligence" (Pascale, Millemann, & Gioja, 2000, p. 253).

operation. All leaders and participants must be able to respond to these questions without evasion and must recognize the hard facts of success or failure.

This highly reflective and effective process was begun by the National Training Center in the Mojave Desert after the Vietnam War. Combat units would come to the desert; plan to engage the enemy, role-played by U.S. forces; engage them; and then debrief immediately following an intense simulated combat that commenced at dawn and was usually over by 1100 hours. Visitors seldom won, and the AAR was designed to help them learn from their actions and mistakes.

During an AAR all participants listen and record in notebooks what they need to do differently next time. Says Brigadier General W. Scott Wallace, former commander of the National Training Center, "The After Action Review has democratized the Army. *It has instilled a discipline of relentlessly questioning everything we do* [italics added]. Above all, it has re-socialized many generations of officers to move away from a command-and-control style of leadership to one that takes advantage of distributed intelligence" (Pascale, Millemann, & Gioja, 2000, p. 253).

General Wallace has given us an amazing view of the contemporary army, where "relentlessly questioning everything we do" becomes the norm. Imagine life as a private in a combat zone raising questions about goals, strategies, tactics, resources, and validity of intelligence findings. During my service in the U.S. Navy, it hardly ever occurred to me to question my superiors' judgment, at least not to their faces.

Now, what does this mean for us in education?

How many times have you sat with colleagues to analyze a program or initiative that might not have been as successful as it could or should have been? Indeed, how many times do we engage in what General W. Scott Wallace called for, that is, "relentlessly questioning everything we do"?

Not enough, I imagine.

"WHAT METRICS DID YOU USE TO MEASURE IT?"

Sergey Brin, cofounder of Google, asked this question of someone applying for a job at the then start-up company in 1999. He was asking a future marketing manager to identify a project he'd worked on and what observable criteria he had used to assess success (Edwards, 2011, p. C5).

We know from our curricular plans that we've outlined specific metrics, that is, evidence that students have met our objectives for understanding and growth. And we know that not all students did superbly well. Not everybody was a Jennifer in Lorraine Radford's kindergarten or a Rachel in Pat Burrows's eighth-grade literature and writing class that focused so intently on critical thinking. So like our friends in the business world, we want to ask the logical follow-up questions, such as, What changes do we need to make in our plans to achieve these intended outcomes?

FLEXING AND ADJUSTING

One of the first things I learned about effective teachers was that they were flexible and could adjust their plans to meet the circumstances. They were constantly assessing the instructional environment and modifying their approaches to meet the performance indicators we specify in our scoring guidelines or rubrics.

This means more than what we outlined in Chapter 6 on formative assessment. That is, we need to know more than where Jennifer or Rachel are on a list of subtopics under the performance indicator of inquiry or critical thinking.

We need to think of how we will alter our approaches when we discover that some students are just not getting what we want them to understand. That's the fourth question of the AAR.

Here the basic principle is, Don't do the same thing over again!

Do not subject students to exactly the same ways of teaching that have not lead to understanding in the past. We need to think of alternative methodologies, resources, social arrangements/groupings, and learning experiences.

Let us consider the following:

objectives,

strategies,

resources,

organization, and

means of assessment.

Objectives

If students are not making adequate progress toward our goals, one of the questions we need to ask is, Should we revise these goals and objectives?

Have we set the bar too high, for example? Are students struggling because of lack of prior knowledge or lack of developmental readiness? We cannot, for example, expect Lorraine's students to reach Pat's levels for critical thinking because they are not ready for the kinds of abstract thinking evidenced by Rachel. (However, some of their time travel questions did challenge *my* preconceptions.)

By the same token, some of the evidence from students in all four of the major case studies here (see Chapters 7–10) suggest that students might be able to achieve at levels higher than we had anticipated.

We do not wish to suffer from the preconception of low expectations.

Strategies

We have witnessed here a wide array of instructional approaches—including investigating crime scenes, building accurate models of roller coasters, and writing persuasive essays to the town fathers. What links all of them is the common thread of problematic situations we need to think about.

It's hard for me to imagine that confronting students with intriguing problematic situations such as those you have read about would not succeed in helping students become better at inquiry, problem solving, and critical/creative thinking.

But perhaps we need to tinker with them. Were they

age appropriate?

interesting to our students? and

accessible in the time available for students to mess around with them, that is, to ask good questions, get some feedback, and begin to dig deeper?

Remember Harry in Shauna Ullman's third-grade class and his progressively more challenging questions about plant growth. He succeeded because Shauna provided a wide variety of learning experiences for him and his classmates: She formed literary circles for research, held discussions, and continually "revisited [their] tracking sheets" on which were recorded their initial questions. She provided them iPads with which to communicate and to find answers to their questions, immediately. Eventually, most classrooms will avail themselves of smart phones, iPads, and cloud computing to ask, seek, and find, thereby breaking down those four walls and liberating all children's vivid imaginations.

A similar restructuring occurred under fifth-grade teacher Crystal Martin's leadership (Heights Elementary, Ft. Myers) when she created inquiry circles wherein students read articles related to the unit of study (current events), classified them, divided themselves into inquiry and research groups of interest, and eventually shared their findings in what she called a "grand conversation." One of the methods she used to track and monitor students' thinking was their use of sticky notes on which were notated, "a Question, a Connection, and/or a Learning." Each sticky note had a Q, a C, or an L in one corner. These "notes were used as 'evidence of inquiry' which allowed me to visualize their individual inquiry process and the learning resulting from inquiry methods" (Martin, 2011). Restructuring could occur thereafter.

Another element is how students organize themselves (or are organized). Many of our teachers have used small-group investigations and problem solving to reach their objectives, such as solving the crime scene investigation or building the roller coaster. One thing Mary Darr in Sandusky did after the initial science, technology, engineering, and math project was to alter the teams' organization. Instead of having teachers appoint CEOs as they did the first time, she allowed students to self-organize, select their own teams. How did this work? According to several students with whom I spoke, they appreciated working with their friends. "We didn't have to get to know them first. We knew what they were good at."[2]

Strategies are merely ways to accomplish a task. I often remember what I think was a Hindu concept of God—at the top of the mountain with many pathways upward. When we get caught in doing things one way, that's when we need an AAR and creative problem solving to generate multiple possibilities. Here's where I remember what my father always used to say when he was pioneering the development of a new contraption called a computer: "There's no such word as CAN'T."

> "There's no such word as CAN'T" (Ralph J. Barell).

When our data, our evidence of growth, suggests that kids are not improving at inquiry, problem solving, and critical thinking, then we need to flex and adjust.

Resources

Sometimes teachers ask me about age-appropriate resources for a unit on ecology or U.S. history. Here we need to plan for and rely on our experts in the media center. At Parkside Elementary School in Austin, I saw stacks of books all ready for the young investigators about to descend, searching for answers to questions from the inquiry unit. Planning had ensured that resources were available.

Lorraine Radford had the luxury of taking her students to one of the finest aquariums in the land. When I used to work at the American

Museum of Natural History (Barell, 2003), I was always thrilled to see so many New York City students taking advantage of the incredible resources in the Hayden Planetarium, the Hall of Planet Earth, the Milstein Hall of Ocean Life, and the many cultural halls.

Not everybody can visit these sites in person. But at least you can visit the American Museum of Natural History online at www.amnh.org, where you will find all of the permanent and temporary halls displayed together with hall guides for teachers and students. There are also more active resources; for example, view science bulletins online at www.amnh .org/sciencebulletins/ for films of today's scientists working with brown dwarfs, Mt. Etna, coral reefs, and dolphins.

And for young investigators there is Ology, www.amnh.org/ology, where you can learn more about archeology, anthropology, astronomy, biodiversity, the human brain, and many more topics—all on exhibit at American Museum of Natural History.

With what Shauna Ullman's kids (and increasingly many more!) are doing with iPads in the classroom, they will become excellent museum researchers in no time.

Assessments

And maybe we're just not getting the kinds of information we need to show growth in the 21st century capacities. If we're relying on standardized tests, these would need to be testing for the skills of critical thinking precisely.

But we've seen too many other kinds of information gathering:

teacher's wonder journals;

Evidence of Inquiry forms;

students' written work;

student projects such as films of their journeys to Mars (Sandusky);

students' reflections, orally and in writing, on their work;

students' inquiry or travel journals;

teachers' observations, notes, and journals; and

students' use of iPads, Google Docs, wikis, and other online means of communication and record keeping.

Perhaps we need to expand our ways of helping students share what they are thinking. During the writing of this book I read somewhere that one innovator was figuring out ways to make our clothing into computing and communicating devices. Maybe all we'll have to do one day is talk out loud, and our thoughts will be recorded. And then, soon thereafter, there will be the imThinking pad that records our thoughts without displaying them to the public.

CONNECT TO THE WORLD BEYOND THE CLASSROOM

But perhaps we have considered curriculum from too narrow a focus. Maybe we're bound by our walls and need to step out.

At Normal Park Elementary School in Chattanooga, where travel journals are used, many of the students' projects become museum exhibits because of the many museums in the city. And students regularly interact with adults in the community. For a stirring account of such an experience, read Robin Cayce's story in *Why Are School Buses Always Yellow?* (Barell, 2007), describing the time when a World War II vet came to school, told the story of his escape from the Germans, and then displayed his captured Nazi flag. "There wasn't a dry eye in the room" (p. 11–13), recalled Robin Cayce.

Once again, here is Jesse Mackay of Edmonton:

> Invite the broader community to voice their opinions (parents, students and staff) by posting a kind of graffiti board outside of the classroom. This is very powerful for children to see that philosophical questions often address issues that affect many people, which roots this kind of questioning to "real life." This activity sort of puts students on an even playing field with adults and with my students this year it created a monumental shift in thinking for many of the kids. I did see many things change, including the way they dealt with disagreements and conflicts to feeling free to ask questions about ANYTHING. Eaves dropping on their conversations became very rewarding. (J. Mackay, personal communication, July 2011)

Of course, we have seen how Jesse's "broader community" in the science, technology, engineering,

"Invite the broader community to voice their opinions (parents, students and staff) by posting a kind of graffiti board outside of the classroom. This is very powerful for children to see that philosophical questions often address issues that affect many people, which roots this kind of questioning to 'real life'" (J. Mackay, personal communication, July 2011).

and math projects included specialists, lawyers, architects, Cedar Park representatives, and members of the Cleveland Indians baseball team.

I can hardly imagine anything more powerful for a seventh grader than presenting his or her ideas before such an esteemed group of professionals.

And in the schools of today and tomorrow, we know our students will be communicating with peers and other resource persons all across the globe, asking, seeking out information, and drawing reasonable conclusions. The school will be an open-air exploratorium of opportunity and challenge, not bound by textbooks too heavy to lift.

My own experience (Barell, 2011) was similar: writing to a world-famous polar explorer, Admiral Richard E. Byrd, and having him respond to each and every one of my questions about his expeditions and about the possibility then, years ago, of finding oil in Antarctica. "You're entirely right," he said. Words do not do justice to the feeling of pride and the enlargement of self-esteem when somebody you admire greatly, a world-famous person who has experienced four ticker tape parades up Broadway, tells you, a seventh grader, "You're right!"

Go and do likewise.

CONCLUSION

I feel as if we've been on a long journey to some of the greatest educational environments on the North American continent, led by pioneers of 21st century learning. At times it's been very cold up in Edmonton and really warm down in Arizona. Regardless of the climate, these educators brought to their professions deep passion, commitment, intelligence, and willingness to take risks and venture into unknown territories. Here is where we learn, where we grow and thrive. These teachers are all persons of incredibly bold stripes!

And those newer worlds have no stronger testament than that expressed by one student in Jasmin Ramzinsky's third-grade class this year who, on being challenged to question and think about the solar system in new and dynamic ways, asked her, "Mrs. Ram, I bet your kids kinda got bored with finding the answers to your questions. Why would you ask questions about my planet? You weren't doing the research, I was."

Indeed.

As that wandering explorer Ulysses so famously said in Tennyson's poem,

> Come, my friends,

> 'Tis not too late to seek a newer world.

Set your sights high and higher.

...all experience is an arch wherethrough

Gleams that unravelled world, whose margin fades

For ever and for ever when I move.

How dull it is to pause, to make an end,

To rust unburnished, not to shine in use!

As though to breathe were life...

Come, my friends,

'Tis not too late to seek a newer world...

To strive, to seek, to find, and not to yield.

(Alfred, Lord Tennyson, "Ulysses," 1842, www.victorianweb.org/authors/
tennyson/ulyssestext.html)

ENDNOTES

1. Other descriptions of the After Action Review include the logical fourth step, "What will we do now to improve?"

2. As you might imagine, not all faculty members shared the students' point of view in this regard.

REFERENCES

Barell, J. (2003). *Developing more curious minds.* Alexandria, VA: Association for Supervision and Curriculum Development.

Barell, J. (2007). *Why are school buses always yellow? Teaching inquiry preK–5.* Thousand Oaks, CA: Corwin.

Barell, J. (2011). *Quest for Antarctica: A journey of wonder and discovery* (2nd ed.). Lincoln, NE: iUniverse.

Edwards, D. (2011, July 16–17). The beginning. *The Wall Street Journal,* p. C5.

Fullan, M. (2001). *Leading in a culture of change.* San Francisco, CA: Jossey-Bass.

Martin, C. (2011). *Using inquiry, current events, and NGSSS to make meaningful learning connections.* (Unpublished Capstone Project in partial fulfillment of requirements for master's degree). Florida Gulf Coast University, Ft. Myers.

Pascale, R., Millemann, M., & Gioja, L. (2000). *Surfing the edge of chaos.* New York: Crown Business.

Index

CORWIN

A SAGE Company

The Corwin logo—a raven striding across an open book—represents the union of courage and learning. Corwin is committed to improving education for all learners by publishing books and other professional development resources for those serving the field of PreK–12 education. By providing practical, hands-on materials, Corwin continues to carry out the promise of its motto: **"Helping Educators Do Their Work Better."**